Tuscany

& Umbria Guide

Travel G

OPEN R
YOUR GU
Whether you're going a
Open Road along on your jo
Leisure, The Los Angeles
Report, Endless Vacation
many other magazines and
Don't just see the worl

About the Author

Having spent over eight years living in Italy and exploring the country, Douglas E. Morris has compiled his extensive travel experiences into Open Road's *Tuscany & Umbria Guide*. With this book he gives you the most accurate, up-to-date, and comprehensive information about hotels, restaurants, nightlife, sights and activities in Tuscany and Umbria. His other travel books include *Italy Guide* and *Rome Guide* published by Open Road Publishing, and *Become a Travel Writer* from fabjob.com.

Doug in Italia!

Open Road - Travel Guides to Planet Earth!

Open Road Publishing has guide books to exciting, fun destinations on four continents. As veteran travelers, our goal is to bring you the best travel guides available anywhere!

No small task, but here's what we offer:

• All Open Road travel guides are written by authors with a distinct, opinionated point of view – not some sterile committee or team of writers. Our authors are experts in the areas covered and are polished writers.

• Our guides are geared to people who want to make their own travel choices. We'll show you how to discover the real destination – not just see some place from a tour bus window.

• We're strong on the basics, but we also provide terrific choices for those looking to get off the beaten path and experience the country or city – not just see it or pass through it.

• We give you the best, but we also tell you about the worst and what to avoid. Nobody should waste their time and money on their hard-earned vacation because of bad or inadequate travel advice.

• Our guides assume nothing. We tell you everything you need to know to have the trip of a lifetime – presented in a fun, literate, no-nonsense style.

• And, above all, we welcome your input, ideas, and suggestions to help us put out the best travel guides possible.

Tuscany
& Umbria Guide

Travel Guides to Planet Earth!

DISCARDED

Douglas Morris

BY

Open Road Publishing

Open Road Publishing

We offer travel guides to American and foreign locales. Our books tell it like it is, often with an opinionated edge, and our experienced authors always give you all the information you need to have the trip of a lifetime. Write for your free catalog of all our titles.

Catalog Department, Open Road Publishing
P.O. Box 284, Cold Spring Harbor, NY 11724

E-mail:
Jopenroad@aol.com

Acknowledgments

Many people assisted in the development of this book, but I wish to extend special gratitude to my departed parents, Don and Denise, for being the world travelers and citizens of the world that they were. Without them I would never have lived in Italy and developed the experience to write this book. My brother Dan, his wife Sue, and her parents Brendan and Judy Reilly offered valuable insights into Florence. Alain deCocke's editorial assistance, in both English and Italian, was much appreciated. I am also indebted to Anamaria Porcaro, Theresa Luis and the MMI class of '76 for their thoughtful insights about how to travel in Italy as women. And most of all this book is better for the invaluable suggestions and feedback offered by our many readers including: Jack and Joan Sawinski, Pamela A. Motta, Donna and Mike Lareau, Steve and Sheila Cech, Hugh L. Curtin, Senator Paul Simon, and many others. Special thanks to Karin Denniss for inspiring me to visit Umbria, and to Sukey and Malcolm Denniss for their input. Please forgive me if I did not include you here. And please keep your e-mails coming to *Roma79@aol.com.*

Tuscany & Umbria Guide

contents

6. Basic Information   66

7. Shopping   79

Sidebars

Maps

Sidebars

Tuscany

& Umbria Guide

Chapter 1

Tuscany & Umbria, nestled next to one another in central Italy, are lands magically transported out of time, allowing visitors to witness the tapestry of medieval and Renaissance life woven through the picturesque hills, vibrant cities, stunning architecture, delectable cuisine, and the profusion of high quality art and archaeological artifacts – all of which are brought to life by the heart-warming, friendly and passionate people.

Tuscany, and especially Florence, has been a tourist destination for centuries, for good reason. Florence contains more world-renowned art work and architecture per square foot than anywhere else in the world. Her piazzas overflow with the passion of Italian life. But there is more to Tuscany than Florence, as seasoned travelers to this region are well aware.

Siena is home to the annual Palio horse races and stunning medieval pageantry. Tuscany is also home to the romantic ramparts of Lucca, the leaning tower of Pisa, the peace and tranquility of Fiesole, the towers of San Gimignano, the timelessness of Montepulciano and Cortona, and the seaside splendor of the Isola del Giglio.

The same can be said for Umbria – the land of truffles! – though even more so, because Umbria is not as heavily touristed. From the bustling capital of Perugia with its undulating streets and overpasses, to the tranquility of Todi, Gubbio, Orvieto, and Spoleto, to the pilgrimage stop of Assisi, Umbria will put you under her spell.

Whichever destinations you choose in Tuscany or Umbria, you'll be entering a world outside of time, far away from the hectic pace and pressures of modern day life. *Buon Viaggio!*

Chapter 2

Tuscany and Umbria are located in Central Italy. Both regions are easily accessible from airports in Rome (if you're flying in from the US), and Florence or Pisa (if you're flying in from Europe).

Tuscany

Central Italy is that part of the peninsula that includes and extends north of Rome through the Tuscany region. Although only a small part of the area is composed of lowlands, central Italy plays an important role in farming and in some branches of industry, specifically wine growing. **Florence** is the main tourist city in Tuscany and, along with Rome, contains the best museums, the best churches, and the best sights to see, not only in Italy but some would say the world over.

There are a few sights that if you don't see you can't really say you've been to Florence. The first of which, the Duomo with its campanile and baptistery, is hard to miss. The next, the Ponte Vecchio, is a gem of medieval and Renaissance architecture and is filled with gold and jewelry shops. And if you miss Michelangelo's David in the Accademia you shouldn't show your face back in your home town. That work of art is as close to sculpted perfection as any artist will ever achieve.

Last but not least is the art collection in the Uffizzi Gallery. To actually do this museum justice you may need to spend close to one day wandering through its many rooms. And don't forget to shop at the San Lorenzo Market or browse through the local Mercato Centrale.

There are countless other wonderful sights to see and places to go in Florence. Walking the streets is like strolling

through a fairy tale. But if you haven't seen the items above, you haven't been to Florence!

One small, often overlooked town that shouldn't be missed while visiting Florence is **Lucca**. One of only two completely walled medieval cities left in Europe, the ramparts and battlements that surround the city have been converted into the most romantic tree-lined walkway you will find anywhere. Feast your eyes on the Roman amphitheater, ancient churches and towers, beautiful gardens, and the amazing city walls and imposing entry gate. For romantics, Lucca is a must-see.

In **Pisa**, the main event of course is the Piazza dei Miracoli, which has the church, baptistery and leaning tower. Don't miss the colorful market of Piazza Vettovaglie near the river and just off of the Borgo Stretto, the street with the famous covered sidewalk. It's well worth the visit.

Located about an hour and a half from Florence, **Siena** is a perfect day trip. Here you have the famous Campo, a tower that rises above the city for great photos, quaint medieval streets and plenty of ambiance to spare. If you can get to Siena while the Palio is being held, you simply must do it. The pageantry, the horse race, the costumes, the intensity all evoke a time long gone and will sweep you back through the centuries. Held biannually on July 2 and August 16, plan well in advance to get a place to stay and a ticket to the horse race. Among other great sights, visit the **Torre del Mangia** – if you're in good shape, the 112 meters and 400-plus small confined steps can be taken easily. Once at the top you will be treated to the most amazing panoramic view over the town and the surrounding countryside.

The ancient town of **Fiesole**, once the Roman Empire's dominant town in Tuscany, is a great place to stay if you're looking for a nearby country retreat from Florence. Fiesole's archaeological excavations are well worth a visit, as are the churches, gardesn, and the panoramic view of Florence.

We round out our coverage of Tuscany with the towers and stunning beauty of the small hill town of **San Gimignano**, with its earthen-colored walls and famous towers; the wonderful churches and markets of **Cortona**; the Renaissance palazzi and churches of **Montepulciano**, not to mention the town's summer festival season; and the seaside splendor of the **Isola del Giglio**, the mostly undeveloped and little-touristed island just off the Tuscan coast in the Mediterranean.

Umbria

The quaint and colorful medieval hill towns of **Umbria** are on the periphery of the well-worn tourist path. Since many of Umbria's cities are not on strategic rail lines, Italy's main form of inter-city transportation, getting to many locations can be time-consuming. But once you are here, Umbria is a beautiful slice of mother nature's paradise, little visited by tourists with the exception of Assisi. Covered with lush green forests, manicured fields and wonderful medieval hill towns like Perugia, Gubbio, Assisi, Spoleto, Orvieto and Todi, Umbria is an ideal destination.

Spreading majestically over the tops of a series of hills, **Perugia**, the regional capital, is interlaced with winding cobblestones streets, an aqueduct turned walkway, ancient palazzi, Etruscan and Roman arches, and pictur-esque piazzas. Or take in the rustic charm of **Gubbio**, a hill town growing in popularity. There is also the heavily visited **Assisi**, a pilgrimage stop as well as a rewarding tourist destination. Two of my Umbrian favorites are **Orvieto**, with its splendid cathedral and fascinating Etruscan necropolises only a fifty minute train ride from Rome. In the old core of **Spoleto** atop its hill, you can bathe in the beauty and charm of medieval life. Of itself that is wonderful, but what makes Spoleto special is that only a five-minute walk away, over an ancient aqueduct spanning a scenic gorge, you are transported into a pristine, untouched, forested natural setting – a combination that cannot be duplicated in too many other places. Another ancient and stunningly beautiful city featuring medieval walls and quaint winding streets, **Todi** rises up among green hills above where the Naia flows into the Tiber. All of Umbria is remote from the concerns of the bustling urban pace of big Italian cities.

Experience History

Home to the ancient world's most powerful empire, Italy is awash in history. Daily life revolves around ruins thousands of years old. Modern buildings incorporate ancient structures into their walls. Medieval streets snake through almost all cities and many towns. In Italy you can see the tapestry of history woven directly in front of you. Museums abound with ancient artifacts, beautiful paintings, and stunning sculpture. You can easily spend an entire trip roaming through museums – or for that matter inside the beautiful churches where you'll see some of the most exquisite paintings and sculptures anywhere on earth!

A Feast for the Eyes!

Even though you could spend an entire trip inside museums or churches, if you decided to do so you would miss out on what makes Italy such a wonderful vacation: its ancient beauty, charm, and ambiance. Being in Italy is like walking through a fairy tale, and this is especially true in Tuscany and Umbria. The old winding streets, twisting around the quaint refurbished buildings, leading to a tiny piazza centered with a sparkling fountain seems like something out of a dream.

Food & Wine

But a feast for the eyes is not all you'll get. Italy has, arguably (pipe down, you Francophiles!) the best food you'll find anywhere in the world. In most cases it's simple food, but with a bountiful taste. Since Italy is surrounded on almost all sides by water you can also sample any flavor of seafood imaginable. Usually caught the same day, especially in the small towns along the sea, the seafood in Italy will have you coming back for more.

You'll find all shapes and sizes of pasta covered with sauces of every description and variety. Regions are known for certain pasta dishes and when there you have to sample them all. The area around Bologna is known for the production of the best ham in the world, Prosciutto di Parma. To make this ham so succulent, the pigs are fed from the scraps of the magnificent cheese they make in the same region, Parmigiano Reggiano. Both of these foods feature prominently in spaghetti alla bolognese making it a favorite in the region and throughout Italy.

To wash down all these savory dishes you need look no further than the local wine list. Italian wines may not have a reputation as being as full-bodied and robust as French or California wines, but they have an intimate, down to earth, abundant flavor. Order from the wine list or get a carafe of the house wine, which is usually delicious and more often than not comes from the local vineyards located just outside the city.

Open Road's Tuscany & Umbria

Besides offering the many sights to see, museums and churches to visit, and places to go, I've also listed the best sights to see while visiting a certain destination. In conjunction I've detailed for you the best hotels from each star category, as well as the restaurants where you'll find the best atmosphere and most satisfying cuisine. And to help you plan the perfect vacation and find everything the instant you arrive, this book offers you the **most complete set of city maps** you'll find in virtually any travel guide to Italy.

Chapter 3

l a n d & p e o p l e

Land

From the top of the boot to the toe, Italy is a little more than 675 miles (1,090 kilometers) long. The widest part, in the north, measures about only 355 miles (570 kilometers) from east to west. The rest of the peninsula varies in width from 100 to 150 miles (160 to 240 kilometers) making it an easily traveled country, at least side to side. In total the peninsula of Italy fills an area of about 116,000 square miles (300,400 square kilometers).

A mountainous country, Italy is dominated by two large mountain systems – the **Alps** in the north and the **Apennines** which run down the center of the peninsula. The Alps, which are the highest mountains in Europe, extend in a great curve from the northwestern coast of Italy to the point where they merge with Austria and Slovenia in the east. Just west of the port city of Genoa, the **Maritime Alps** are the beginning of the chain. Despite mighty peaks and steep-sided valleys, the Alps are pierced by modern engineering marvels of mountain passes that have allowed commerce between Italy and its northern neighbors to flow freely. These highway and railroad tunnels provide year-round access through the mountains encouraging trade, tourism and transit.

The Apennine mountain system is an eastern continuation of the Maritime Alps. It forms a long curve that makes up the backbone of the Italian peninsula. The Apennines extend across Italy in the north, follow the east coast across the central region, then turn toward the west coast, and, interrupted by the narrow Strait of Messina, continue into Sicily.

There are numerous smaller mountains in Italy, many of volcanic ancestry, most of which are thankfully extinct. But that does not mean mother nature remains dormant in Italy. Because of the volcanic nature of the peninsula, which is caused by the earth plates shifting, Italy is prone to earthquakes. In the summer of 1997 an earthquake hit Umbria and destroyed not only towns and villages but some of Giotto's precious frescoes in the cathedral in Assisi. The region was still active for months and aftershocks were felt in Rome in November of that year. I can personally attest to that since the aftershocks woke me up at 3 o'clock one November morning.

Tuscany stretches from the coast well inland to the edge of Umbria and Lazio on its central and southern borders. Tuscany is the home of Florence, but is also the land of medieval towns, undulating hills, seaside delights, and beautiful valleys.

Called the "**Green Heart of Italy**," Umbria is a beautiful slice of mother nature's paradise, with its rolling hills and lush valleys. Covered with lush green forest and manicured fields, Umbria is located in the center of Italy and is bordered by Tuscany and Lazio, the provinces that are home to Florence and Rome. Umbria is one of the smallest regions of Italy at only 8,500 square

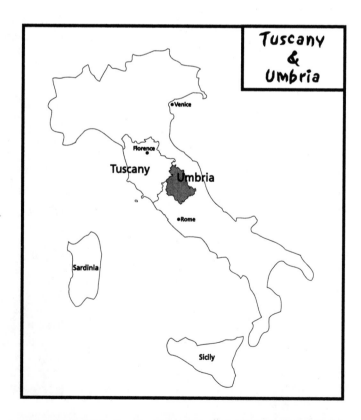

kilometers. Even though it is one of only a few Italian provinces not bordered by the sea, Umbria's mountains offer plenty of scenic splendor.

People

The Italian people are now considered to be one of the most homogeneous, in language and religion, of all the European populations. About 95 percent of the Italian people speak Italian. For more than seven centuries the standard form of the language has been the one spoken in Tuscany. However, there are many dialects, some of which are difficult even for Italians to understand. Two of these principal dialects, those of Sicily and Sardinia, sound like a foreign language to most Italians. Because of these differences, if you have lived in Italy for a while, it is easy to discern the different accents and dialects and pinpoint where someone is from. Just like it is easy for us to figure out if someone is from New England or the South based on their accent.

But all this is just about where they live and how they speak. What are the Italians like?

Shakespeare was enamored with Italians and things Italian, as is evidenced by having many of his plays take place in Italy. And when he wrote "All the world's a stage," he definitely had Italy in mind. Filled with stunningly beautiful architecture and ancient ruins, Italy's physical landscape is a perfect backdrop for the play of Italian life. In Italy everyone is an actor, dramatically emphasizing a point with their hands, facial expressions leaving no doubt about what is being discussed and voices rising or falling based on what the scene requires.

Play in the Piazza

Italians are some of the most animated people in the world and watching them is more than half the fun of going to Italy. These people relish living and are unafraid to express themselves. There is a tense, dramatic, exciting directness about Italians which is refreshing to foreigners accustomed to Anglo-Saxon self-control. In Italy most travelers find, without even realizing it was missing, that combination of sensuality, love and sincerity that is so lacking in their own lives.

In every piazza, on every street, there is some act being played. Whether it's two neighbors quarreling, vendors extolling the virtues of their wares, a group of older ladies chatting across the street as they lean out their windows, lovers whispering hands caressing each other as they walk, a man checking his reflection in the mirror primping for all to see, there is something about the daily street scenes all over Italy that make this country seem more alive, more animated than the rest or the world. Italians really know how to enjoy the production of living; and they love to watch these everyday scenes unfold.

Seats are strategically placed in cafés to catch all that occurs. And it is easy, even for the uninitiated, to see what is transpiring a distance away because

Italians are so expressive. On the faces of Italians it is easy to read joy, sorrow, hope, anger, lust, desire, relief, boredom, despair, adoration and disappointment as easily as if they were spoken aloud. When Italians visit Northern Europe, England, or America they seem lost since they seldom know what is going on, as everyone is so expressionless.

Fashion, Art & Warfare?

Virtually all Italians share a love for fashion. The Italians are some of the best dressed people in the world, and they love to prance around like peacocks displaying their finery. 'Style over substance' is an adage that well describes Italians; but they live it with such flair that it can be forgiven. Along with the finery they wear, the beauty of the Italian people is unparalleled. All manner of coloration, including the stereotypical sensual brown eyed and brown haired beauties abound. Besides fashion Italians love art. If you ask an Italian to take your photograph expect to be posed and re-posed for at least five minutes. All Italians imagine themselves to be Federico Fellini, the famous film producer. They want to get the light just right, the shading perfect and the framing ideal. They'll pose you until you're almost blue in the face, but you'll get a great picture.

They also love architecture. What happened in the United States where beautiful buildings were destroyed all over the country to erect parking lots would never happen in Italy, where you'll also never see garish strip malls or ugly suburban sprawl. For example, the McDonalds' in Italy do not stand out the way they do in America with the golden arches glowing the location for all to see. The store signs have been blended to the architecture of the building in which they are located. A balance has been found between commercialism and aesthetic appeal that has been forgotten in America.

Their love for style over substance is why Italians have always excelled in activities where appearance is paramount, like architecture, decorating, landscaping, fireworks, opera, industrial design, graphic design, fashion and cinema. It could be conjectured that because of this pursuit of such 'effeminate' pastimes, warfare has never been Italy's forte.

During the Renaissance, battles were mere window dressing. Well paid condottieri headed beautifully appointed companies of men, resplendent in their finest silks, carrying colorful flags bearing the emblem of the families who were paying them. Martial music was played, songs were sung, and bloodcurdling cries were bellowed. But there was not much war being made. There were limited casualties, and when blood was shed it was usually by accident. "Armies" would pursue each other back and forth for weeks in a pageantry of color and celebration until a settlement was decided by negotiation, not bloodshed. This may seem to be a ludicrous form of warfare, but it is a brilliant expression of life, and an appreciation for living.

Religion & Family

In all, the best way to describe Italians is that they are fun. They will "live while they have life to live, and love while they have love to give." But they are also very traditional in their religion. As the center of Roman Catholicism, Italy is a shining example of Christian piety, even though many of the saints they worship are only decorated pagan gods dating back to the pre-Christian era. The Pope is revered as if he truly is sitting on the right hand of God. Virtually every holiday in Italy has some religious undertones and the people perform the necessary rites and rituals associated with those holidays with vigor and enthusiasm.

Christmas is a prime example of religion's effect. In Italy it is not as garish and commercial an activity as it is in America. Religion takes precedence over mass consumption. Having a lavish dinner with family and friends is more important than going into debt to show people you love them through product purchases. Most decorations are of religious figures, not the commercial icons like Santa Claus and Rudolph.

Religion may guide the people and present a foundation for living, but the family is paramount. In a society where legal authority is weak, the law is resented and resisted (estimates place the number of people that actually pay income tax at around 20%) and the safety and welfare of each person is mainly due to the strength of the family. Family gatherings, especially over meals are common. Knowing your third cousins is not rare. And many family members live and die all in the same small neighborhoods where they were born, even in the large cities of Florence, Venice, Naples and Rome. Family traditions are maintained, strengthened and passed on. The young interact, learn from, and respect their elders. The family is the core of Italian society, strong and durable; and from it grows a healthy sense of community.

Useful Phrases

If you want to take a few virtual language lessons before you go, visit the "Foreign Language for Travelers" website at *www.travlang.com/languages*. It's helpful and fun.

Pronunciation

Even though Italian is basically pronounced the way you see it, there are few pronuciation idiocyncrasies you should be aware of before attempting to speak the language.

In Italian you pronounce every letter. Vowels are pronounced differently in Italian than in English. In general **e** is pronunced 'ay,' **i** is 'ee,' **a** is 'ah,' **o** is always 'oh,' and **u** is 'oo.' Which would make our vowel list, a-e-i-o-u pronounced ah-ay-ee-o-oo. Alos, an 'e' at the end of a word is always pronounced. And 'e' and 'i' when used with consonants are soft.

Also, and this is important, the second to last syllable is stressed. This is different from English where the first syllable is usually stressed. For example, we pronounce 'rodeo' with the stress on the 'RO' part. The Italians would put the stress on the 'E' part. We would say **RO**deo. They would say rod**E**o. And would pronounced the **e** as 'ay.'

Other than that, Italian is pretty simple. What you see is how it is pronounced. Sure there are exceptions to that rule, but in general simplicity is the rule. Listed below should not be a considered a comprehensive pronunciation guide for each letter, but it should serve you well.

a - as in father

au - as the 'ow' in cow

b - same as in English

c, cca, ca, cco, co, cchi and **cu** - as the hard 'k' in keep

cci, ci and **ce** - as the 'ch' in cheap

(**c** is the toughest letter with many variations, including: **ca** - ka, **ce** - chay, **ci** - chee, **chi** - key, **che** - kay)

d - same as in English

e - as the 'ay' in day

f - same as in English

g, ga, go, gh and **gu** - as the hard 'g' in gate

ge and **gi** - as the soft 'g' in jar

gl - as the 'll' in million

gn - as the 'ni' in onion

h - silent. OK so not everything is as it appears.

i - as the 'ee' in keep

j - in rare appearances is soft like a 'y' in you.

k/l/m/n - same as in English

o - as the 'o' in float

p/q - same as in English

r - same as in English except for a rolling of the letter. Think of cat purring.

s - majority of cases is as the hard 's' in sit. Between two vowels is soft 's' as in hose.

sc, sca, sco, scu - as the hard sound 'sc' in scout

sce and **sci** - as the soft sound 'sh' in sheep

t - same as in English

u - preceded by a cosonant is pronounced as a 'w'

u - all other occurrences pronounced 'oo' (as in an exlamation over fireworks, oooh)

v - preceded by a consonant is pronounced as a 'w. All other times as in English.

z - like the 'ts' sound in cats

Italian is really easy when you grasp the simple pronunciation rules. Yes these rules are different from those in English, but that helps make the Italian language sound so lyrical.

General
• Excuse me, but ....
Mi scusi, ma .... (This is a good introduction to virtually any and all inquiries listed below. It is a polite way of introducing your questions.)
• Thank you
Grazie
• Please
Per favore
• If you are in trouble, yell "Help"
Aiuto (eyeyootoh)

If you are looking for something, a restaurant, a hotel, a museum, simply ask "where is ...:"
• Where is the restaurant(name of restaurant)
Dov'é il ristorante_____?
• Where is the hotel (name of hotel)
Dov'é l'hotel _____?
• Where is the museum (name of museum)
Dov'é il museo _____?
Note: *(Dov'é* is pronounced "Dove [as in the past tense of dive] -ay")

Travel-Trains
• Where is track number ...
Dov'é binnario ...

1	*uno*	11	*undici*
2	*due*	12	*dodici*
3	*tre*	13	*tredici*
4	*quatro*	14	*quatordici*
5	*cinque*	15	*quindici*
6	*sei*	16	*sédici*
7	*sette*	17	*diciassette*
8	*otto*	18	*diciotto*
9	*nove*	19	*dicianove*
10	*dieci*	20	*venti*

• Is this the train for Florence (Roma)?
E questo il treno per Firenze (Roma)?
• When does the train leave?
Quando partira il treno?

• When is the next train for Naples/Milan?
Quando e il prossimo treno per Napoli/Milano?

Travel-Cars
• Where is the next gas station?
Dov'é la prossima stazione di benzina?
• I would like some oil for my car.
Voglio un po di olio per il mio automobile.
• Can you change my oil?
Puo fare un cambio dell'olio per me?
• I need a new oil filter.
Voglio un nuovo filtro dell'olio.

Travel-Public Transport
• Where is the (name of station) metro station?
Dov'é la stazione di Metro _____?
• Where can I buy a Metro ticket?
Dov'é posso prendere un biglietto per il Metro?
• How much is the ticket?
Quanto costa il biglietto?
• Where is the bus stop for bus number ___.
Dov'é la fermata per il bus numero ___?
• Excuse me, but I want to get off.
Mi scusi, ma voglio scendere.
• Where can I catch a taxi?
Dov'é posso prendere un tassi?

Purchasing
The following you can usually get at a drug store (*Farmacia*).
• Where can I get...?
Dov'é posso prendere ...?
• toothpaste
dentifricio
• a razor
un rasoio
• some deodorant
un po di deodorante
• a comb
un pettine
• rubbers
dei profilattici
• a toothbrush
un spazzolino

- some aspirin
  un po di aspirina

The following you can usually get at a *Tabacchaio:*
- stamps
  francobolli
- a newspaper
  un giornale
- a pen
  una penna
- envelopes
  buste per lettere
- some postcards
  dei cartoline

The following you can usually get at an *Alimentari:*
- some mustard
  un po di senape
- some mayonnaise
  un po di maionese
- tomatoes
  tomaté
- olive oil
  olio d'oliva
- I would like ... *Voglio ...*
- 1/4 of a pound of this salami
  un etto di questo salami
- 1/2 of a pound of Milanese salami
  due etti di salami milanese
- 3/4 of a pound of this cheese
  tre etti di questo formaggio
- a small piece of mozzarella
  un piccolo pezzo di mozzarrella
- a portion of that cheese
  una porzione di quel' formaggio
- a slice of ham
  una fetta (or una trancia) di prosciutto
- one roll
  un panino
- two/three/four rolls
  due/tre/quatro panini
- How much for the toothpaste, razor, etc?
  Quante costa per il dentifrico, il rasoio, etc.

- How much for this?
  Quante costa per questo?
- Excuse me, but where I can find a ...?
  Mi scusi, ma dov'é un ... ?
- pharmacy
  Farmacia
- tobacconist
  Tabacchaio
- food store
  Alimentari
- bakery
  Panificio

Communications
- Where is the post office?
  Dov'é l'ufficio postale?
- Where is a post box?
  Dov'é una buca delle lettere
- Where is a public telephone?
  Dov'é una cabina telefonica?
- May I use this telephone?
  Posso usare questo telefono?

Hotel
- How much is a double for one night/two nights?
  Quanto costa una doppia per una notte/due notte?
- How much is a single for one night/two nights?
  Quanto costa una singola per una notte/due notte?
- Where is the Exit/Entrance?
  Dov'é l'uscita/l'ingresso?
- What time is breakfast?
  A che ora e prima colazione?
- Can I get another....for the room?
  Posso prender un altro ... per la camera?
- blanket
  coperta
- pillow
  cuscino
- bed
  letto

Miscellaneous
- Where is the bathroom?
  Dov'é il cabinetto?
- What time is it?
  Che oré sono?
- Sorry, I don't speak Italian.
  Mi scusi, ma non parlo italiano.
- Where can I get a ticket for ...?
  Dov'é posso prendere un biglietto per ...?
- a soccer game
  una partita di calcio
- a basketball game
  una partita di pallacanestro
- the theater
  il teatro
the opera
  l'opera
- You are truly beautiful.
  Tu se veramente bella (spoken to a woman informally)
  lei e veramente bella (spoken to woman formally)
  Tu se veramente bello (spoken to a man)
  lei e veramente bello (spoken to man formally)
- Can I buy you a drink?
  Posso comprarti una bevanda?
- Do you speak any English?
  Parli un po d'Inglese?
- Do you want to go for a walk with me?
  Voi andare a una passeggiata con me?
- Is there anyplace to go dancing nearby?
  Ch'é un posto per ballara vicino?

a short history

Chapter 4

A short Italian history is a contradiction in terms. So much has occurred in that narrow strip of land which has affected the direction of the entire Western world, that it is difficult to succinctly describe its history in a brief outline. We've had the Etruscans, Romans, Greeks, 'Barbarian' hordes, Holy Roman Emperors, the Papacy (although not the whole time – the seat of the Catholic Church was moved to Avignon, France from 1305 until 1377), painters, sculptors, the Renaissance, the Medici family, Crusaders, Muslim invaders, French marauders, Spanish conquistadors, Anarchists, Fascists, American soldiers, Communists, Red Brigades, and much more.

What follows is an attempt at a brief outline of the major events on the Italian peninsula as they relate primarily to Tuscany and Umbria.

Etruscans

Long before Romulus and Remus were being raised by a she-wolf to become the founders of Rome, Italy was the home of a people with an already advanced civilization – the **Etruscans**. This powerful and prosperous society almost vanished from recorded history because not only were they conquered by Rome but were also devastated by marauding **Gauls**. During these conquests once from the south, the other from the north, it is assumed that most of their written history was destroyed, and little remains of it today. The **Eugubine Tablets**, the Rosetta Stone for Central Italy, are the best link we have to understanding the Etruscan language. These tablets have corresponding Umbrian language text, which evolved from the Etruscan, and a corresponding rudimentary form of Latin.

Because of the lack of preserved examples of their language, and the fact that the inscriptions on their monuments has been only partially deciphered, archaeologists have gained most of their knowledge of the Etruscans from studying the remains of their city walls, houses, monuments, and tombs.

From their research, archaeologists have been able to ascertain that the Etruscans were a seafaring people from Asia Minor, and that as early as 1000 BCE (Before the Common Era) they had settled in Italy in the region that is today **Tuscany** and **Lazio**. An area basically from Rome's Tiber River north almost to Florence's Arno River. Their influence eventually embraced a large part of western Italy, including Rome.

As a seafaring people, the Etruscans controlled the commerce of the Tyrrhenian Sea on their western border. After losing control of Rome, they strengthened their naval power through an alliance with Carthage against Greece. In 474 BCE, their fleet was destroyed by the Greeks of Syracuse. This left them vulnerable not only to Rome, but the Gauls from the north. The Gauls overran the country from the north, and the Etruscans' strong southern fortress of **Veii** fell to Rome after a ten-year siege (396 BCE). But as was the Roman way, the Etruscans were absorbed into their society, and eventually Rome adopted many of their advanced arts, their customs, and their institutions.

The Etruscan Kings of Early Rome

When Greece was reaching the height of its prosperity, Rome was just beginning its ascent to power. Rome didn't have any plan for its climb to world domination; it just seemed to evolve. There were plenty of setbacks along the way, but everything seemed to fall into place at the right time; and the end result was that at its apex, Rome ruled most of the known world.

The early Romans kept no written records and their history is so mixed with fables and myths that historians have difficulty distinguishing truth from fiction. The old legends say that **Romulus** founded the city in 753 BCE when the settlements on the seven hills were united. But this date is probably later than the actual founding of the city. As is the case with many emerging societies, the founders are mythical figures, as was Romulus, but there is some evidence that the kings who followed him in the ancient stories actually existed.

Shortly before 600 BCE, Rome was conquered by several Etruscan princes. The Etruscans were benevolent conquerors, an attitude that Rome would itself adopt, and set about improving the native lifestyles to match their own.

The Etruscans built Rome into the center of all Latium, their southern province. Impressive public works were constructed, like the huge sewer **Cloaca Maxima**, which is still in use today. Trade also expanded and prospered, and by the end of the 6th century BCE Rome had become the largest and richest city in Italy.

The Native Roman Population Revolts

But in spite of all this progress and development, the old Latin aristocracy wanted their power back from the Etruscans. **Junius Brutus** led a successful revolt around 509 BCE, which expelled the Etruscans from the city. That was when the people of Rome made themselves a **republic**.

Rome's successful thwarting of the Etruscans helped the young republic gain the confidence it needed to begin its long history of almost constant conquest. At the time Rome was only a tiny city-state, much like the city-states that were flourishing at the same time in Greece, with a population of roughly 150,000. But in a few centuries this small republic would eventually rule the known world.

Roman Conquest of Italy

The Latin League started to develop a dislike for the growing power and arrogance of their ally and attempted to break away from its control; but Rome won the two year war that followed (340-338 BCE) and firmly established their dominance. The truce that was made between Rome and the Latin League was broken a few years later (326 BCE) by the **Samnites**, and a wild-fought struggle ensued, with a variety of interruptions, until the decisive battle of **Sentinum** (295 BCE), which made Rome supreme over all central and northern Italy.

Southern Italy, still occupied by a disunited group of Greek city-states, still remained independent. Alarmed at the spread of Roman power, the Greek cities appealed to **Pyrrhus**, king of Epirus in Greece, who heeded their warning and inflicted two telling defeats on the Roman army. He then crossed to Sicily to aid the Greek cities there in eliminating Carthaginian rule. Unfortunately this was a classic example of spreading your forces too thin and trying to fight a war on two fronts. Encouraged by the arrival of a Carthaginian fleet to combat the Greeks, Rome renewed its struggle for the Greek city-states in southern Italy, and in 275 BCE defeated Pyrrhus in the battle of **Beneventum** and a new phrase was born: a Pyrrhic victory – where you win the war but at excessive cost. Eventually, one by one the Greek cities were taken, and just like that Rome was ruler of all Italy.

Keeping the Conquered Lands Happy

Rome gradually wove the lands conquered into the fabric of a single nation, contented and unified. Rome could have exploited the conquered cities of Italy for its own interests, but instead made them partners in the future success of the entire empire.

Rome also set about establishing colonies of its citizens all over Italy. Almost one sixth of all Italy was annexed and distributed among these colonizing Roman citizens. By encouraging this colonization, a common interest in the welfare of Rome spread throughout the Italian peninsula. The

Roman republic eventually gave way to the Roman empire, which brought about two centuries of peace and prosperity known as the **Roman Peace** (*Pax Romana*).

But all was not well at home. The rich amused themselves by giving splendid feasts. The poor had their circuses where free bread and wine was distributed. Slave labor had degraded the once sturdy peasantry to the status of serfs or beggars, and the middle class, who once had been the backbone of the nation, had almost disappeared. A welfare mentality overcame the population. And Roman governors of the provinces once again began to concentrate on siphoning off as much money as possible during their short term of office, instead of keeping abreast of the economic and political climate.

The Fall of the Roman Empire

Political decay, economic troubles, and decadent living were sapping the strength and discipline of the Roman Empire. At this time, German 'barbarians,' who were a violent people living on the fringes of the empire and led by warrior chiefs, began to attack the edges of the empire in the 4th century CE (Common Era). These **Goths, Vandals, Lombards, Franks, Angles, Saxons,** and other tribes defeated unprepared Roman garrison after garrison, and sacking and pillaging the decadent and crumbling empire. In 330 CE, when the Roman emperor **Constantine** moved the capital to **Constantinople** (today's Istanbul in Turkey), the Western Roman Empire began a gradual decline. Order made way for chaos and rival governors fought over fragments of Italian territory to increase their power.

With the fall of the Western Roman Empire in CE 476, this was the beginning of the period called the **Dark Ages**. They were so called because Roman civilization and law collapse along with its artistic and engineering achievements. Order was lost, well developed distribution trade routes evaporated, people went back to the way life was like prior to Roman rule and in most cases it was a step backward in time. Coordinated agriculture was lost, the roads fell into ruin, irrigation system were not maintained, public health measures were ignored and the resulting poor hygiene set the stage for coming of the Black Plague.

What the 'barbarians' did bring with them, however, an aspect of their freedom and independence that helped shape the future of Western civilization, was their belief that the individual was important, more so than the state. In contrast, the Romans believed in the rule of the state over the people – in despotism, or the concept of a benevolent dictator. The 'barbarians' gave us a rudimentary form of personal rights, including more respect for women, government by the people for the people, and a system of law which represented the needs and wishes of the people being governed. In essence, these 'barbarians' lived under the beginnings of democracy in Europe.

After the Roman Empire

Even **Charlemagne**, who had conquered the Lombard rulers and had himself crowned emperor of the **Holy Roman Empire** in 800 CE, could not stop the disintegration of everything the Roman Empire had built. To maintain a semblance of order, the Holy Roman Empire became a union between the Papacy and Charlemagne in which management of the empire was shared.

But Charlemagne's Holy Roman Empire fell apart after his death, only to be refounded by the Saxon **Otto I** in 962 CE, bringing Italy into a close alliance with Germany. From that time until the 1800s, the Holy Roman Empire took on many shapes, sizes, and rulers. It included at different times France, Germany, Luxembourg, the north of Italy (because the Muslims, and then the Normans had taken control of Italy south of Naples), Austria, Switzerland, and more. It had rulers from the Saxon Line, Franconian Line, Hohenstaufen Line, Luxembourg Line, and the Hapsburg Line. It may have been constantly in flux but it did last over 1,000 years in some shape or form.

While the Holy Roman Empire expanded and contracted, it eventually contracted itself outside of Italy, leaving Italy an amalgamation of warring city-states. Florence, Venice, Milan, and the Papacy became the strongest of these contending powers and they came to dominate the countryside while feudalism declined. They drew their riches from the produce of their fertile river valleys and from profits generated in commerce between the Orient and Europe. This trade flowed in through Venice, Pisa, Genoa and Naples and passed through to other European cities on its way across the Alps.

The Italian Renaissance

Under the patronage of the Papacy and of the increasingly prosperous princes of the city-states, such as the **Medici** of Florence, the scholars, writers, sculptors and painters created the masterpieces of literature, art, and science that made the **Italian Renaissance** one of the most influential movements in history. In this period many splendid churches, palaces, and public buildings were built that still inspire awe in Italians and visitors alike. But at the same time as this resurgence in artistic expression, almost completely lost after the fall of the Roman Empire the dominant city states in Italy – Florence, Pisa, Siena, Venice, Perugia, Milan, the Papal States and more – were filled with social strife and political unrest.

Pawn of Strong Nations

While Italy was being torn by struggles between the local rulers and the Papacy, and among themselves, strong nations were developing elsewhere in Europe. As a result of this, Italy became an area of conquest for the other powers struggling for European supremacy. French and Spanish rivalry over Italy began in 1494. **Charles VIII of France** valiantly fought his way through the peninsula to Naples, but by 1544 **Charles I of Spain** had defeated the French three times and had become ruler of Sicily, Naples, and Milan.

For centuries the city-states of Italy remained mere pawns in other nations' massive chess games of power. Italian city-states passed from one to another of Europe's rulers through war, marriage, death, or treaty. The **Papacy** was, however, usually strong enough to protect its temporal power over the areas in central Italy known as the **States of the Church**, or the **Papal States**.

Movement for Political Unity

Eventually hatred of foreign rule mounted, and with it grew the **Risorgimento**, or movement for political unity. Such secret societies as the Carbonari (charcoal burners, the name given from their use of charcoal burners' huts for meeting places), plotted against the Austrians, but the **Carbonari Revolts** were crushed in 1821 and again in 1831 by Austrian troops.

Then the idealistic republican leader, **Giuseppe Mazzini**, organized his revolutionary society, **Young Italy**, and called upon **Charles Albert**, king of Sardinia-Piedmont and a member of the ancient House of Savoy, to head a movement to liberate Italy. By early 1848, revolts had broken out in many regions, and constitutions had been granted to Naples, Piedmont, and Tuscany. But when Mazzini drove out the pope and set up a short-lived republic in Rome the French came to the pope's aid, and Austria quelled the revolt in the north. Despite this outside interference, the ball was rolling, and when Charles Albert abdicated his rule in Sardinia-Piedmont to his son **Victor Emmanuel II**, the stage was set for a run at independence.

Under the able leadership of the shrewd diplomat **Count Camillo di Cavour**, Victor Emmanuel's minister, Sardinia-Piedmont grew strong in resources and in alliances. Cavour was also aware that no matter how real Italian patriotic fervor was, the country would never be unified without help from abroad, so he cleverly forged an alliance with **Napoleon III** of France. Then in the spring of 1859 Austria was goaded into declaring war against Sardinia-Piedmont and France, and was defeated by the combined French and Italian forces. Italy claimed the lands of Lombardy for a united Italy, but France kept as its bounty the kingdom of Venezia.

To consolidate their power, Cavour and Victor Emmanuel lobbied the peoples of Tuscany, Modena, Parma, and Emilia who eventually voted to cast out their princes and join Sardinia-Piedmont as parts of a unified Italy. Napoleon III consented to such an arrangement, but only if Savoy and Nice voted to join France. (Politics is too complicated. I'll stick to travel writing).

Garibaldi To The Rescue

The second step toward a united Italy came the next year, when the famous soldier of fortune **Giuseppe Garibaldi** and his thousand red-shirted volunteers stormed the island of Sicily and the rest of the Kingdom of Naples on the mainland. The people everywhere hailed him as a liberator, and the hated Bourbon king was driven out.

In February 1861 **Victor Emmanuel II** was proclaimed king of Italy, and he began working closely with Garibaldi. Now only the Papal States and Venezia remained outside of the new Italian nation. Venezia joined in 1866 after Prussia defeated Austria in alliance with Italy. The Papal States and **San Marino** were now the only entities on the peninsula outside the Italian kingdom. Not yet as small and isolated as it is today, San Marino was then about the size the current region of Lazio making it a valuable prize for a unified Italy.

Vatican Captured - Kingdom of Italy United

Since French troops still guarded the pope's sovereignty, Victor Emmanuel, being the apt pupil of Cavour (who had died in 1861), did not want to attack the French and perhaps undo all that had been accomplished. Then, miraculously in 1870, the **Franco-Prussian War** forced France to withdraw its soldiers from Rome, at which time Italian forces immediately marched in.

Pope Pius IX, in his infinite lack of wisdom and understanding, excommunicated the invaders and withdrew behind the walls of the Vatican. There he and his successors remained 'voluntary prisoners' until the **Concordat of 1929**, or **Lateran Treaty**, between Italy and the Holy See, which recognized the temporal power of the pope as sovereign ruler over Vatican City (all 108.7 acres of it, or about 1/6 of a square mile!). The rest of the Papal States was absorbed into the new unified Italy, as was San Marino, except for the small, fortified town on top of a butte-like hill that remains independent today.

Modern Italy - The Beginning

Staggering under a load of debt and heavy taxation, giant steps needed to still be taken for Italy to survive. Leaders of the various regions, always trying to gain an edge, were in constant disagreement – even in active conflict. At the same time citizens, used to the ultimate control of despotic rule, found it difficult to adopt the ways of parliamentary government. As a result, riots and other forms of civil disorder were the rule in the latter half of the 19th century.

Despite all of these problems, in the typical Italian mode of functioning despite complete political chaos, an army and navy were developed; railroads, ports, and schools were constructed; and a merchant marine was developed. At the same time, industrial manufacturing started to flourish as it was all over the world.

But then, in 1900, **King Umberto I** (son of Victor Emmanuel II) was assassinated by anarchists – in what was to turn out to be a string of assassinations during that time period all over Europe – and his son, **Victor Emmanuel III**, rose to the throne. Although having joined with Germany and

Austria in the **Triple Alliance** in 1882, by the early 1900s Italy began to befriend France and England. With Austria's invasion of Serbia in 1914 after the assassination of Archduke Ferdinand of Austria, Italy declared its neutrality despite being Austria's ally. In April 1915, Italy signed a secret treaty with the **Allies** (Russia, France, and England), and the next month it stated that it had withdrawn from the Triple Alliance. On May 23, 1915, the king of Italy declared war on Austria.

When World War I ended in 1918, the old Austro-Hungarian Empire was broken up. Italy was granted territory formerly under Austrian rule, including "unredeemed Italy" of the Trentino in the north and the peninsula of Istria at the head of the Adriatic.

Mussolini & Fascism

The massive worldwide depression after World War I brought strikes and riots, which were fomented by anarchists, socialists, and Communists. The government of Victor Emmanuel III seemed powerless to stop bands of former servicemen lawlessly roaming the country. In these bands, **Benito Mussolini** saw his opportunity to gain power. With his gift of oratory he soon molded this rabble into enthusiastic, organized groups in many communities all over Italy, armed them, and set them to preserving the order which had been had destroyed. These bands formed the nucleus of his black-shirted **Fascist** party, whose emblem was the *fasces*, the bundle of sticks that had symbolized the authority of the Roman Empire.

On Oct. 28, 1922, the **Blackshirts**, meeting in Naples, were strong enough, well enough prepared, and willing to march on Rome and seize the government. The king, fearing civil war and his own life, refused to proclaim martial law, forced the premier to resign, and asked Mussolini to form a shared government. Within a few years Mussolini, *Il Duce* (The Leader), had reorganized the government so that the people had no voice at all. Mussolini first abolished all parties except his own Fascist party, and took from the Chamber of Deputies the power to consider any laws not proposed by him. The king remained as a figurehead because he was revered by the people and had the support of many wealthy and important families. In 1939 when Mussolini replaced the Chamber of Deputies with the Chamber of Fasces and Corporations, composed of all his henchmen, no semblance of popular rule remained.

Intimidation or violence crushed all opposition. Suspected critics of the regime were sentenced to prison by special courts or were terrorized, tortured or murdered by Blackshirt thugs. News was censored and public meetings could not be held without the government's permission. The new Fascist state was based on the doctrine that the welfare of the state is all-important and that the individual exists only for the state, owes everything to it, and has no right of protection against it. It was a return to the despotism of the later Roman Empire.

A Return to The Roman Empire?

Mussolini, like other Italian leaders before him, longed to create a new Roman empire and to bring back Italy's lost glory. So, in 1935, with his large army and recently expanded navy, he attacked and conquered the weak, backward, and poorly defended African country of Ethiopia.

In October 1936, at Mussolini's invitation, the **Rome-Berlin Axis** was formed between Italy and Nazi Germany to oppose the power of France and England. At this time Mussolini was considered the stronger ally of the two. In April 1939, Italy invaded Albania, and which that time Italy and Germany became formal military allies.

But when Germany's program of aggression plunged it into war with England and France on September 3, 1939, Italy at first adopted the position of a non-belligerent. But on June 10, 1940, Italian forces attacked southeastern France in an invasion coordinated with German forces in the north.

Defeat in World War II

Italy lacked the military power, resources, and national will to fight a large-scale modern war. Within six months, Italian armies met defeat in Greece and North Africa. In fact a running joke during World War II was that Italian tanks had only one gear: reverse. Italy then humbly accepted the military assistance of Germany. This soon grew into complete economic and military dependence, and Italy was forced to let Germany occupy it, control its home affairs, and Mussolini became a German puppet.

The end of the war found Italy with the majority of its industry and agriculture shattered. During its occupation, the Germans had almost stripped Italy's industry bare by commandeering supplies. Italian factories, roads, docks, and entire villages were ruined by the Allied bombing raids and during the invasion. To make things worse, as the Germans retreated they had wrecked whatever industries and transportation remained.

Even with the Allies contributing substantial quantities of food, clothing, and other supplies, the people were cold, hungry, and jobless. After the war, the United Nations Relief and Rehabilitation Administration gave more aid to Italy than to any other country. Reconstruction lagged, however, because of internal political turmoil, a situation that has become something of a theme in postwar Italian politics.

Postwar Political Changes

On June 2, 1946, the Italian people voted to found a republic. They then elected deputies to a Constituent Assembly to draft a new constitution. On February 10, 1947, the peace treaty between Italy and the Allies was ready to be signed. The treaty stripped Italy of its African 'empire' of Libya, Italian Somaliland, and Eritrea. The pact also ceded the Dodecanese Islands to

Greece, placed Trieste under UN protection, made minor boundary changes with France, and gave about 3,000 square miles to Yugoslavia, including most of the Istrian peninsula.

Italy had to pay $360 million in reparations, and was also forced to restore independence to Ethiopia and Albania. One lone gain was that **South Tyrol**, which Austria had been forced to cede after World War I, remained with Italy; and eventually, in 1954, **Trieste** was given to Italy through a pact with Yugoslavia.

On January 1, 1948, Italy's newly formed constitution became effective. It banned the Fascist party – though today there are a number of political parties in Italy that go by another name but informally call themselves *Fascisti* – and the monarchy. Freedom of religion was guaranteed, though Catholicism remained the state religion.

But a constitution alone cannot recreate a country. Italian leaders had the double task of creating a stable parliamentary system of government while at the same time restoring the economy. (They still haven't solved the first problem.) The main economic hindrance was the poverty-stricken, agriculturally dependent south contributing little to the improving industrial economy of the north. As a result there were many riots and moments of intense civil unrest.

Land Reform

One of the reasons that the south of Italy was so poor was because much the lands there, as well as in Sicily and Sardinia were among the last aristocratic strongholds of large-scale landowners. The estates of these landowners covered many thousands of acres and employed only small numbers of laborers, mostly at harvest time. These landless peasants, who had no work during much of the year, lived in nearby villages and small towns and barely made ends meet all year. These people either stayed peaceful and subservient, contributed to civil unrest, or emigrated to find better employment and living conditions elsewhere.

In the early 1950s, the Italian parliament passed special land reform laws that divided large private estates into small farms and distributed them to the peasants. The new owners were given substantial government support for their first years on the land, and the previous owners received cash compensation. Thousands of new small farms were created in this way during the 1950s, and farm production, as a result of the land reform and other measures, rose quickly.

The Italian government not only invested large sums of money in land reform but at the same time also started to develop the infrastructure in the south to help the farmers. New roads were built to help carry produce to market, and new irrigation systems, needed during the long, dry summers, were constructed. Warehouses and cold storage facilities for farm products were provided, and the government also helped to introduce new crops.

Chaos Mixed With Stability

Even with the south's new-found prosperity, Italy's economic development was mainly due to spectacular gains in industrial production in the north. But then during the mid-1960s, Italy began to suffer from severe inflation. A government austerity program to combat this trend produced a decline in profits and a lag in investments. To add insult to injury, devastating floods – the worst in 700 years which were caused by severe soil erosion – hit the country in 1966, ravaging one third of the land and causing losses of more than $1.5 billion. To make matters even worse, some of the priceless art treasures of Florence were irreparably damaged when the flood waters poured through that city.

In 1971 Italy had its largest economic recession since the country's post-World War II recovery. Strikes affected nearly every sector of the economy as Italian workers demanded social reforms. The problems of inflation, unemployment, lack of housing, and unfavorable balance of payments continued in the 1970s.

When Italy was about to pull out of its economic problems, political terrorism escalated, culminating in March 1978, when **Aldo Moro**, leader of the Christian Democratic party and former premier, was abducted in Rome by the **Red Brigades**, an extreme left-wing terrorist group. During the two months that Moro was held, Rome was like an armed camp, with military roadblocks everywhere. I was living there at that time and the memory of sub-machine guns being pointed at me still lingers. Eventually Moro was found murdered and left in the trunk of his car.

In 1980, in Italy's worst natural disaster in more than 70 years, an earthquake killed more than 3,000 persons in the Naples area. As if things could only get worse, in May 1981 a Turkish political dissident tried to kill Pope John Paul II in St. Peter's Square. Also in 1981, a corruption scandal involving hundreds of public servants who were allegedly members of a secret society erupted and brought down the government.

Economic conditions in the early 1980s were affected by growing recession and rising inflation. The Vatican Bank and the Banco Ambrosiano of Milan, Italy's biggest private banking group, were involved in a major banking scandal that forced the liquidation of Banco Ambrosiano in 1982. Two more natural disasters, an earthquake and a landslide, caused widespread damage in the regions of Perugia and Ancona in late 1982.

In 1989, another bank became involved in a scandal when it was revealed that an American branch of the Banca Nazionale del Lavoro had loaned billions of dollars to Iraq. Then severe drought occurred throughout Italy in the winter of 1989 and in Venice some canals were unusable because water levels had dropped so low. And still, into the late 1990s, the Italian government is under intense investigation for rampant corruption which includes officials taking bribes from, or actively colluding with members of the Mafia.

Despite all of this, the Italian economy continues to improve, to the point where it is one of the more successful in Europe. Throughout all of this chaos, Italy perseveres. It's almost as if without a reasonable amount of disorder, Italy could not survive.

Most recently, a separatist political party has emerged, called the **Northern League** (La Lega Nord) is attempting to create the 'federal republic of Padania' in the industrial north of Italy. Founded in 1984, the party is now gaining support and popularity because most northern Italians feel that they pay a disproportionate share of the country's taxes. Taxes which they say go to support the impoverished south and keep the bloated government functioning in Rome.

This idea of splitting Italy in two is not so far fetched when you realize that only in the last century has the peninsula been one unified country. There have always been glaring differences in culture between south and central Italy and their northern cousins. And to emphasize this point, in the last local elections, the Northern League won over 10% of the vote.

What's New?

Italy has raced into the 21st century along with the rest of Europe by adopting a new currency, the **Euro**, which will join the economies of a number of countries and help the Europeans counterbalance the economic power of America and the almighty dollar. The jury is still out on the impact this will have.

To get to the point where they could be included in this economic gambit, Italy had to pass some rather unpopular laws. The ones which were most controversial were the those associated with food production. Italy is home to some of the world's most diverse food products, all made with time-honored tradition, but sometimes these traditions did not meet hygienic standards required by the European Union. Despite the outcry over having to change the way their beloved food is made, since these standards were imposed food poisonings have decreased all over Italy and the quality and taste of the food products have stayed the same.

Immigration is another issue Italy shares with its European brethren. The economies of Third World countries are not keeping pace with those in the First World. As a result all of Europe is experiencing unparalleled immigration pressure from Africa, the Middle East, Asia, and Eastern Europe. Italy is being especially overrun with refugees from the Balkans, who initially came to avoid the recent war there, but are now escaping their stagnant economies as well.

All of these changes seem to have enhanced the pleasant chaos that is life in Italy.

planning your trip

Chapter 5

Climate & Weather

The climate in Italy is as varied as the country itself, but it never seems to get too harsh. As a result any time is a good time to travel to Italy since most of the country has a Mediterranean type of climate, meaning cool, slightly rainy winters and warm, dry summers.

The summers are mild in the north, but winters there tend to be colder because these regions are in or near the Alps. The Alps do play a role in protecting the rest of Italy from cold northern winds. Because Italy is a peninsula and thus surrounded by water, the entire country never seems to get too hot except for the south and Sicily.

Winter is the rainy season, when stream beds that remain empty during much of the year fill to overflowing. Rome has the mildest climate all year round, although the *sirocco* – a hot and humid red sand tinged wind blowing from North Africa – can produce stifling weather in August every other year or so. The climate in Tuscany and Umbria is very similar to Rome's, although winters are colder in Florence. But winters are very moderate with snow being extremely rare; still, it is wise to dress warmly.

When to Go

Basically, anytime is good time to travel to Italy. The climate doesn't vary greatly making Italy a pleasant trip any time of year. Then again I'm biased – I spent eight wonderful years in Italy and I think it's fantastic all year. The busiest tourist season is from May to October, leaving the off-season of spring and autumn as the choice times to have Italy all to yourself.

I do believe though that the best time to go is the off-season, when there are less tourists around. More specifically, October and November and March and April are perfect times not only because of the weather but also because of the lack of tourists. December is also fun because there are so many festivals during the Christmas season.

Most people come during the summer making many of the most popular tourist cities like Rome, Florence and Venice over crowded. Then in August the entire country literally shuts down, since most Italians abandon the cities to vacation at the beach or in the mountains. Personally I find August a wonderful time to visit too, since the cities become sparse with people. Granted many restaurants, shops and businesses are closed during this time, but the country is still as scenic and beautiful.

The early summer months, though packed with people in the cities, are great months to come and visit the hiking trails of the Alps and Appenines. Remember to bring clothing for colder weather even though it is summer.

The sidebar below offers you a breakdown by season of the best regions to visit during those times.

What to Pack

One suitcase and a carry-on should suffice for your average ten day trip. Maybe the best advice for shoppers is to pack light and buy clothes while you're there, since there are countless clothing stores from which you can buy yourself any needed item. Also if you pack light it will be easier to transport your belongings. A suitcase with wheels is important, but since there are endless numbers of stairs even the wheels won't relieve the burden of lifting your bag every once and awhile. And even if there are no stairs, because of the uneven state of Italian pavements, and in some cases non-existent sidewalks, pulling a wheel suitcase can be cumbersome. I prefer a wheeled carry-on, but if you're the rugged type, a back pack is the best choice.

You can always find a local Tintoria (dry cleaner) if your hotel does not supply such a service. If you want to clean your own clothes, it's best to look for a Lavanderia – coin operated laundromat – instead. Remember also to pack all your personal cosmetic items that you've grown accustomed to, since, more than likely, they're not available in Italian stores. The Italian culture just hasn't seemed to grasp the necessity of having 400 types of toothpaste, or 200 types of tampons. If you take medication remember to get the drug's generic name because name brands on medications are different all over the world.

An important item to remember, especially if you're traveling in the winter time, is an umbrella, a raincoat, and water-proof shoes. You never know when the rain will fall in the winter. You should also bring a small pack, or knapsack to carry with you on day trips. A money belt is also advised, because of pick pockets though I've never had any problems. The same can be said for handbags and purses to thwart the potential risk of purse snatchers.

But most importantly, bring a good pair of comfortable walking shoes or hiking boots. A light travel iron is not a bad idea if you cannot abide wrinkles; but a more sensible option is to pack wrinkle free clothes. And in the summer, if you want to get into most of the churches, remember to pack long pants or something to cover your legs. Tank tops and halter top type shirts are also not considered appropriate attire.

And finally, an important item to remember if you are sexually active are condoms. They can be expensive in Italy so remember to bring along your own.

Public Holidays

Offices and shops in Italy are closed on the dates below. So prepare for the eventuality of having virtually everything closed and stock up on picnic snacks, soda, whatever, because in most cities and towns there is no such thing as a 24 hour a day 7-11. The Italians take their free time seriously. To them the concept of having something open 24 hours a day is, well, a little crazy. Florence's feast day is June 24th; St. John the Baptist is the patron saint.
• **January 1**, New Year's Day
• **January 6**, Epiphany
• **April 25**, Liberation Day (1945)
• **Easter Monday**
• **May 1**, Labor Day
• **August 15**, *Ferragosto* and Assumption of the Blessed Virgin (climax of Italian family holiday season. Hardly anything stays open in the big cities through the month of August)
• **November 1**, All Saints Day
• **December 8**, Immaculate Conception
• **December 25/26**, Christmas

Listed below are some dates that may be considered public holidays in different areas of Italy, so prepare for them too:
• **Ascension**
• **Corpus Christi**
• **June 2**, Proclamation of Republic (celebrated on the following Saturday)
• **November 4**, National Unity Day (celebrated on following Saturday)

Making Airline Reservations

Since airfares can vary so widely it is advised to contact a reputable travel agent and stay abreast of all promotional fares advertised in the newspapers. Once you're ticketed getting there is a breeze. Just hop on the plane and 6-8 hours later you're there. Italy's two main international airports are Rome's **Fiumicino** (also known as **Leonardo da Vinci**) and Milan's **Malpensa**, which handle all incoming flights from North America and Australia.

There are other, smaller regional airports in Bologna, Florence, Pisa and Venice that accept flights from all over Europe as well as the United Kingdom, but not from North America or Australia. See later in this chapter, *Getting to Tuscany & Umbria,* for details.

Fares are highest during the peak summer months (June through mid-September) and lowest from November through March (except during peak Christmas travel time). You can get the best fares by booking far in advance. This will also assure you a good seat. Getting a non-stop flight to Italy at the last minute is simply an impossibility during the high season. If you are concerned about having to change your schedule at the last minute, and do not want to book far in advance, look into some special **travel insurance** that will cover the cost of your ticket under such circumstances. Check with your travel agent about details and pricing since these, like ticket prices, change almost on a daily basis.

Passport Regulations

A visa is not required for US or Canadian citizens, or members of the European Economic Community, who are holding a valid passport, unless that person expects to stay in Italy longer than 90 days and/or study or seek employment. While in Italy, you can apply for a longer stay at any police station for an extension of an additional 90 days. You will be asked to prove that you're not seeking such an extension for study or employment, and that you have adequate means of support. Usually permission is granted almost immediately.

When staying at a hotel, you will need to produce your passport when you register; and most likely the desk clerk will need to keep your passport overnight to transcribe the relevant details for their records. Your passport will most likely be returned that same day. If not, make sure you request it since it is an Italian law that identification papers be carried at all times. Usually a native driver's license will suffice but I always carry my passport. If you are concerned about pickpockets, keep your passport in the front pocket of your pants. I keep mine in a small zip lock bag so it won't get moist with perspiration.

To find out all the information you need to know about applying for a US Passport go to the State Department website at *http://travel.state.gov/ passport_services.html.*

If you have failed to renew your passport and you need one right away try **Instant Passport***, Tel. 800/284-2564, www.instantpassport.com.* They promise to give you 24-hour turnaround from the time they receive your passport pictures and requisite forms. They charge $100 plus overnight shipping on top of all fees associated with passport issuance.

Another company, **American Passport Express***, Tel. 800/841-6778, www.americanpassport.com,* offers three types of service – expedited (24 hours), express (three to four business days) and regular. Prices range from $245 to $135.

For **Canadian travelers**, the Canadian Passport Office *(www.dfait-maeci.gc.ca/passport/menu.asp)* also offers an excellent web site to help walk you through the steps to apply for the passport.

For **British travelers**, the United Kingdom Passport Agency *(www.ukpa.gov.uk)* offers a similar level of exemplary service on their web site.

Vaccinations

No vaccinations are required to enter Italy, or for that matter, to re-enter the U.S., Canada, or any other European country. But some people are starting to think it may be wise, especially for Hepatitis A. One of those people is Donna Shipley, B.S.N, R.N. and President of Smart Travel, an international health service organization. She says, "Even though the perception is that Italy is safe and clean, it is still not like North America. In other words it is better to be safe than sorry. Prevention makes sense."

For information about vaccinations contact:
• **Smart Travel**, *Tel. 800/730-3170*

Travel Insurance

This is the most frequently forgotten precaution in travel. Just like other insurance, this is for 'just in case' scenarios. The beauty of travel insurance is that it covers a wide variety of occurrences, such as trip cancellation or interruption, trip delay/missed connection, itinerary change, accident medical expense, sickness medical expense, baggage and baggage delay, and medical evacuation/repatriation. And to get all that for a week long trip will only cost you $25. You'll spend more than that on the cab ride from the airport when you arrive.

For travel insurance look in your local yellow pages or contact the well-known international organization below:
• **Travelex**, *Tel. 800/228-9792*

Customs Regulations

Duty free entry is allowed for personal effects that will not be sold, given away, or traded while in Italy: clothing, bicycle, moped no bigger than 50cc, books, camping and household equipment, fishing tackle, one pair of skis, two tennis racquets, portable computer, record player with 10 records, tape recorder or Dictaphone, baby carriage, two still cameras with 10 rolls of film for each, one movie camera with 10 rolls of film (I suppose they mean 10 cassette tapes now), binoculars, personal jewelry, portable radio set (may be subject to small license fee), 400 cigarettes, and a quantity of cigars or pipe tobacco not to exceed 500 grams (1.1 lbs), two bottles of wine and one bottle of liquor, 4.4 lbs of coffee, 6.6 lbs of sugar, and 2.2 lbs of cocoa. This is Italy's official list, but they are very flexible with personal items. As well they should be, since technology is changing so rapidly that items not listed last year could be a personal item for most people this year (i.e. Sony Watchmans, portable video games, etc.).

Getting to Italy

FLYING TO ITALY

Alitalia is Italy's national airline. As you probably know, most international carriers have amazing service, pristine environments, serve exquisite food and overall are a joy to travel – but to be honest Alitalia is not one of them. If you want to experience the chaos of Italy at 30,000 feet, fly Alitalia. Despite all of this rhetoric, Alitalia does have the most frequent direct flights from North America to Italy, and as such they are the most convenient carrier to take to Italy.

Airlines

Below is a list of some other major carriers and their flights to Italy:
- **Alitalia**, *Tel. 800/223-5730 in US, www.alitalia.it/eng/index.html. Toll free in Italy 800/1478/65642. Address in Rome – Via Bissolati 13.* Flights from the United States, Canada, and the United Kingdom.
- **Air Canada**, *Tel. 800/776-3000; www.aircanada.com. Toll free in Italy 800/862-216. Rome address – Via C. Veneziani 58.* Flights from Canada to London or Paris, then connections on another carrier to Rome or Milan.
- **American Airlines**, *Tel. 800/433-7300; www.americanair.com. Rome Tel. 06/4274-1240, Via Sicilia 50. Italy E-mail: abtvlaa@tin.it.* Direct flights from Chicago to Milan.
- **British Airways**, *Tel. 800/247-9297; www.british-airways.com. Toll free in Italy 1478/12266. Rome address – Via Bissolati 54.* Connections through London's Heathrow to Rome, Milan, Bologna, Venice, and Palermo.

Registration by Tourists
This is usually taken care of within three days by the management of your hotel. If you are staying with friends or in a private home, you must register in person at the nearest police station within that three day period. Rome has a special police information office to assist tourists, and they have interpreters available: *Tel. 461-950 or 486-609.*

- **Delta**, *Tel. 800/221-1212; www.delta-air.com. Toll free in Italy 800/864-114. Rome address – Via Po 10.* Direct flights from New York to Rome or Milan.
- **Northwest**, *Tel. 800/2245-2525; www.nwa.com. KLM in Rome 06/652-9286.* Flights to Amsterdam connecting to KLM and onto Rome or Milan.
- **TWA**, *Tel. 800/221-2000; www.twa.com. Toll free in Italy 800/841-843. Rome address – Via Barberini 59.* Direct flights from New York's JFK to Rome or Milan.
- **United**, *Tel. 800/538-2929; www.ual.com. Rome Tel. 06/4890-4140, Via Bissolati 54.* Direct flights from Washington Dulles to Milan.
- **US Airways,** *Tel. 800/622-1015; www.ual.com. Toll free in Italy 800/870-945.* Direct flights from Philadelphia to Rome.

Discount Travel Agents

The best way to find a travel agency for your travel to Italy is by looking in your local yellow pages; but if you want to get the same flights for less, the three organizations below offer the lowest fares available. I have had the best service and best prices from *www.lowestfare.com*, but the others are good also.

- **Fly Cheap**, *Tel. 800/FLY-CHEAP*
- **Fare Deals, Ltd.**, *Tel. 800/347-7006*
- **Lowestfare.com**, *Tel. 888/777-2222*
- **Airdeals.com**, *Tel. 888/999-2174*

In conjunction, listed below are some online travel booking services that offer great fares. Online travel searching can be cumbersome, since there is a registration process and each has a different approach to the reservation and booking process. In essence, what you learn from these services is what your travel agent goes through when they work with reservation systems like Apollo, Worldspan and System One. Also, if you shop here to find out what prices and availability are and then book your flights the regular way, from the airline or a live travel agent, these online service do not like that. Some will even terminate your registration if you shop too frequently without buying.

With that said, here are some websites:
- **Internet Travel Network**, *www.itn.net*
- **Preview Travel**, *www.previewtravel.com*
- **Expedia**, *www.expedia.com*
- **Travelocity**, *www.travelocity.com*

Courier Flights

Acting as an air courier – whereby you accompany shipments sent by air in your cargo space in return for discounted airfare – can be one of the least expensive ways to fly. It can also be a little restrictive and inconvenient. But if you want to travel to Italy, at almost half the regular fare, being a courier is for you.

The hassles are (1) that in most cases you have to get to the courier company's offices before your flight, (2) most flights only originate from one city and that may not be the one where you are, (3) since you usually check in later than all other flyers you may not get your choice of seating, (4) you can only use a carry-on since your cargo space is being allocated for the shipment you are accompanying, (5) your length of stay is usually only 7-10 days – no longer, and (6) courier flights don't do companion flights, which means you fly alone.

But contrary to the common impression, as a courier you usually do not even see the goods being transported and you don't need to check them through customs. Also you are not legally responsible for the shipment's contents – that's the courier company's responsibility – according to industry sources and US Customs. All this aside, if you are interested in saving a large chunk of change, give these services a try:
- **Halbart Express**, *Tel. 718/656-8189*
- **Now Voyager**, *Tel. 212/431-1616. Fee of $50*
- **Discount Travel International**, *Tel. 212/362-8113*
- **Airhitch**, *Tel. 212/864-2000; www.airhitch.org.* Air hitching is the least expensive but they are also the most restrictive. You really need to be very flexible, i.e. can travel at the drop of a hat.

For more information about courier flights, listed below are some books you can buy or organizations you can contact:
- **"Insiders Guide to Air Courier Bargains"** *by Kelly Monaghan. Tel. 212/ 569-1081.* Contact: The Intrepid Traveler, *Tel. 212/569-1081; www.intrepidtraveler.com.* Company is owned by Monaghan.
- **International Association of Air Travel Couriers**, *Tel. 561/582-8320, www.courier.org.*
- **"A Simple Guide to Courier Travel,"** *Tel. 800/344-9375*

Getting to Tuscany & Umbria

There are a number of ways to get to Tuscany and Umbria. One of which is to fly directly into Rome, non-stop, then take the train where you want to go. Other options include flying into another location in Europe, then flying into either the airport in Florence or Pisa. These airports are smaller than Leonardo da Vinci in Rome and do not accommodate transatlantic flights. See information about airports below.

THE FLORENCE AIRPORT

Florence's **Aeroporto Amerigo Vespucci**, *www.airport.florence.it/*, has an information desk in the arrival terminal which is open from 7:30am to

11:30pm everyday. It provides tourist information, *Tel. 055/315874*, and information on flight arrivals and departures, *Tel. 055/3061300*, as well as information on lost baggage, *Tel. 055/30061302*. The information desk can also be reached by fax at *055/315874* or E-mail: *infoaeroporto@safnet.it*. Automated flight information is available also: domestic flights *Tel. 055/306-1700*, international flights *Tel. 055/306-1702*.

Taxi Service

The bus service is the best and least expensive way to get to Florence from the airport, but if you want to go by taxi, there is a taxi stand outside the main exit from the airport. *Tel. 055/4242, 4798, 4390, 4499*.

Bus Service

The SITA station (Via Caterina da Siena 17- Florence, *Tel. 055/214-721, Toll-free in Italy 800/373-760, 800/424-500*, is located next to the train station in Florence. Buses leave frequently between the bus station and the airport, typically once or twice an hour for most of the day.

Car Rental
• **Avis**, *Tel. 055/315-588* (open 8:00am-11:30pm)
• **Hertz**, *Tel. 055/307-370* (open 8:30am-10:30pm; Saturday-Sunday 9:30am-10:30pm)
• **Maggiore/National**, *Tel. 055/311-256* (open 8:30am-10:50pm)

THE PISA AIRPORT

Pisa's **Aeroporto Galileo Galilei,** *www.pisa-airport.com/* (in Italian), has an information office open every day from 8:00am until 10:00pm, *Tel. 050/500-707*. They dispense tourist information, flight information, and can store your bags for you.

Taxi Service

At the airport the taxi stand is right outside the exit of the airport. To call a radio taxi: *Tel. 050 541600*.

The train station in Pisa is about five minutes from the airport; the taxi stand is located directly in front of the station, *Tel. 050/41252*. In town, there's a taxi stand in the Piazza Duomo, *Tel. 050/561-878*.

Train Schedule

You can take a train from the Pisa Airport directly into Florence in a little over an hour and a half. Trains leave frequently for other destinations throughout Tuscany and the rest of Italy, for the most part once an hour or more every day for most of the day.

Car Rental
- **Avis**, *Tel. 050/42028, 42028*
- **Hertz**, *Tel. 050/43220, 49156*
- **Maggiore**, *Tel. 050/ 42574, 42574*
- **Thrifty** (Italy by Car), *Tel. 050/45490, 45356*

Hotel Accommodations
What to Expect at Hotels

Don't be surprised by hotel taxes, additional charges, and requests for payment for extras, such as air conditioning that make your bill larger than expected. Sometimes these taxes/service charges are included in room rates but you should check upon arrival or when you make your reservation. Remember to save receipts from hotels and car rentals, as 15% to 20% of the value-added taxes (VAT) on these services may be refunded if you are a non-resident. For more information, call **I.T.S. Fabry**, *Tel. 803/720-8646* or see Chapter 8, *Shopping*, Tax-Free Shopping section.

The Italian Tourist Board categorizes all of the hotels in Italy with a star rating. A five star deluxe hotel (*****) is the best, a one-star hotel (*) is the least desirable and usually the least expensive too. The term *Pensione* is in the process of being phased out, and these smaller, bed-and-breakfast type inns are being replaced with a designation of one-star (*), two-star (**), or three star (***) hotel.

Making Reservations

I recommend faxing the hotel(s) of your choice inquiring about availability for the dates you are interested in, as well as the rate for those dates. Faxing is preferable to calling since you can quickly and easily communicate your information, reducing any long distance telephone charges. Obviously if the hotel listed has an e-mail address, that form of communication is preferable.

Also, since most Italians who run hotels speak English, it is possible to write your fax or e-mail in English; but if you want to practice your Italian, they usually appreciate any effort at communicating in their own language. Personally, I write my requests in both English and Italian so that there is no confusion as to the information imparted.

When writing the dates you are interested in, make sure you spell out the month, since here in America we transpose the month and day in numeric dates. For example, in the US January 10, 2001 would appear numerically as 1/10/01. In Europe, it would appear as 10/01/01. See where the confusion could come in?

Expect a reply to your communication within a few days. If you do not get a reply send another message. Sometimes faxes get lost in the night shift. To book your room you will need to send the hotel a credit card number with expiration date in a reply communication. This will ensure that you show up.

So if you have to cancel your trip for whatever reason, make sure you contact the hotel and cancel your room – otherwise you will be charged.

Hotel Prices

The prices that are listed sometimes include a range, for example E50-75. The first number in the range indicates what the price is during the off-season, the second price is the going rate during high season. If there is no range, then the hotel doesn't raise its rate for the off-season.

The high season is generally April through September, with Christmas and New Year's week thrown in. Other high seasons will include local festivals, like the **Palio** in Siena or **Calcio in Costume** in Florence. Also, the high season for the ski areas will be winter, not summer, so it is important to inquire up front about what the actual rates will be.

Hotel Rating System

The star rating system that the Italian Tourist Board officially uses has little to do with the prices of the hotels, but more to do with the amenities you will find. The prices for each category will vary according to the locale, so if it's a big city, a four star will be super-expensive; if it's a small town, it will be priced like a three star in a big city.

In the ambiguous way of the Italians, nothing is ever as it seems, which means that even the amenities will be different for each star category depending on whether you are in a big city or a smaller town. But basically the list below is what the ratings mean by star category:

*****Five star, deluxe hotel**: Professional service, great restaurant, perfectly immaculate large rooms and bathrooms with air conditioning, satellite TV, mini-bar, room service, laundry service, and every convenience you could imagine to make you feel like a king or queen. Bathrooms in every room.

****Four star hotel**: professional service, most probably they have a restaurant, clean rooms not so large, air conditioning, TV (usually via satellite), mini-bar, room service, laundry service and maybe a few more North American-like amenities. Bathrooms in every room.

***Three star hotel**: a little less professional service, most probably do not have room service, should have air conditioning, TV and mini bar, but the rooms are mostly small as are their bathrooms. Some rooms in small town hotels may not have bathrooms.

Two star hotel: Usually a family run place, some not so immaculate and well taken care of as higher rated hotels. Mostly you'll only find a telephone in the room, and in big cities you'll be lucky to get air conditioning. About 50% of the rooms have either a shower/bath or water closet and sometimes not both together. Hardly any amenities, just a place to lay your head. The exception to this is in small towns, where some two stars are as well appointed as some of the best three stars.

*One star hotel: Here you usually get a small room with a bed, sometimes you have to share the rooms with other travelers. The bathroom is usually in the hall. No air conditioning, no telephone in the room, just a room with bed. These are what used to be the low-end *pensiones*. Definitely for budget travelers.

Agriturismo

If you have ever wanted to work on a farm, Italy has a well organized system where you can do just that. Initially the idea behind **Agriturismo** started as a way for urban Italians to re-connect with their old towns and villages, and through that to the earth again; but every year it has grown in popularity. Traditionally you would rent rooms in family farmhouses, but some accommodations have evolved into more hotel type, bed-and-breakfast like situations with separate buildings on the farms for agriturists. Since there is such a large demand for agriturism, two separate competing bodies have published directories to assist people trying to reconnect with mother nature.

Both of the books sold by these groups are also available at selected bookstores, like the Feltrinelli Bookstores listed in this guide:

- **Agriturist**, Via Vittorio Emanuele 89, 00186 Roma, Tel. *06/658-342*. Open Monday-Friday 10:00am-noon and Tuesday, Wednesday, Thursday 3:30-5:30pm. Closed Saturday and Sunday.
- **Turismo Verde** (Green Tourism), Via Mariano Fortuny 20, 00196 Roma, Tel. *06/361-1051*.

Mountain Refuges

There are a number of mountain refuges (*rifugi*) available for rent in the Alps and Apennines, many of which are run by the **Club Alpino Italiano (CAI)**. If you are a member, you can get maps and information about hiking, and all necessary information about the *rifugi*. The CAI has offices all over Italy, but there is limited centralization of resources and information, and most offices are run by volunteers and/or avid hikers. Contact the CAI offices listed below, or the local tourist office in the city nearby where you want to go hiking, for any available information.

Even if you are not a member, they are usually rather flexible about accommodating your needs. And if they are not, you can join CAI at any of their offices by simply bringing a photo of yourself and E50. With that you will receive a tessera (identification document) which is valid for discounts on all CAI merchandise and on stays in the *rifugi* for a year. You can renew by mail.

The *rifugi* are generally dormitory style and meals are available at a cost of around E12 per person. There are private *rifugi* which charge rates comparable to about one or two star hotel accommodations. All rifugi are

usually only open from July to September and are booked well in advance.
- **CAI–Milano**, Via Silvio Pellico 6, *Tel. 02/8646-3516.*
- **CAI–Roma**, 305 Corso Vittorio Emanuelle II, 4th floor, *Tel. 06/686-1011, Fax 06/6880-3424, www.frascati.enea.it/cai*

Renting Villas & Apartments

One of the best ways to spend a vacation in Italy is in a rented villa in the country or in an apartment in the center of town. It makes you feel as if you actually are living in Italy and not just passing through. Staying in "your own place" gives your trip that little extra sense of belonging.

The best way to find a place of your own in Italy is to contact one of the agencies listed below that specialize in the rental of villas and apartments in Italy:
- **At Home Abroad, Inc.**, 405 East 58th Street, New York, NY 10022. *Tel. 212/421-9165, Fax 212/752-1591*
- **Astra Maccioni Kohane** (CUENDET), 10 Columbus Circle, Suite 1220, New York, NY 10019. *Tel. 212/765-3924, Fax 212/262-0011*
- **B&D De Vogue International, Inc.**, 250 S. Beverly Drive, Suite 203, Beverly Hills CA. *Tel. 310/247 8612, 800/438-4748, Fax 310/247-9460*
- **Better Homes and Travel**, 30 East 33rd Street, New York, NY 10016. *Tel. 212/689 6608, Fax 212/679-5072*
- **CIT Tours Corp.**, 342 Madison Ave #207, New York, NY 10173. *Tel. 212/697-2100, 800/248-8687, Fax 212/697-1394*
- **Columbus Travel**, 507 Columbus Avenue, San Francisco, CA 94153. *Tel. 415/39S2322, Fax 415/3984674*
- **Destination Italia, Inc.**, 165 Chestnut Street, Allendale, NJ 07401. *Tel. 201/327-2333, Fax 201/825-2664*
- **Europa-let, Inc.** 92 N. Main Street or P.O. Box 3537, Ashland, OR 97520. *Tel. 503/482-5806, 800/4624486, Fax 503/482-0660*
- **European Connection**, 4 Mineola Avenue, Roslyn Heights, NY 11577. *Tel. 516/625-1800, 800/345 4679, Fax 516/625-1138*
- **Four Star Living, Inc.**, 640 Fifth Avenue, New York, NY 10019. *Tel. 212/518 3690, Fax 914/677-5528*
- **Heaven on Hearth**, 44 Kittyhawk, Pittsford, NY 14534. *Tel. 716/381-7625, Fax 716/381-9784*
- **Hidden Treasure of Italy**, 934 Elmwood, Wilmette IL 60091. *Tel. 708/853-1313. Fax 708/853-1340*
- **Hideaways International**, P.O. Box 1270, Littleton, MA 01460. *Tel. 508/486-8955, 800/8434433, Fax 508/486-8525*
- **Homes International**, Via L. Bissolati 20, 00187 Rome, Italy. *Tel. 39/06/488-1800, Fax 39/06/488-1808. E-mail: homesint@tin.it*
- **Home Tours International**, 1170 Broadway, New York, NY 10001. *Tel. 212/6894851, Outside New York 800/367-4668*

- **Interhome Inc.**, 124 Little Falls Road, Fairfield, NJ 07004. *Tel. 201/882-6864, Fax 201/8051 742*
- **International Home Rentals**, P.O. Box 329, Middleburg, VA 22117. *Tel. 703/687-3161, 800/221-9001, Fax 703/687-3352*
- **International Services**, P.O. Box 118, Mendham, NJ 07945. *Tel. 201/545-9114, Fax; 201/543-9159*
- **Invitation to Tuscany**, 94 Winthrop Street, Augusta, ME 04330. *Tel. 207/622-0743*
- **Italian Rentals**, 3801 Ingomar Street, N.W., Washington, D.C. 20015. *Tel. 202/244-5345, Fax 202/362-0520*
- **Italian Villa Rentals**, P.O. Box 1145, Bellevue, Washington 98009. *Tel 206/827-3964, Telex: 3794026, Fax 206/827-2323*
- **Italy Farm Holidays**, 547 Martling Avenue, Tarrytown, NY 10591. *Tel. 914/631-7880, Fax 914/631-8831*
- **LNT Associates, Inc.**, P.O. Box 219, Warren, MI 48090. *Tel. 313/739-2266, 800/582 4832, Fax 313/739-3312*
- **Massimo Carli**, *www.incentro.it*
- **Overseas Connection**, 31 North Harbor Drive, Sag Harbor, NY 11963. *Tel. 516/725-9308, Fax 516/725-5825*
- **Palazzo Antellesi**, 175 West 92nd Street #1GE, New York NY 10025. *Tel. 212/932-3480, Fax 212/932-9039*
- **The Parker Company**, 319 Lynnway, Lynn MA 01901. *Tel. 617/596-8282, Fax 617/596-3125*
- **Prestige Villas**, P.O. Box 1046, Southport, CT 06490. *Tel. 203/254-1302.* Outside Connecticut: *Tel. 800/336-0080, Fax 203/254-7261*
- **Rent a Home International, Inc.**, 7200 34th Avenue. N.W. Seattle, WA 98117. *Tel. 206/789-9377, 800/488-RENT, Fax 206/789-9379, Telex 40597*
- **Rentals In Italy**, Suzanne T. Pidduck (CUENDET), 1742 Calle Corva, Camarillo, CA 93010. *Tel. 805/987-5278, 800/726-6702, Fax 805/482-7976*
- **Rent-A-Vacation Everywhere, Inc**. (RAVE), 585 Park Avenue, Rochester, NY 14607. *Tel. 716/256-0760, Fax 716/256-2676*
- **Unusual Villa Rentals**, Tel. 804/288-2823. Fax 804/342-9016. *E-mail: johng@unusualvillarentals.com; www.unusualvillarentals.com*
- **Vacanze In Italia**, P.O. Box 297, Falls Village, CT 06031. *Tel. 413/528-6610, Fax 413/528-6222. E-mail: villrent@taconic.net. Web: www.homeabroad.com*
- **Villas and Apartments Abroad, Ltd.**, 420 Madison Avenue. New York, NY 10017. *Tel. 212/759-1025. 800/433-3021 (nationwide), 800/433-3020 (NY)*
- **Villas International**, 605 Market Street, Suite 610, San Francisco, CA 94105. *Tel. 415/281-0910, 800/221-2260, Fax 415/281-0919*

Youth Hostels

Youth Hostels (ostelli per la gioventu) provide reasonably priced accommodations, specifically for younger travelers. A membership card is needed that is associated with the youth hostel's organization, i.e. a student ID card. Advanced booking is a must during the high season since these low priced accommodations fill up fast. Hundreds of youth hostels are located all over Italy. Contact the Tourist Information office when you arrive in the city to locate them.

Getting Around Italy

Italy is connected by an extensive highway system **(Autostrada)**, a superb train system, a series of regional airports, and naturally, since Italy is virtually surrounded by water and has a number of islands, a complete maritime service involving ferries, hydrofoils, and passenger liners. The mode of transportation you select will depend on how long you're staying in Italy and where you are going.

In general, if you have plenty of time on your hands, there will be no need to fly around Italy, and travel by train and car will suffice. If you are going to rural, off-the-beaten path locations, you'll need a car, because even if the train did go to where you're going, the **Locale** would take forever since it stops at every town along the way.

By Air

You can fly between many Italian destinations quite easily. If you are on business, using air travel makes sense to fly from Milan to Rome, but not if you are a tourist. You could enjoy a relaxing three hour train ride in the morning to Florence, spend a day shopping and sightseeing, then get on another three hour train ride to Rome and get there in time for dinner. And the entire cost would only be around $100, a lot less than if you had flown.

But if you insist on flying, here is a list of towns that have airports that receive service from the larger venues in Rome and Milan: Alghero, Ancona, Bari, Bologna, Brindisi, Cagliari, Catania, Firenze, Genoa, Lamezia Terme, Lampedusa, Napoli, Olbia, Pantelleria, Pescara, Pisa, Reggio Calabria, Torino, Trapani, Trieste, Venice, Verona.

By Bicycle

You may think that riding a bicycle among Italian drivers would be ludicrous, but they are actually very respectful and courteous of bicyclists. Cycling is a national sport in Italy, so your reception in Italy will be more as a hero than a villain, as you can all too often be viewed in North America. And if you get tired, one benefit of the Italian train system is that many trains have bicycle cars to accommodate travelers such as us. So if you get to one location and feel like you want a breather, or if you want to make better time, you can hop on trains to your next destination.

Another way to hike or bike around Italy is with an organized tour group. Two such organizations are **Ciclismo Classico**, and **BCT Scenic Walking**. They offer magnificent tours all over Italy, from Sardinia to Tuscany, to Venice and beyond. Their guides are extremely knowledgeable and professional and speak impeccable English. And with Ciclismo you stay at fine hotels, eat fantastic food, meet wonderful people, and constantly interact with the locals – all while seeing Italy up close and personal on a bicycle. I find this to be a truly authentic way to appreciate and experience Italy.

To get more information, contact **Ciclismo Classico**, 13 Marathon Street, Arlington MA 02174, *Tel. 800/866-7314 or 781/646-3377, Fax 617/641-1512, E-mail:info@ciclismoclassico.com, Web: www.ciclismoclassico.com.* **BCT Tours**, 2506 N. Clark St #150, Chicago, IL 60614, *Tel. 800/736-BIKE, Fax 773/404-1833, E-mail: adventure@cbttours. Web: www.cbttours.com.*

If you are an avid hiker, and enjoy seeing a country from the perspective of the back roads or trails, contact this excellent organization, **BCT** (British Coastal Trails) **Scenic Walking**, which offers some great walking tours of Italy, England and the rest of the European continent. **BCT Scenic Tours**, 703 Palomar Airport Road, Suite 200, Carlsbad CA 92009, *Tel. 800/473-1210 or 760/431-7306. Web: bctwalk.com.*

By Bus

Most long distance travel is done by train, but the regional bus systems can be beneficial for inter-city trips to smaller towns not serviced by rail lines, and the Pullman buses can be perfect for a very long trip. If you're not a rental car person, and you simply have to get to that beautiful little medieval hill town you saw from the train window, the only way you're going to get there is by regional bus. Also, if you're going from Florence to Bari to catch the ferry to Greece, it is more convenient to catch a direct bus since you won't have to stop in the Rome or Naples train station to pick up other passengers.

Conveniently, most bus stations are next door to or near the train station in most towns and cities. The Italian transportation system is something to be admired since they make it so convenient, and comfortable too. Hopefully one day Americans will wake up and learn that having a multiplicity of transportation options is better than being completely dependent on the automobile. In Italy, most long range buses are equipped with bathrooms and some have televisions on them (not that you'd understand what was on). The regional inter-town buses are a little less comfortable but still palatial compared to the same type of bus in Central America.

I suggest sticking to the trains, unless the trains don't go where you want to go – which is about everywhere.

By Car

The world's first automobile expressways were built in northern Italy during the 1920s. Today, Italy and Germany have the most extensive networks of fast, limited-access highways in Europe. Motorists can drive without encountering traffic lights or crossroads – stopping only for border crossings, rest, or fuel – from Belgium, Holland, France, or Germany across the Alps all the way to Sicily. Unlike in America, where our highways were designed for short trips with access every other mile or less, in Europe the highways are for long distance travel.

Two highway tunnels through the Alps, under the Great St. Bernard Pass and through Mont Blanc, enable motor vehicles to travel between Italy and the rest of Europe via car regardless of weather. The expressways, called *Autostrada*, are superhighways and toll roads. They connect all major Italian cities and have contributed to the tremendous increase in tourist travel.

Driving is a good way to see the variety of Italy's towns, villages, seascapes, landscapes, and monuments. The Italian drivers may be a little *pazzo* (crazy), but if you drive confidently and carefully you should be fine. If you remain aware and keep your eyes on the car in front of you, you should be fine. Still, be alert on Italy's roadways, because Italian drivers are like nothing you have ever experienced.

Driver's Licenses

US, British, and Canadian driving licenses are valid in Italy, but only when accompanied by a translation. This translation is obtainable from **AAA**, the offices of the **Touring Club Italiano** in Italy, at the offices for the **Italian Government Tourist Office**, and at the Italian frontier. Even if your native driver's license is accepted, it is strongly recommended that you apply for and receive an 'International Drivers Permit,' which you can get from the Italian Government Tourist Offices listed below:
• **Touring Club Italiano**, Via Marsala 8, 00185, Roma, *Tel. 06/49 98 99*
• **Italian Government Tourist Office** – in the US: 500 N. Michigan Ave, Chicago, IL 60611, *Tel. 312/644-0990;* 630 Fifth Ave, Suite 1565, New York, NY 10111, *Tel. 212/245-4822, Fax 212/586-9249;* 360 Post Street, Suite 801, San Francisco CA 94109, *Tel. 415/392-6206;* in Canada: Store 56, Plaza 3, 3 Place Ville Marie, Montreal, Quebec, *Tel. 514/866 7667. Web: www.italiantourism.com.*

Car Rental

In all major cities there are a variety of car rental locations, and even such American stalwarts as Avis and Hertz (see each city's individual section for specifics). All you need to do to rent a car is contact the agency in question, or have the management of your hotel do it for you. Remember to have had your driver's license translated prior to your arrival (see above). From your car rental place, you will be able to pick up detailed maps of the area in which you want to drive.

Driving through the back roads of Italy can offer you some of the best access to secluded little hill towns, clear mountain lakes, snow capped mountains and more; but it can also be one of the most expensive items on your trip, not only because of the exorbitant cost of the rental itself, but also because of the price of gasoline, which can run up to $6 or more per gallon. Naturally, there are ways to keep the cost down, one of which is to make the best use of your car.

Don't rent a car for your entire trip, allowing it to sit in a garage when you are in a big city and you are getting around on foot or by bus, metro, or taxi. Use a rental car to travel through the isolated hills and valleys in between the big cities and drop off the car once you arrive at your destination. Compared to the cost of the rental, drop-off charges are minimal. And of course, make sure you have unlimited mileage, otherwise the cost will creep up by the kilometer.

But always be aware of the wild Italian drivers. Unless you are from Boston and are used to aggressive driving tactics, driving a car to get around Italy should be avoided. So think twice about renting a car. Italian drivers are like nothing you've ever seen.

Another caveat against car rental is that it will isolate you from many experiences while traveling. Going by train or bus allows you to become a part of the daily lives of the locals. You experience living from their perspective. Behind the glass and steel of an automobile you tend be isolated from pure cultural experiences.

Since 1945 in America we have not really known anything other than getting around by automobile, but in Europe, and especially in Italy, there are a multiplicity of other transportation options, whether it is inter or intra-city. The inter-urban Italian train system is one of the best in the world, and where trains don't go, frequent bus service exists. So think twice about car rental because there are many other transportation options to choose from in Italy, unlike here in America.

If you do choose to rent a car, Hertz and Avis have offices all over Italy. To book a car in advance, contact their toll free numbers: **Hertz**, *Tel. 800/654-3001*; **Avis**, *Tel. 800/331-1084*.

Road Maps

If you're going to be our of Rome you are going to want adequate maps, and the only place to get really good maps is from the **Touring Club Italiano**. Your rental company will supply you something that will enable you to get the car out of their parking lot, but after that you are on your own. My recommendation to you would be to contact the **Touring Club Italiano**, Via Marsala 8, 00185, Roma, *Tel. 06/49 98 99*, well prior to your visit, or visit their store in Rome at Via del Babuino 19-21, *Tel 06/3609-5834* near the Piazza del Popolo. Here you can get all the maps they have available.

By Hiking

If you are an avid hiker, and enjoy seeing a country from the perspective of the backroads or trails, contact this excellent organization, **BCT** (British Coastal Trails) **Scenic Walking**, which offers some great walking tours of Italy, England and the rest of the European continent. **BCT Scenic Tours** (see page 59 for details).

By Train

The Italian railroad system is owned by the government and provides convenient and extensive transportation throughout the country. Train is by far the simplest, easiest, and least expensive way to get around Italy. Ferries link the principal islands with the mainland, and those that travel between southernmost Italy and Sicily carry trains as well as cars, trucks, and people. To get schedule and ticket information call the offices for the **Italian Rail Agency** (CIT) in North America, *Tel. 800/248-7245*. A great web site that contains everything you need to know about rail travel in Italy is for the Italian Rail Company (**Ferrovie dello Stato** – FS) at *www.fs-on-line.com*.

The railroad system is more extensive in north and central Italy, but main lines run along both coasts, and other routes cross the peninsula in several places. The **Simplon Tunnel**, one of the world's longest railroad tunnels, connects Italy and Switzerland. Other rail lines follow routes across the Alps between Italy and France, Austria, and Slovenia.

Taking the train is by far the most expedient, most relaxing, and by far the best way to travel throughout Italy. Trains go almost every place you'd like to visit, they are comfortable, run on time, and free you from having to drive. This efficiency of the railway system in Italy can be directly attributed to Mussolini. You may have heard the saying, "He may not have done much else, but he got the trains to arrive on time." Well, it's true.

When traveling by train, one thing to remember is that you must **always stamp your ticket before boarding the train**. Otherwise you may incur a fine of E20. The machines to stamp your ticket with the time and date are at the head of every track platform.

Types of Train Tickets

There are two different levels of seating on most every train in Italy: **first class** and **second class**. The difference in price is usually only a few dollars, but the difference in convenience is astounding. First class ticket holders can make reservations in advance, while second class ticket seating is on a first come first serve basis.

In conjunction, the seating quality is light-years apart. An example of the price difference between first class and second when traveling between Rome and Florence is $35 for first class, $22 for second class. But in first class you will have an air-conditioned car and separate cloth seat, while in second class you will have not A/C, and you'll be in a compartment with five other people sitting on sweat-inducing plastic seats.

Ticket Discounts

The Italian Railway System offers a variety of discounts on its tickets. Check out their web site for more details (*www.fs-on-line.com*). These tickets are can be purchased through the Italian Government Travel Offices (see numbers listed above under Driver's License section) and through authorized travel agencies.

- **Silver Card for Seniors**: Available to all people 60 years and older. It allows for a 20% reduction on the basic fare for all first class and second class tickets on national routes. For day trains for inter-city routes the discount is 40%. A one year pass costs E5; A two year pass costs E9; a permanent pass costs E12.
- **Green Card for Youth Travel**: Available to all persons from 12 to 26 years of age. It allows for a 20% reduction on all first and second class tickets. A one year pass costs E5; a two year pass costs E9.
- **Italy Flexi Rail Cards**: An excellent option for rail travel in Italy. There are many rules and regulations associated with these cards, but they do not hinder the bearer in any way. Example of some rules: cannot be sold to permanent residents of Italy, card is not transferable, card must be validated at any Italian State Railway station's ticket office before travel can commence, validation slip must be kept separate from card (kind of like the validation slip for travelers checks), and lost or stolen cards cannot

Eurostar Style

A feather in the cap of the Italian rail system is the **Eurostar trains**. These are very comfortable, luxurious and fast. Travel between Rome and Florence (and Venice and Florence) has been reduced to less than two hours each way. The seats on these trains are large and accommodating in both first and second class. In first class they serve you a snack with free beverage service, and offer you headphones that you can keep. A truly wonderful way to travel. So if you are going by train and want to enjoy luxury on the rails, try the Eurostar. The price might be expensive for some at E55 (about $55) each way, but is well worth it.

Train Departure (Partenze) Board Description

- When the train is scheduled to depart
  - Number of the Train
    - Classes of Service available
      - Main Stops and Destinations
- Special Services Available
  - Track from which the train will depart

Ora	Treno	Classi Servizi	Principali Fermate e Destinazione	Servizi Diretti e Annotazione	Bina rio
11:35	9412	1-2	Firenze (13:11) Bologna (14:13)		9

PARTENZE

be refunded or replaced unless bearer has validation slip. Rules, rules, rules. Here are the prices for the Flexi Railcards:

Validity	1st Class	2nd Class
• 4 days of travel within 9 days of validity	$170	$116
• 8 days of travel within 21 days of validity	$250	$164
• 12 days of travel within 30 days of validity	$314	$210

• **Italy Rail Card** or the "BTLC Italian Tourist Ticket:" all travel and any type of train is unlimited and free, except for the special **TR450 or Eurostar** trains where a supplemental fee will be required. The time period begins on the first day of its use. Here are the prices for the Unlimited Rail Pass:

Validity	1st Class	2nd Class
• 8 days	$226	$152
• 15 days	$284	$190
• 21 days	$330	$220
• 30 days	$396	$264

Types of Trains
• **Eurostar**: Top notch services and speed. Air-conditioned, comfortable seats, snacks served at your seat and head phones available for use.
• **IC-Intercity**: Both first and second class seating is available with most first class compartments air-conditioned. Dining cars are also available.
• **EC-Eurocity**: These are the trains that are used in international rail service.
• **EXPR-Expresso**: Ordinary express trains usually carry first and second class

passengers. No supplemental fare and reservations are necessary, but I recommend you make them. Food and drink service is available. These are the trains to take. Hardly any stops at all. Kind of like the MetroLiner Service on Amtrak between Washington DC and New York.

- **DIR-Diretto**: Semi-express trains that make plenty of stops. They often have second class seating only. During off-peak hours they are not crowded, but at peak hours they're sardine-city.
- **Locale**: These trains stop everywhere on their route and take forever, but to get to rural locations these are the only options.

Boarding the Right Train

When taking a train in Italy the ultimate destination that is listed on the train schedule and the departure listing by the track may not be the same city or town to which you are going. To get to Pisa, for example, sometimes you have to board a train whose ultimate destination is Livorno. To make sure you're boarding the proper train, consult one of the large glass-enclosed schedules (see graphic on page 64) located in the information offices and usually at the head of the tracks. Match your intended departure time with the time printed on the sheet. Then check directly to the right of the time to see the list of all the destinations for the train. If the name of your destination is listed, you've found your train. Next write down the ultimate destination of the train so you can check the main board at the station that lists **partenze** (trains leaving) to see which **binnario** (track) you should board.

If that still doesn't soothe your concerns, ask someone waiting at the track or inside the train if it is going to your destination. Ask at least two people. Whatever the case, to ask someone politely in Italian whether the train is going to your destination – for example, Lucca – say **"Scusa, ma questo treno va a Lucca?"** ("Excuse me, but does this train go to Lucca?")

Finally, if you're standing on the platform waiting for the train to come and you suddenly see all the Italians moving away en masse, that usually means that the public address announcer just declared a track change. Ask one of the departing Italians "Has the track for the train to Lucca changed?" **(E cambiato il binnario per il treno per Lucca?)** If the answer is yes (si), either get the number and go there or simply follow them, and as you pass the board that lists the trains leaving, you'll see the change already officially noted.

basic information

Chapter 6

Business Hours

Store hours vary all over Italy, but as a rule they are open from Monday through Friday, 9:00am to 1:00pm, then re-open at 3:30 or 4:00pm to 7:30/8:00pm, and Saturdays from 9:00am to 1:00pm. In large towns, mainly to cater to tourists, stores are open on Saturday afternoons and Sundays as well. Most stores everywhere else in Italy are closed on Sundays, and everywhere they are closed on national holidays. Don't expect to find any 24-hour convenience stores just around the corner in Italy. If you want some soda in your room after a long day of touring you need to plan ahead.

Food stores (alimentari) keep their own hours entirely but generally follow the regular business hours listed above. Alimentari also close at least one other day of the week besides Sunday. Usually this day is Thursday (Giovedi), but it varies region to region, and even city to city within the region. There is a sign outside each alimentari that you can check to see which day they are closed (chiuso).

Basically, you must plan on most stores being closed from 1:00pm to 4:00pm, since this is the Italian siesta time. During that time, the only places open are restaurants, and most of those close at 3pm.

Banking

Banks in Italy are open Monday through Friday, 8:30am to 1:30pm and from 2:45pm to 4:00pm, and are closed all day Saturday and Sunday and on national holidays. In some cities the afternoon open hour may not even exist, and in some cities, like Rome, banks may open on Saturday mornings and extend longer on Thursdays.

Once again, bank hours, like business hours, vary region to region and even city to city within the region. Check outside of banks for their posted hours of operation. Even if the bank is closed, most travelers' checks can be exchanged for Italian currency at hotels as well as shops and at the many foreign exchange offices in railway stations and at airports.

Shop around for the best exchange rate. Each bank offers a different rate and exchange fee, as do the **Casa di Cambio**, smaller exchange establishments. Sometimes the rate charged to exchange your money is a set fee, which is best when you change a large amount of money. Other places charge a percentage of the total which is generally more beneficial for smaller amounts.

Lost or Stolen Travelers Checks & Credit Cards

The toll free numbers listed below should be called if your credit cards or traveler's checks are stolen:

American Express, *Tel. 800/872-000* (travelers checks)
American Express, *Tel. 800/874-333* (credit cards)
Diner's Club, *Tel. 800/864-064*
Mastercard, *Tel. 800/870-866*
Thomas Cook/Mastercard, *Tel. 800/872-050* (traveler's checks)
VISA, *Tel. 800/874-155* (traveler's checks)
VISA, *Tel. 800/877-232* (credit cards)

Currency - The Euro

On January 1, 2002, the official currency for all participating members of the European Community, to which Italy belongs, became the **Euro**. (In this book the Euro is represented by a capital 'E.') It took about two months to become seamlessly adopted in each participating country, and now the lira is no longer in circulation.

The Euro will have far reaching economic and political effects, but the impact is also grammatical. In most European languages, the name of the old currency was a feminine word, such as the now extinct Italian lira, which ends in an 'a.' But the word 'Euro' is masculine since it ends in an 'o.' Another grammatical conundrum is the plural. In Italian a masculine plural is usually represented by an 'i.' But with the Euro all of Europe has adopted the English way by adding an 's' - i.e. 'Euros.'

The Euro comes in coin denominations of 50, 20, 10, 5, 2 and 1 cent, and bill denominations of 500, 200, 100, 50, 20, 10, 5, 2, and 1 Euro.

Dollar-Euro Exchange Rates

Following is a conversion table showing what one Euro is approximately valued at in US dollars As you can see it is almost a one-to-one transfer which should make purchases easier for us now. We will no longer have to deal with tens of thousand of lire and wonder how much that is in dollars. Now it is straightforward. This rate changes all the time. Please check your local paper for up-to-date exchange rates.

Euro (E)	US Dollar ($)
1	1.01
2	2.01
5	5.03
10	10.06
20	20.12
50	50.29
100	100.59
200	201.17
500	502.93

Electricity

The standard electric current in Italy is 220v, but check with your hotel before you plug in an appliance to find out what the current is, because it's not always 220v! If you want to use your blow dryer, electric razor, radio, or plug in your laptop you are going to need a hardware adapter to switch your appliance from a two prong to a three prong insert. These can be found at most hardware stores. Also check before you leave to see if your appliance automatically changes the voltage from 110v to 220v. If it doesn't, you will need to purchase a converter.

If you can't find these devices at your hardware store, you can order them from the **Franzus Company**, Murtha Industrial Park, PO Box, 142, Beacon Falls, CT 06403, *Tel. 203/723-6664, Fax 203/723-6666.* They also have a free brochure *Foreign Electricity Is No Deep Dark Secret* that can be mailed or faxed to you.

Express Couriers

• **DHL**, Via Lucrezia Romana 87a, *Toll free in Italy 800/345-345, Fax 06/7932-0051, E-mail: dhl@dhl.com, Web: www.dhl.it*
• **UPS**, Via della Magliana 329, *Toll free in Italy 800/822-054, Fax 06/5226-8200.*

Health Concerns

A wonderful "just in case..." option is Personal Physicians Worldwide. This organization can provide you with a list of physicians and hospitals at your destination. If you have a medical condition that may need treatment, or you just want to be safe, they can help. Your personal medical history will be confidentially reviewed by the Medical Director, Dr. David Abramson. He will then contact screened and qualified physicians at your destination to see if they will agree to be available and to care for you if the need arises, while you are in their location.

This is a great service since you never know where you'll be when you need the care of a competent doctor. To find out more information, contact:

- **Personal Physicians Worldwide**, *Tel. 888/657-8114, Fax 301/718-7725; E-mail: myra@personalphysicians.com* (for Myra Altschuler, Director) *or doctors@personalphysicians.com* (for Dr. David Abramson, Medical Director); *Web: www.personalphysicians.com.*

Newspapers & Magazines

At most newsstands in Italy you can find the world renowned *International Herald Tribune,* which is published jointly by The Washington Post and The New York Times and printed in Bologna. You will also be able to find a condensed version of *USA Today.* Besides these two, you can also find newspapers from all over the world at almost any newsstand.

If you want an insight into what may be going on in the English language community of the city you are visiting, simply stop into any local English-language bookstore. There should be a list of local events posted, or itemized in a newsletter.

Pets

If you're bringing your precious pooch (your dog will have to be on a leash and wear a muzzle in public in Italy) or kitty into Italy with you, you must have a veterinarian's certificate stating that your pet has been vaccinated against rabies between 20 days and 11 months before entry into Italy, and that your pet is in overall good health. The certificate must contain the breed, age, sex, and color of your pet and your name and address. This certificate will be valid only for 30 days. The specific forms that the vet needs to fill out are available at all Italian diplomatic and consular offices.

Parrots, parakeets, rabbits, and hares are also subject to health certification by a vet, and will also be examined further upon entry into Italy. Also Customs officials may require a health examination of your pet if you have just come from a tropical region or that they suspect the pet to be ill. All this means that they can do whatever they want whenever they want, so it might be wise to leave your pet at home.

Postal Service

Stamps can be purchased at any post office or tabacchi. If you send a letter airmail with insufficient postage it will not be returned to sender, but will be sent surface mail, which could take months. So make sure you have the correct postage. Air mail prices for post cards is E1.3 to the US and Canada. Air mail letters cost 1.5. And if you put your coorespondence in a red post box, remember to put it in the right hand slot which reads "Per tutte le altre desinazione" (for all other destinations other – other than the city where you are).

The main post office in each city is generally open from 8:30am to 6:00 or 7:00pm Monday through Friday and Saturday they close at noon. Smaller post offices are only open from 8:30am to 2:00pm Monday through Friday.

Restaurant Hours

Restraurants in Italy keep rather rigid hours, which are usually 12:30 or 1:00pm for lunch until 3:00 or 3:30pm. The dinner hours start at either 7:30 or 8:00pm and usually run until 10:00pm. Some late night restaurants, stay open until the early morning hours.

Safety & Avoiding Trouble

Italian cities are definitely much safer than any equivalent American city. You can walk almost anywhere without fear of harm, but that doesn't mean you shouldn't play it safe. Listed below are some simple rules to follow to ensure that nothing bad occurs:
• At night, make sure the streets you are strolling along have plenty of other people. Like I said, most cities are safe, but it doesn't hurt to be cautious.
• Always have your knapsack or purse flung over the shoulder that is not directly next to the road. Why? There have been cases of Italians on motor bikes snatching purses off old ladies and in some cases dragging them a few blocks.
• Better yet, have your companion walk on the street side, while you walk on the inside of the sidewalk with the knapsack or purse.
• Better still is to buy one of those tummy wallets that goes under your shirt so no one can even be tempted to purse-snatch you.
• Always follow basic common sense. If you feel threatened, scared, or alone, retrace your steps back to a place where there are other people.

Staying out of trouble with the law is paramount, because in Italy you are guilty until proven innocent, unlike in the States where it's the other way around. And most importantly, if arrested you are not simply placed in a holding cell. The Italian officials take you directly to a maximum security prison and lock you up. And that's where you'll stay for as long as it takes your traveling partners to figure out where you are, bribe your case to the top of the local judge's pile, and have your case heard. That whole process can sometimes take months.

So if you like your drinks strong and your nights long, remember to keep your temper in check. And don't even think about smuggling any banned substance into the country, or God forbid, buying something illicit when you're in Italy. If you are approached to buy some hashish or something else, say politely – No Grazie (no thank you) – and walk away.

Diplomatic & Consular Offices In Italy

These are the places you'll need to contact if you lose your passport or have some unfortunate brush with the law. Remember that the employees of these offices are merely your government's representatives in a foreign country, not God. They cannot fix your problems in the blink of an eye, but they will do their best on your behalf.

Embassies & Consulates in Rome

- **Australia** - Via Alessandria 205, *Tel. 06/852-721*
- **Canadian Embassy** - Via GB de Rossi 27, *Tel. 06/445-981*
- **Great Britain** - Via XX Settembre 80a, *Tel. 06/482-5441, www.grbr.it*
- **Ireland** - Piazza di Campitelli 3, *Tel. 06/697-912*
- **New Zealand** - Via Zara 28, *Tel. 06/441-7171, nzemb.roma@flashnet.it*
- **South Africa** - Via Tanaro 1, *Tel. 06/852-541, sae@flashnet.it*
- **United States** - Via Veneto 199, *Tel. 06/46741*

US Consulates

- **Florence** - Lungarno Amerigo Vespucci 38. 1 50123 Firenze, *Tel. 055/239-8276*

Canadian Consulates

- **Milan** - Via Vittor Pisani 19, 20124 Milano, *Tel. 02/669-7451 and 669-4970 (night line)*

UK Consulates

- **Florence** - Palazzo Castelbarco, Lungarno Corsini 2, 50123 Firenze, *Tel. 055/21 26 94, 28 41 33 and 28 74 49*
- **Genoa** - Via XII Ottobre 2, 16121 Genova, *Tel. 010/48 33-36*
- **Milan** - Via San Paolo 7, 1-20121 Milano, *Tel. 02/80 34 42*

Finally, you may have the misfortune of being confronted with a pack of gypsies whose only interest is to relieve you of your wallet and other valuables. These situations are rare but they do happen. Gypsies are not violent, and usually you will only encounter women and children, but they tend to swarm all around you, poke pieces of cardboard in your midsection and generally distract you to the point where they are able to pilfer your pockets, fanny packs, back packs, or knapsacks. So if you are swarmed by gypsies, do not be polite, push back if you need to, make a scene, yell, scream, start running, do anything you can to get out of their midst. Gypsies will not harm you, but if you do not act quickly you will lose your valuables.

Taxis

Taxi service is widely available in all major cities in Italy, and a little less so in smaller cities such as Pisa or Lucca, and almost non-existent in remote towns and villages. Rates are comparable to those charged in your large American cities, which means expensive. Generally taxis locate themselves in special stands located at railway stations and main parts of the city, but many can be waved down as they cruise the streets for fares. At these taxi stands there are usually telephones that you can call directly from your hotel, but remember, in Italy, if called, the meter starts at the point of origin, so you'll be paying the cabby to come pick you up. The same goes for radio taxis if called to come pick you up.

Fares will vary from city to city, but basically when you get in the cab there will be a fixed starting charge of approximately 2,800 to 6,400 lire, and a cost per kilometer of approximately 1,000 to 1,250 lire. If you are stuck in traffic, every minute another Euro 50 cents or so will be added to the fare. Some extra charges may come into play, like the **nighttime supplement** (between 10:00pm and 6:00am), a **Sunday and public holiday supplement**, as well as a **per item luggage charge**. You will also be charged for every piece of luggage. All of these vary from city to city.

On long trips, like from airports, it is advised to agree upon a price before heading out. Ask at the information booth inside each airport what the expected charge should be.

Telephones & Fax
Calling Italy

Even when making local calls the area code must be used. In conjunction, before it was necessary to discard the leading zero of the area code (for example Rome's area code is 06), but now you need to use the leading zero in all area codes.

To dial Rome from the United States, first dial the international prefix, **011**, then the country code, **39**, then the city code for Rome, **06**, then the number you wish to reach.

Long Distance Calling From Italy

The days of the 'gettone' phones is long past. Most pay phones in Italy only use **phone cards** (which you can buy in denominations of E2.5, E5 or E7.5) but some use a combination of cards and coins. You can buy phone cards at any tabacchi (the stores with the **T** out in front of them), newsstand, post office and some bars. You will need these cards to be able to use public pay phones

Listed below are some of the major telecommunications carriers for North America and their access numbers:

AT&T – *Tel. 172-1011* (a toll free number in Italy) to gain access to an AT&T operator (or English language prompts) for efficient service. You can bill your AT&T calling card, local phone company card, or call direct.

Canada Direct – *Tel. 172-1001* (a toll free number in Italy) and you will be connected to the Canadian telephone network with access to a bilingual operator. You can bill your *Calling Card, Call Me*™ service, your *Hello!* Phone Pass or call collect.

MCI – *Tel. 172-1022* (a toll free number in Italy) for MCI's World Phone and to use your MCI credit card or call collect. All done through English speaking MCI operators.

Sprint – *Tel. 172-1877* (a toll free number in Italy) for access to an English speaking Sprint operator who can charge your phone card or make your call collect.

Modem or Fax Usage In Italy

To connect you modem or fax to the wall you will need an adapter. These too can be bought from a hardware store or from the **Franzus Company** (see above under Electricity). Many hotels in Italy are starting to use the American standard phone plug, so this may not be a concern. When making your reservations, inquire about the type of plugs in use to insure you can communicate with home without a problem.

Phone Cards

An inexpensive option for international calling is to buy an international phone card (carta telefonica internationale) which are sold at most tabacchi. You can get cards for E10 which have 100 minutes available on them. This translates to about 10 cents a minute, a steal for international calling.

These cards can be used in your hotel room or at public phone booths simply by following the directions on the back. This usually entails calling a toll free number, receiving instructions in a variety of languages, including English, punching in the number of your specific card (usually found on the back after rubbing off a covering), then keying in the number you wish to call. Your connection is crisp and clear. Discerning travelers concerned with spending an arm and a leg to call home, use this option.

Renting Cell Phones for Use in Italy

Italy has the third highest number of cell phone subscribers in the world. In all 53.9 per cent of 56 million Italians use cellular phones, which accounts for more than 31.3 million subscriptions. Despite the proliferation of cell phones, don't think you can use your North American cell phone over here. Italy, like most of the rest of the world, uses GSM while most of the U.S. uses a standard known as AMPS.

So, if you want to use a cell phone in Italy you will have to rent one. To achieve this you will find vendors in most Italian airports, offices in downtown locations, and websites that are more than willing to sign you up. However, some people have encountered a problem getting their deposits back if they rent a phone while in Italy. One individual in particular, who rented a cell phone at the **World in Touch/Nolitel** office at Malpensa airport, is still encountering difficulties getting his money back, even months after he has returned from Italy.

My recommendation would be to rent a cell phone before you go. There are companies that can outfit you with a phone, adapters, and accompanying service for your travels. The costs usually break down into an equipment rental charge ($50-$75 for a week), plus per-minute calling charges. This basic rental charge should include equipment delivery to your office and back to the service. Some services will also charge an activation fee, which for most phones will average around $15.

Be warned, cell phone calling rates are not cheap. You will find that it will generally cost over $2 per minute to call the United States from abroad. While this may be somewhat comparable to hotel calling rates, they are significantly more than calling cards. For example, using an AT&T calling card, a call to the U.S. from France costs 49¢ per minute, with an 89¢ per call handling fee. And pre-paid calling cards bought in Italy (see *Phone Card* section above) cost only between 5¢ and 10¢ per minute. So renting a cell phone is a convenient but expensive option.

Also, if you will be having people call you from the local area, find out where the phone you will be using is registered. If the majority of people will be calling you from Italy, the phone should be registered there. Otherwise whoever will be calling you will incur a long distance charge when they do so.

Some websites for cell phone rental companies to consider include:
• *www.cellhire.co.uk*
• *www.planetfone.com*
• *www.globalphone.net*

Time

Italy is **six hours ahead of Eastern Standard Time** in North America, so if it's noon in New York it's 6:00pm in Rome. Daylight savings time goes into effect each year in Italy usually from the end of March to the end of September.

Tipping
Hotels
A service charge of 15-18% is usually added to your hotel bill, but it is customary to leave a little something else, whatever you deem sufficient, but anything over E1-2 per service rendered can be extravagant.

Restaurants
A service charge of around 15% is usually automatically added to all restaurant bills. But if you felt the service was good, it is customary to leave a little something. There is no set percentage, and a good rule of thumb is to leave whatever change is returned, as long as it is not above between 5-10%.

The same applies in cafés and bars. For example, around two hundred lire is normal if you're standing at the counter drinking a soda, cappuccino, etc. If you have an alcoholic beverage, something to eat, etc. at the counter, the tip should be Euro 50 cents or more. Leaving change in this manner is a good way to rid myself of burdensome coins.

Theater Ushers
They get E1 or more if the theater is very high class.

Taxis
Give the cabby 5% of the fare, otherwise they just might drive away leaving you without your luggage. (Just kidding).

Sightseeing Guide & Driver
Give E1 minimum per person for half-day tours, and E2 minimum per person for full day tours.

Service Station Attendant
Give Euro 50 cents or more for extra service like cleaning your windshield, or giving you directions while also filling up your tank.

Weights & Measures
Italy uses the metric system, where everything is a factor of ten. The table on the next page gives you a list of weights and measures with approximate values.

Websites of Interest
Before you head off to Italy, I've listed some websites below that you may find interesting or useful. Some of them are featured elsewhere in this book.

Airfare
• www.bestfares.com

Metric Conversions

Weights

Italy	14 grams	Etto	Kilo
US	1/2 oz	1/4 lb	2 lb 2oz

Liquid Measure

Italy	Litro
US	1.065 quart

Distance Measure

Italy	Centimeter	Meter	Kilometer
US	2/5 inch	39 inches	3/5 mile

• *www.lowestfare.com*
• *www.cheaptickets.com*
• *www.airdeals.com*
• *www.lastminutetravel.com*

Currency
• *www.oanda.com/converter/travel* – to create a pocket currency conversion chart to bring with you, visit this website

General Information
• *www.italiantourism.com* – website for the Italian government tourist office; filled with lots of great information
• *www.itwg.com* – an all-inclusive website featuring loads of useful information about Italy
• *www.travel.it/welcome.html* – another all encompassing website produced by yet another Italian government agency
• *www.enjoyrome.com* – offers walking tours of Rome
• *www.mondoweb.it/livinginrome* – the complete guide to living in Rome for foreigners

Hotels
• *www.venere.it* – you can get hotel reservations for thousands of hotels all over Italy at this site, including many that are in this book

Language
• *www.travlang.com/languages* – if you want to take a few virtual language lessons before you go, visit the *Foreign Language for Travelers* website
• *www.arcodidruso.com* – Italian language and culture for foreigners

Medical
- *www.personalphysicians.com* – provides you with a list of physicians and hospitals at your destination; if you have a medical condition that may need treatment, or you just want to be safe, they can help

Passport
- *www.instantpassport.com* – this website promises to give you 24-hour turnaround from the time they receive your passport pictures and requisite forms; they charge $100 plus overnight shipping on top of all fees associated with passport issuance.
- *www.americanpassport.com* – this site offers three types of service: expedited (24 hours), express (three to four business days) and regular; prices range from $245 to $135.
- *www.travel.state.gov* – you can download passport application forms, international travel advisories, and listings of embassies and consulates worldwide

Weather
- *www.washingtonpost.com/wp-srv/weather/historical/historical.htm* – if you want to obtain the average temperature, temperature ranges and rain accumulation totals by month for Rome or other destinations in Italy visit this website

Women Travelers

As stated in the Safety section above, Italy is a safe country, but generally women traveling alone will find themselves the recipients of unwanted attention from men. In most cases the attention you receive will be limited to whistles, stares, comments (in Italian which you will probably not understand), catcalls and the like. This may happen whether you are in groups or alone. But usually if you are with a male companion this type of unwanted attention doesn't occur.

If you choose to be alone, whether it's going for a walk, seeing a sight, or stopping for a coffee, don't expect to be alone for long. Since foreign women have a reputation for being easy, ignoring unwanted suitors won't work because they think they can charm their way into your heart and elsewhere. My suggestion is to politely tell them you are waiting for your boyfriend (aspetto mio fidanzato) or husband (marito). If that doesn't work, raise your voice, look them in the eye angrily and tell them to" lascia mi stare" (lash-ah me star-ay), which means "leave me alone."

If these ploys do not work, simply walk away. If the man continues to badger you, find a local policeman for assistance, but always remain in a populated area. In the vast majority of cases there is truly nothing to fear. Most Italians just want to get lucky and when rebuffed they will go find easier prey.

In conjunction, most of the attention falls into the nuisance category, but like I said in the Safety section, please use common sense. Avoid unpopulated areas, avoid walking alone on dark streets, avoid hitchhiking alone and things like that. Just be smart. Italy is much safer than America and is not even remotely as violent, but it's better to be safe than sorry.

In general too, the further south you go, the more you will be hassled. Something about the warm climate must heat the male's blood or stimulate their libido. Also in port cities women traveling alone will be pegged as targets for petty theft. So be extra careful in those types of cities.

And all over the country, when you ride public transportation you may very well be confronted with wandering hands, especially when the bus or train is crowded. To avoid this, keep your back to the wall. If someone does start to fondle your posterior or elsewhere, make a loud fuss – otherwise it will continue unabated.

Yellow Pages

There is an excellent **English Yellow Pages (EYP)** in Italy. It is the annual telephone directory of English-speaking professionals, organizations, services and commercial activities in Rome, Florence, Milan, Naples, Genoa and Bologna. The EYP is a well-known resource and reference source among the international community in Italy, from which you can easily find numbers for airlines and embassies, English-speaking doctors and dentists, international schools and organizations, hotels, moving companies, real estate agents, accountants, attorneys, consultants, plumbers, electricians, mechanics and much more. Listings are complete with address including zip code, phone and fax numbers, e-mail and web sites.

You can find copies at embassies, international organizations (FAO, IFAD, WWF, etc.) schools & universities, social and professional associations, English-language churches, foreign press offices, local events within the expat community and various businesses that deal directly with an international clientele. And copies of it are on sale at most international bookstores. This is a great resource for any resident or visitor to Italy. Their website is *www.eyp.com*.

Chapter 7

Store hours are usually Monday through Friday 9:00am to 1:00pm, 3:30/4:00pm to 7:30/8:00pm, and Saturday 9:00am to 1:00pm. In major cities like Florence and Rome, shops will also open in the afternoons on Saturday, but everywhere in Italy they will be closed on Sunday.

The big Italian chain stores are **La Rinascente**, **Coin**, **UPIM**, and **STANDA**. In Coin, UPIM, and STANDA, you will also find supermarkets filled with all manner of Italian delectables. At the end of this chapter I'll make some suggestions about what you could buy at a local Italian Supermercato or Alimentari (smaller food store) to bring home with you so you can make a fine Italian meal with authentic ingredients!

Besides food and clothing, Italy has a wide variety of handicrafts. Any one of Italy's crafts would be a perfect memento of your stay. Works in alabaster and marble can be readily found in and around Florence, Milan, and Venice. Wood carvings are the specialty of many of the cities in the south, such as Palermo and Messina. Beautiful glasswork is at its best in and around Venice and Pisa. Embroidery and lace work can be found all over Italy, and rugs from Sardinia rival those of most other European countries. Sardinia is also known for its straw bags, hats, and mats, as is Florence.

Exquisite gold and silver jewelry is a specialty of Florence, where, on the Ponte Vecchio, you'll find shop after shop of jewelry stores. In other parts of Tuscany you can find hand-wrought iron work as well as beautiful tiles.

And finally, the main fashion centers in Italy are, of course, Milan, Florence and Rome, with Florence specializing in shoes and gloves, and Milan and Rome everything else. I will describe for you specific places to shop to find the most exquisite and authentic regional handicrafts.

Tax-Free Shopping

Italian law entitles all non-European Union residents to a **VAT (IVA) tax refund** with a minimum purchase exceeding E150. Ask for an invoice (fattura in Italian) or a **Tax-Free Check** when completing a purchase. Upon departure from Italy, purchased goods must be shown to a customs agent at the airport or border station and a customs stamp must be obtained no later than three months after the date of purchase. The stamped invoice must be returned to the store or the VAT Refund Companies Office in Italy no later than four months after the date of purchase.

Direct refunds at the airport or the border are offered albeit at a lower rate. There are also a number of tax-free services, such as **Cashback, Global Refund Italia, Tax-Free for Tourists**, etc. and each have a different window at the airport. Be aware of this when you make your purchases so that your time spent in lines at the airport getting refunds is lessened. You will usually see the tax back signs in most upscale stores.

Little Italian Stores

Since there are no 24-hour pharmacies or convenience stores that carry everything under the sun like we have in North America, shopping for the basic necessities can be a little confusing. Listed on the next few pages are specific types of shops and what you can find in them.

Cartoleria

Shopping at a cartoleria brings you face to face with Italian make-work programs, since most are not self-service. Some products you can pick out

Tax Rebate on Purchases

If you acquire products at the same merchant in excess of E150 (about $150), you can claim an **IVA** (purchase tax) **rebate**. You must ask the vendor for the proper receipt **(il ricetto per il IVA per favore)**, have the receipt stamped at Italian customs, then mail no later than 90 days after the date of the receipt back to the vendor. The vendor will then send you the IVA rebate. You can also do this at the airport, but will receive less money in return. If you spend a fair chunk of money in Italy on clothing or other items, this is a good way to get some money back. Also be aware that there is more than one tax free service available.

what you want, others you will have to enlist a stockboy/girl to help you get it. But you don't bring the products up to the register. In most cases you will have the cost of your purchases tabulated for you by the stockperson. You bring this receipt and your desired products up to the register, where another person rings them up for you.

Things sold in cartoleria include:

- pen   penna
- pencil   mattita
- notebook   quaderno
- paper   carta
- envelope   borsa per una lettera
- binder   classificatore
- calendar   calandra
- wrapping paper carta da regalo

Alimentari

When shopping at an alimentari some products are self-service and some have to be prepared for you. Most meats, cheeses and breads are not pre-packaged and therefore you will have to talk to someone behind a glass counter to get you what you want. Other goods, like mustard and water, are self-service. When ordering meats, cheeses or breads, you will get the products and the receipt for the products from the person behind the counter. Bring the receipt and all your other products to the cashier where you pay.

Typical items in alimentari include:

- mustard   senape
- mayonnaise   maionese
- tomatoes   tomaté
- olive oil   olio d'oliva
- salami   salame (the best types are Milanese or Ungherese)
- cheese   formaggio
- mineral water aqua minerale
- wine (red/white) vino (rosso/bianco)
- beer   birra
- potato chips   patate fritte
- cookies   biscotti
- roll   panino
- bread   pane
- butter   burro

Sometimes alimentari do not have bread. If that is the case you'll need to find a panificio (bakery). Same type of service here as in an alimentari.

Farmacia

Shopping in a pharmacy is full service. You do not have access to anything. If you want anything you have to ask the pharmacist or his/her assistant.

This is what you'll buy in farmacia:

- toothpaste   dentifricio
- razor   rasoio
- deodorant   deodorante
- comb   pettine
- rubbers   profilattici
- toothbrush   spazzolino
- aspirin   aspirina
- tampon   tampone

Tabacchaio

Most everything but the tobacco products and stamps are self-service in a tabacchaio.

The tabacchaio sell:

- stamps   francobolli
- newspaper   giornale
- pen   penna
- envelopes   buste per lettere
- postcards   cartoline
- cigars   sigaro
- cigarettes   sigarette
- cigarette paper   cartina
- pipe tobacco   tabacco da pipa
- matches   fiammiferi
- lottery ticket   biglietto di lotteria
- lighter   accendino

Clothing Sizes

The chart below is a comparison guide between US and Italian sizes. Many sizes are not standardized, so you will need to try everything on anyway. Generally if you are above 6'2" and weigh over 200 pounds you may have trouble finding clothing in Italy because the Italians just are not big people. The following conversions should help you out in your shopping quest:

WOMEN'S CLOTHING SIZES

US	2	4	6	8	10	12	14	16
Italy	36	38	40	42	44	46	48	50
Continued								
	18	20	24					
	52	54	56					

WOMEN'S SHOE SIZES

US	5 1/2	6 1/2	7	7 1/2	8	8 1/2	9	10
Italy	35	36	37	38	38 1/2	39	40	41

WOMEN'S HOSIERY SIZES

US	Petite	Small	Medium	Large
Italy	I	II	III	IV

MEN'S SUITS, OVERCOATS, SWEATERS, & PAJAMAS

US	34	36	38	40	42	44	46	48
Italy	44	46	48	50	52	54	56	58

MEN'S SHIRTS

US	14	14 1/2	15	15 1/2	16	16 1/2	17	17 1/2
Italy	36	37	38	39	40	41	42	43

MEN'S SHOES

US	6	6 1/2	7	7 1/2	8	8 1/2	9	9 1/2
Italy	30	40	40 1/2	41	41 1/2	42	42 1/2	43

Continued

10	10 1/2	11-11 1/2
43 1/2	44-44 1/2	45

MEN'S HATS

US	6 7/8	7	7 1/8	7 1/4	7 3/8	7 1/2	7 5/8	7 3/4
Italy	55	56	57	58	59	60	61	62

CHILDREN'S SIZES

US	1	2	3	4	5	6	7	8
Italy	35	40	45	50	55	60	65	70

Continued

9	10	11	12	13	14
75	80	85	90	95	100

CHILDREN'S SHOES

US	4	5	6	7	8	9	10	10 1/2
Italy	21	21	22	23	24	25	26	27

Continued

11	12	13
28	29	30

Key Shopping & Bargaining Phrases

Italian	English
Quanto costa?	How much is this?
E Troppo	That's too much
No Grazie	No thank you
Voglio paggare meno	I want to pay less
Che lai questo pui grande?	Do have this in a bigger size?
..... pui piccolo	..... in a smaller size
..... in nero	..... in black
..... in bianco	..... in white
..... in roso	..... in red
..... in verde	..... in green

When to Bargain

In all stores, even the smallest shops, bargaining is not accepted, just like here in North America. But you can bargain at any street vending location, even if they have placed a sign indicating the price. Don't be afraid to bargain, or you'll end up spending more than you (ahem) 'bargained' for.

Most Italian vendors see foreigners as easy marks to make a few more lire because they know it is not in our culture to bargain, while in theirs it is a way of life.

The best way to bargain, if the street vendor doesn't speak English, is by writing your request on a piece of paper. This keeps it subdued in case you're embarrassed about haggling over money. Basically while in Italy try to let go of that cultural bias. Anyway, you and the vendor will probably pass the paper back and forth a few times changing the numbers before a price is finally agreed upon. And of course, the Italian vendor will be waving his arms about, jabbering away, most probably describing how you're trying to rip him off, all

Italian Soccer Attire

If you or someone you know is a soccer nut, you may want to get them a jersey, hat, or scarf from one of the local teams. Most cities and towns in Italy have a soccer team, whether in the **Serie A** (First Division) or in the three lower divisions. The games are played from September to June and are the best places to get low cost, high quality merchandise.

Outside of most games vendors are selling everything from key rings to official soccer jerseys, all at a low price. The Italian soccer teams are starting to open their own stores featuring their specially-licensed products, like **Milan Point**, for one of the teams in Milan, but those prices will be about four times as much as at the stadium.

in an effort to get you to pay a higher price. Remember, this is all done in fun – so enjoy it.

What You're Allowed to Bring Back Through Customs

See Chapter 5, *Planning Your Trip,* for more details, but in short you can bring back to the US $400 worth of goods duty free. On the next $1,000 worth of purchases you will be assessed a flat 10% fee. These products must be with you when you go through customs.

You can mail products duty free, providing the total value of each package sent is not more than $50 *and* no one person is receiving more than one package a day. Also, each package sent must be stamped "Unsolicited Gift" and the amount paid and the contents of the package must be displayed. They'll be able to tell you all this again at the post office.

What you cannot bring back to North America are any fruits, vegetables, and in most cases meats and cheeses, even if they're for your consumption alone, and even if they are vacuum sealed. Customs has to do this to prevent any potential parasites from entering our country and destroying our crops. Unfortunately, this means all those great salamis and cheeses you bought at those quaint outdoor food markets and had on one of your picnics will not be let back into North America.

But there are some things you can buy. In most supermarkets you can find salamis and cheeses that have been shrink-wrapped, which customs should let through. At the same time all the hard cheeses, like Parmigiano Reggiano and Pecorino, will be let through because they have been cured long enough.

**c
u
l
t
u
r
e
&
a
r
t
s**

Chapter 8

From Etruscans to the Renaissance

Italy is perhaps best known for its great contributions to painting and sculpture; and many art lovers have described the country as one vast museum. Italy gave birth to such world renowned artists as Giotto, Donatello, Raphael, Michelangelo, Leonardo da Vinci, and Botticelli, who are revered the world over.

The oldest works of art in Italy are those of the **Etruscans**, and they date back to the 9th century BCE. This mysterious society's main cities and art centers were in the middle of the peninsula, between Rome and Florence, mainly in the province now know as Tuscany (the region was named after them ... Etruscans ... Tuscany). In Tarquinia, Volterra, Cerveteri, and Veio, the Etruscans have left behind magnificent temples, sculptures, and bronzes as well as other fascinating testimonies to their presence. In Florence, the must-see museum for you Etruscan fans is the **Archaeological Museum**.

Italy is also known for being a repository of ancient Greek art. During the time of the Etruscans, the Greeks established colonies in the south of modern-day Italy as well as Sicily.

After the Greeks and Etruscans, the Roman Empire left its lasting impression all over Italy. There are still roads, bridges, aqueducts, arches, and theaters built by the Romans still in use today, some of which are over 2,000 years old.

After the fall of the Roman Empire, the Byzantine Empire ruled many parts of the southern and eastern regions of Italy. This period left behind many churches, with their glorious mosaics.

Then after the Dark Ages, when the Roman Empire's progress reverted back to tribalism, the Renaissance came. This artistic period, meaning "re-birth," began in Italy in the 14th century and lasted for two hundred years. The Renaissance left us an extensive array of churches, palaces, paintings, statues, and beautiful city squares in almost every city of Italy. The main cities of Florence, Rome, Venice, Milan, and Naples have most of the treasures and beauty of this period, but smaller towns like Ferrara and Rimini also have their share. The best museums for viewing Renaissance art featured in this book are are the **Uffizzi Gallery** and **Pitti Palace** in Florence. If you are traveling to Rom, don't miss the **Vatican Museums** and **Borghese Galleries** (in the Borghese Gardens).

Renaissance Painting

In Italy (with France and Germany soon following suit) during the 14th and 15th centuries, the Renaissance was a period of exploration, invention, and discovery. Mariners from all over Europe set sail in search of new lands. Scientists like **Leonardo da Vinci** studied the mysteries of the world and the heavens. Artists found the human body to be a marvel of mechanics and beauty (but had to secretly study it, as Michelangelo did, lest the Church condemn them for heresy). This was undoubtedly one of Italy's most exciting periods in the history of artistic and scientific advancement.

Many consider the birthplace of Renaissance art to be Florence. It seemed to start with a young painter named **Masaccio**, who began introducing many bold new ideas into his painting. He made his paintings vibrantly interesting by drawing each person completely different from another, as well as making each person as realistic as possible. In conjunction with his ability to express the human form, Masaccio used combinations of colors to give the impression of space and dimension in his landscapes. Now every art student studies how brown makes objects appear closer, and blue makes them appear as if they in the distance.

Paolo Uccello, another Florentine, worked at the same time as Masaccio. A mathematician as well as an artist, he expanded on the mechanical and scientific issues of painting rather than on the human and psychological ones. One of his paintings, *The Battle of San Romano*, circa 1457, celebrated the victory of Florence over Siena some 25 years earlier, and is a brilliant study in **perspective**. His depiction of objects, men, and horses all help to accentuate the sense of real perspective he was trying to achieve. One technique he used, which is now part of any good art school's curriculum, is **foreshortening**. In the left foreground of *The Battle of San Romano* is a fallen soldier with his feet facing the front of the picture. To give this figure a proper perspective, Uccello had to shorten the perceived length of the body, an extremely difficult task, and one not usually seen in other artists' previous works. In conjunction, Uccello drew roads, fields, etc., going back into the painting towards the horizon, to give the impression of distance. Now these are all well used and rather pedestrian artistic techniques, but back then they revolutionized the art world.

But most definitely three of the most influential Renaissance artists were **Raphael, Leonardo da Vinci**, and **Michelangelo**. Raphael was mainly known for his paintings of the Madonna and Child, from which our conceptual image of the Mother of Jesus is largely based. All of his paintings reflect a harmony that leaves the viewer with a warm and positive feeling of contentment.

Leonardo da Vinci is most well known for his *Mona Lisa*, painted in Tuscany in 1505-06 and now hanging in the Louvre, but he was also a versatile architect and scientist as well. Leonardo studied botany, geology, zoology, hydraulics, military engineering, anatomy, perspective, optics, and physiology. You name it, he did it – the original Renaissance Man!

Another versatile artist of the Italian Renaissance, and definitely its most popular then and now – he was always being commissioned to paint or sculpt all the wealthy people's portraits – was Michelangelo Buonarroti. Although he considered himself chiefly a sculptor – he trained as a young boy to become a stone carver – he left us equally great works as a painter and architect. As a painter he created the huge **Sistine Chapel** frescoes in the Vatican, encompassing more than 10,000 square feet in area. As an architect he helped complete the designs for **St. Peter's**, where his world renowned statue, *La Pieta*, currently resides.

Renaissance Sculpture

Besides painting and architecture, Michelangelo was also the pre-eminent sculptor of the Renaissance. By the age of 26 he had carved *La Pieta*, his amazing version of Virgin Mary supporting the dead Christ on her knees; and was in the process of carving the huge and heroic marble *David*. He also created the memorable **Medici tombs** in the Chapel of San Lorenzo, Florence.

Even though Michelangelo was commissioned to create many works by the Popes themselves, he had learned his amazing knowledge of the human anatomy by dissecting cadavers in his home town of Florence as a young man, a crime punishable by death and/or excommunication at the time.

During the Renaissance there were many other sculptors of note, but Michelangelo was truly the best. One of the others was **Lorenzo Ghiberti**, who died a few years before Michelangelo was born. For 29 years he labored to produce ten bronze panels, depicting Biblical episodes, for the doors of the Baptistery of Florence. Michelangelo was said to have been inspired to become a great artist because of these beautiful bronze doors.

Music

Italy also has a great tradition in music. Even today, Italian folk music has made a resurgence, mainly because of the theme song for the *Godfather* movie series. Can't you just hear it playing in your head right now? There are also many opera festivals all over Italy virtually year-round.

Italian Opera

Italian opera began in the 16th century. Over time such composers as Gioacchino Rossini, Gaetano Donizetti, and Vincenzo Bellini created **bel canto** opera – opera that prizes beautiful singing above all else. The best singers were indulged with arias that gave them ample opportunity for a prominent display of their vocal resources of range and agility.

Rossini, who reigned as Italy's foremost composer of the early 19th century, was a master of both melody and stage effects. Success came easily, and while still in his teens he composed the first of a string of 32 operas that he completed by the age of 30. Many of these are comic operas, a genre in which Rossini excelled, and his masterpieces in this form are still performed and admired today. Among them is one you probably recognize, *The Barber of Seville* (1816).

Rossini's immediate successor as Italy's leading operatic composer was **Donizetti**, who composed more than 70 works in the genre. A less refined composer than Rossini, Donizetti left his finest work in comic operas, including *Don Pasquale* (1843) and *Lucia di Lammermoor* (1835).

Although he lived for a shorter time than either Rossini or Donizetti and enjoyed a far briefer career, **Bellini** wrote music that many believe surpassed theirs in refinement. Among the finest of his ten operas are *La Sonnambula* (The Sleepwalker, 1831), *Norma* (1831), and *I Puritani* (The Puritans, 1835), all of which blend acute dramatic perceptions with florid virtuosity.

From these roots came Italy's greatest opera composers of all times, **Puccini** and **Verdi**. Giacomo Puccini lived from 1858-1924 and composed twelve operas in all. Considered by many to be a close second to Verdi in skill of composition, Puccini's music remains alive in the popular mind because of enduring works like *Madame Butterfly* and *La Boheme*. Even though Puccini was the fifth generation of musicians in his family, he was mainly influenced to pursue his career after hearing Verdi's *Aida*.

Giuseppe Verdi lived from 1813-1901, and is best known for his operas *Rigoletto* (1851), *Il Trovatore* and *La Traviata* (both 1853), and what could be the grandest opera of them all, *Aida* (1871). Verdi composed his thirtieth and last opera *Falstaff* at the age of 79.

Opera, Music, Drama, & Ballet Festivals

As the birthplace of opera, Italy offers visitors a variety of choices during the operatic seasons, which are almost year-round. Two of the most spectacular festivals for Italian performing arts are the **Maggio Musicale Fiorentino** with opera, concerts, ballet, and drama performances in Florence from May to June, and the **Festival of Two Worlds** with opera, concerts, ballet, drama performances and art exhibits in Spoleto from mid-June to mid-July. The main opera house in in Florence is **Teatro Communale**, Corso Italia 16, *Tel. 055/ 211-158 or 2729236, Fax 055/277-9410.*

Other events occurring in destinations featured in this book iinclude:
- **Lucca**, April and June: Sacred Music Festival in a variety of churches
- **Marlia (Lucca)**, mid-July to mid-August: Marlia Festival of rare and exotic live performances
- **Perugia**, mid-July to late July: Umbria Jazz Festival. Italy's top jazz festival
- **Siena**, August: musical weeks
- **Torre del Lago Puccini (Lucca)**, August: Puccini opera in the open air theater in Lucca

If you wish to obtain tickets to opera performances, concerts, ballet, and other performances you can either write directly to the theater in question or ask your travel agent to obtain the ticket for you. Currently there is no agency in the US authorized to sell concert and/or opera tickets, so this is the only way. When you are in Italy, your hotel should be able to assist you in obtaining tickets for performances in their city.

Regional & National Folk Festivals

Despite the encroachment of the modern world, the traditional festivals and their accompanying costumes and folk music have survived surprisingly well all over Italy. In many cases they have been successfully woven into the pattern of modern life so as to seem quite normal. Despite all possible modern influences these festivals (both secular and religious) have preserved their distinctive character.

Two of the most famous, the secular festivals of the **Palio** in Siena and **Calcio in Costume** in Florence give foreigners a glimpse into the past customs and way of life of medieval Italians. Both of these festivals pit different sections of their respective cities against each other to see who can earn bragging rights for the year. In Siena, a heated horse race takes place in a crowded city square. In Florence the Piazza della Signorina is turned into a veritable battleground when a game that is a cross between boxing, soccer, rugby, and martial arts is played. And what is most impressive of all in these festivals, besides the competition, is the fact that all participants dress in colorful period garb making each city appear to come alive with the past.

Since Italy is the home of the Catholic church, religious festivals also play a large part in Italian life. Particularly interesting are the processions on the occasion of **Corpus Christi**, **Assumption**, and **Holy Week**. In Italy, holiday times such as Easter and Christmas have not lost their religious intent as they have in most other places, and commercialism takes a back seat to the Almighty. This also means that tradition has not made way for consumerism, allowing us to experience a rich display of costumes, statues, parades, masses and more that evoke a simpler, more peaceful time.

The items below marked by an asterisk are festivals you simply cannot miss; if you can do so, plan your trip around them. The festivals below occur in destinations featured in this book:

JANUARY
- **January 6**, everywhere: Celebration of the Epiphany according to Byzantine rite. Most stores and restaurants are closed.

FEBRUARY/MARCH
- **Both Months**, Pisa: Highlight of the carnival celebrations is the procession of spectacular and colorful floats.
- **19 March**, many places: San Giuseppe (St. Joseph's day)

MARCH/APRIL
- **Palm Sunday**, Many places, particularly Rome and Florence: Blessings of palms, with procession
- **Wednesday before Easter**, Many places: Mercoledi Santo (lamentations, Miserere)
- **Thursday Before Good Friday**, Many places, particularly Rome and Florence: Washing of the Feet, burial of the sacraments
- **Good Friday**, Many places, particularly Rome and Florence: Adoration of the Cross.
- **Easter Saturday**, Many places, particularly Rome and Florence: Lighting of the Sacred Fire
- **Easter Week**, Assisi: Celebration of Spring with rites dating back to ancient times.
- **Easter Day**, Florence: Scopplo dei Carro ("Explosion of the Cart" – A pyramid of fireworks is set off in the Cathedral square to commemorate the victorious return of the first Crusade.

MAY
- **1 May**, * Florence: Calcio in Costume (historical ball game – A Must See; Can't Miss This One)
- **During May**, Florence: Maggio Musicale (Music festival of May)
- **May 15**, Gubbio (Umbria): "Corsa dei Ceri "(procession with candles). Procession in local costumes with tall shrines. They are carried to the church at the top of Mount Ingino.

- **Last Sunday in May**, * Gubbio (Umbria): Palio dei Balestrieri (shooting with crossbows), medieval crossbow contest between Gubbio and Sansepolcro with medieval costumes and arms.
- **Ascension**, Florence: Festival of the Crickets. A lot of fun. You get to take home a cricket in a small cage. Something the Chinese do too, but hey, when in Italy ...
- **Corpus Christi**, Many places, particularly Orvieto (Umbria): Processions.

JUNE

- **First Sunday in June**, Pisa: Gioco del Ponte – medieval parade and contest for the possession of the bridge; *Either Pisa, Genoa, Venice, or the Amalfi Coast: Regatta of the maritime republics. Each year the four former maritime republics of Italy meet to battle for supremacy at sea. The friendly contest takes the form of a historic regatta in which longboats representing each of the republics race for first prize: respect. Site changes between the four cities/regions each year.
- **Mid-June**, Many places: Corpus Domini (Ascension processions)
- **Mid-June to mid-July**, Spoleto (Umbria): International Festival of Music, Dancing and Drama

JULY

- **July 2**, *Siena (Tuscany): Palio delle Contrade (horse race, historical parade). Also held on August 16th.

AUGUST

- **Beginning of August**, Assisi: Perdono (Forgiveness Festival)
- **15 August**, Many places: Assumption (processions and fireworks)
- **16 August**, Siena (Tuscany): Palio delle Contrade (horse-races and processions in medieval costume)

SEPTEMBER/OCTOBER

- **First Sunday in September**, Arezzo (Tuscany): Giostra del Saracino (joust of the Saracen) - Tilting contest from the 13th century with nights.
- **September 7**, Florence: Riticolone (nocturnal festival with lanterns)
- **Second Sunday in September**, Foligno (Umbria): Giostra della Quintane Revival of a 17th century joust with over 600 knights in costume. A historical procession takes place the night before the joust; *Sansepolcro: Palio Balestrieri. Crossbow contest between Sanselpolcro and Gubbio using medieval arms and costumes.
- **September 13**, Lucca (Tuscany): Luminara di Santa Croce

NOVEMBER/DECEMBER

- **November 22**, Many places: Santa Cecilia (St. Cecilia's day)

• **Mid-December to mid-January**, Many places: Christmas crib (Nativity Scenes)

Crafts

Hundreds of thousands of skillful Italian artisans are the heirs to a 2,000-year tradition of craftsmanship. Their products – fashioned of leather, gold, silver, glass, and silk – are widely sought by tourists who flock to Florence, Rome, Milan, and Venice. Cameos made from seashells, an ancient Italian art form, are as popular today as they were in the days of the Roman Empire. The work of Italian artists and artisans is also exported for sale in the great department stores of France, Germany, the United Kingdom, and the U.S.

Italian clothing designers are world famous, especially for precise tailoring, unusual knits, and the imaginative use of fur and leather.

The best place to see Italian artisans at work is in the glass blowing factories of Venice. There you'll be amazed at how easily they can manipulate molten balls into some of the most delicate, colorful, and beautiful pieces you've ever seen.

Literature

Perhaps Italy's most famous author/poet is **Dante Aligheri**, who wrote the *Divine Comedy*, in which he describes his own dream-journey through Hell (*l'Inferno*) Purgatory *(Purgatorio)*, and Paradise *(Paradiso)*. At the time it was extremely controversial, since it is a poem about free will and how man can damn or save his soul as he chooses, which was contrary to church teachings. Even today it sparks controversy since it seems apparent that Dante's description of Purgatory is actually describing the life we all lead on earth, and shows his belief in reincarnation.

Two other notable Italian writers (you should remember these for quality cocktail party conversation) are **Petrarch**, famous for his sonnets to Laura, a beautiful girl from Avignon who died quite young, and is known as the "First of the Romantics;" and **Boccaccio**, the Robin Williams of his time, except he wrote, not performed, his famous *Decameron*, a charming and sometimes ribald series of short stories told by ten young people in a span of ten days. He was sort of like the Chaucer of Italy.

Among contemporary Italian writers, **Umberto Eco** stands out on his own. You may know two of his books that have been translated into English: *The Name of the Rose, Foucault's Pendulum, The Island of the Day Before,* and the just-released (at press time) *Baudolino*. If you are looking for complex, insightful, intriguing, and intellectual reading, Eco's your man. Last but not least, one Italian writer whom children all over the world should know is **Calo Collodi**, who wrote *Pinnochio*.

Chapter 9

Food

Most Italian food is cooked with the freshest ingredients, making their dishes not only healthy but tasty and satisfying. There are many restaurants in Italy of international renown, but you shouldn't limit yourself only to the upper echelon. In most cases you can find as good a meal at a fraction of the cost at any trattoria. Also, many of the upper echelon restaurants you read about are only in business because they cater to the tourist trade. Their food is acceptable, but doesn't warrant the prices charged. I list the best restaurants in every city, where you can get a wonderful meal every time. As you will notice in each regional chapter, I feature some top-of-the-line restaurants as well as many local places, but each are well off the regular tourist path, and each offers a magnificently Italian experience for your enjoyment.

The traditional Italian meal consists of an antipasto (appetizer) and/or soup, and/or pasta and is called primo, a main course called secondo (usually meat or fish), with separately ordered side dishes of contorni (vegetables) or insalata (salad) which come either verdi (green) or mista (mixed), then dolci (dessert), which can be cheese, fruit, or gelato (ice cream). After which you then order your coffee and/or after dinner drink.

Note: Pasta is never served as an accompanying side dish with a secondo. In Italy, it is always served as a separate course. It is time to forget everything you thought you knew about "Italian" food that was learned at some run-of-the-mill restaurant chain.

Many North Americans think that there is one type of Italian food, and that's usually spaghetti and meatballs. As a result they don't know what they are missing. Region by region Italy's food has adapted itself to the culture of the people and land. In Florence you have some of the best steaks in the world, in the south the tomato-based pastas and pizzas are exquisite; in Genoa you

Glossary of Italian Eateries

Bar – Not the bar we have back home. This place serves espresso, cappuccino, rolls, small sandwiches, sodas and alcoholic beverages. It is normal to stand at the counter or sit at a table when one is available. You have to try the **Medalione**, a grilled ham and cheese sandwich available at most bars. A little 'pick-me-up' in the morning is **Café Corretto**, coffee 'corrected' with the addition of **grappa** (Italian brandy) or Cognac.

Gelateria – These establishments offer gelato – ice cream – usually produced on the premises. Italian gelato is softer than American but very sweet and rich.

Osteria – Small tavern-like eatery that serves local wine usually in liter bottles as well as simple food and sandwiches

Panineria – A small sandwich bar with a wider variety than at a regular Italian bar, where a quick meal can be gotten. One thing to remember is that Italians rarely use condiments on their sandwiches. If you want mustard or such you need to ask for it.

Pasticceria – Small pasty shops that sell cookies, cakes, pastries, etc. Carry-out only.

Pizzeria – A casual restaurant specializing in pizza, but they also serve other dishes. Most have their famous brick ovens near the seating area so you can watch the pizza being prepared. There are many excellent featured pizzerias in this book.

Pizza Rustica – Common in central Italy. These are huge cooked rectangular pizzas displayed behind glass. This pizza has a thicker crust and more ingredients than in a regular Pizzeria. You can request as much as you want, since they usually charge by the weight, not the slice.

Rosticceria – A small eatery where they make excellent inexpensive roast chickens and other meats, as well as grilled and roasted vegetables, mainly potatoes. Sometimes they have baked pasta.

Trattoria – A less formal restaurant with many local specialties.

Ristorante – A more formal eating establishment, but even most of these are quite informal at times.

Tavola Calda – Cafeteria-style food served buffet style. They feature a variety of hot and cold dishes. Seating is available. Great places for a quick lunch.

can't miss the pesto sauce (usually garlic, pine nuts, parmiggiano and basil); and don't forget the seafood all along the coast.

Below are each region's specialties, but you'll find examples of different cuisines all over Italy:

- **Piemonte** – fonduta (cheese with eggs and truffles), agnolotti (cheese stuffed pasta), and chocolates and toffees
- **Lombardia** – risotto all milanese (rice with saffron), minestrone (stock and vegetable soup), ossobuco alla milanese (knuckle of pork dish), robiola, gorgonzola, stracchino, Bel Paese (a variety of cheeses)
- **Veneto** – risi e bisi (soup with rice and peas), polenta (corn meal dish) zuppa di pesce (fish soup), scampi (shrimp or prawns)
- **Liguria** – minestrone (stock and vegetable soup), pasta al pesto (pasta with an aromatic garlic basil sauce), torta Pasqualina (Easter pie filled with spinach, artichokes, and cheese)
- **Emilia Romagna** – lasagna verde (lasagna made with spinach), cappelletti alla bolognese (small hats pasta covered with a tomato meat sauce), scallope (scallops) Parmigiano Reggiano (cheese) and a variety of salamis
- **Toscana** – bistecca all Fiorentina (large T-bone steaks grilled), arista (roast pork), cacciucco (fish soup)
- **Lazio** – abbacchio arrosto (roast lamb), porcetta (roast pork), and pastas, including penne all'arrabiata (literally translated it means angry pasta; a spicy hot, garlic-laden, tomato dish; should not be missed) and tortellini alla panna (most of which is cheese stuffed pasta in a heavy cream sauce but sometimes it can be meat stuffed)
- **Campania** – spaghetti alla vongole verace (with a spicy garlic oil sauce.), Fantastic pizzas because of their wonderful cheeses (mozzarella, provola, caciocavallo)
- **Sicilia** – fresh fruits, pastries like cannoli alla Siciliana; caponata di melanzane (eggplant dish), and seafood

Restaurant Listings

The restaurant listings in this book indicate which credit cards are accepted by using the following phrases:

- **Credit cards accepted** = American Express and/or Visa or Mastercard
- **All credit cards accepted** = Everything imaginable is accepted, even cards you've never heard of
- **No credit card accepted** = Only cash or travelers checks (if a listing is left without an indication, that means that no credit cards are accepted.)

Each entry will give a ballpark price for a dinner for two in Euros. For example: "Dinner for two E40." This price represents the cost for two people who choose to eat a full meal of an antipasto, pasta dish and an entrée. In most cases you can get by with one course, which will make the actual price you will

Italian Wines by Region

Piemonte – Barolo (red, dry), Barbera (red, dry), and Asti Spumanti (sweet sparkling wine)

Lombardia – Riesling (white, dry), Frecciarossa (rose wines)

Trentino-Alto Adige – Riesling (white, dry), Santa Maddalena (red, semi-dry), Cabernet (red, dry)

Veneto – Soave (white, dry), Valpolicella (red, dry or semi-sweet)

Liguria – Cinqueterre (named after a section of Liguria you must visit. Cinqueterre is five small seaside towns inaccessible by car or train, you have to walk. They're simply gorgeous.)

Emilia Romagna – Lambrusco (red, semi-sparkling, several kinds going from dry to sweet), Sangiovese (red, dry), Albano (white, dry or semi-sweet)

Tuscany – Chianti (red, dry; look for the Chianti Classico. They're the ones with a black rooster on the neck of the bottle)

Marche – Verdicchio (white, dry)

Umbria – Orvieto (white, dry)

Lazio – Frascati (white, dry or semi-sweet), Est Est Est (white, slightly sweet)

Abruzzi – Montepulciano (red, dry)

Sardinia – Cannonau (red, dry to semi-sweet)

Sicily – Etna (red and white, wide variety), Marsala (white, dry or sweet)

Campania, Apulia, Calabria, Basilicata – Ischia (red and white, several varieties), San Severo (red, dry)

pay less than indicated. With the exchange rate at roughly $1=Euro (E)1, for this example the dollar price would be about $40 for the meal.

Wine

Italy is also famous for its wines. The experts say the reds are not robust enough, and the whites are too light, but I'm not an expert. Personally I think Italian wines are great, one and all. Most importantly, to get a good bottle of wine, you don't have to spend a fortune. You can find some excellent wines straight out of vats in small wine stores in every city in Italy.

At any restaurant, all you'll need to order is the house wine to have a satisfying and excellent wine. (Vino di casa: House Wine; Rosso: Red; Biancho: White). But if you're a connoisseur, or simply want to try a wine for which a certain Italian region is known, in the sidebar above you'll find a selected list of wines and their regions (if you like red wine, try the Chianti, and if it's white you prefer, try Verdicchio or Frascati).

Order Like a Native: Reading an Italian Menu

Here are a few choice words to assist you when you're ordering from a menu while in Italy. Usually, the waiter should be able to assist you, but if not, this will make your dining more pleasurable. You wouldn't want to order octopus, rabbit or horse by surprise, would you?

And if you do not find this list adequate, I can recommend a superb pocket-sized booklet published by Open Road Publishing, *Eating & Drinking in Italy*, by Andy Herbach and Michael Dillon. You will find these ever so useful guides in any bookstore, online or at their website: *www.eatndrink.com*.

ENGLISH	ITALIAN	ENGLISH	ITALIAN
Menu	Lista or Carta	Teaspoon	Cucchiaino
Breakfast	Prima Colazione	Knife	Cotello
Lunch	Pranzo	Fork	Forchetta
Dinner	Cena	Plate	Piatto
		Glass	Bicchiere
Cover	Coperto	Cup	Tazza
Spoon	Cucchiao	Napkin	Tovagliolo

Antipasto

ENGLISH	ITALIAN	ENGLISH	ITALIAN
Soup	Zuppa	Broth	Brodo
Fish Soup	Zuppa di Pesce	Vegetable soup	Minestrone
Broth with beaten egg	Stracciatella		

Pasta

ENGLISH	ITALIAN	ENGLISH	ITALIAN
Ravioli with meat stuffing	Agnolotti	Egg noodles	Fettucine
Large rolls of pasta	Cannelloni	Potato-filled, ravioli-like pasta	Gnocchi
Thin angel hair pasta	Capellini	Thin pasta	Vermicelli
Little hat pasta	Capelletti	Macaroni-like pasta	Penne

Eggs — Uova

ENGLISH	ITALIAN	ENGLISH	ITALIAN
soft-boiled	al guscio	hard boiled	sode
fried	al piatto	omelet	frittata

Fish — Pesce

ENGLISH	ITALIAN	ENGLISH	ITALIAN
Seafood	Frutti di mare	Eel	Anguilla
Lobster	Aragosta	herring	Aringa

Squid	Calamari	Carp	Carpa
Mullet	Cefalo	Grouper	Cernia
Mussels	Cozze/Muscoli	Perch	Pesce Persico
Salmon	Salmone	Clams	Vongole
Octopus	Polpo	Bass	Spigola
Oysters	Ostriche	Mixed fried fish	Fritto Misto Mare

Meat — Carne

Spring Lamb	Abbacchio	Lamb	Agnello
Rabbit	Coniglio	Chicken	Pollo
Small Pig	Porcello	Veal	Vitello
Steak	Bistecca	Breast	Petto
Pork	Maiale	Liver	Fegato
Cutlet	Costellata	Deer	Cervo
Wild Pig	Cinghiale	Pheasant	Fagione
Duck	Anitra	Turkey	Tacchino

Methods of Cooking

Roast	Arrosto	Boiled	Bollito
On the Fire/ Grilled	Ai Ferri Alla Griglia	Spit-roasted	Al Girarrosto
Rare	Al Sangue	Grilled	Alla Griglia
Well Done	Ben Cotto	Medium Rare	Mezzo Cotto

Miscellaneous

French fries	Patate Fritte	Cheese	Formaggio
Butter Sauce	Salsa al burro	Tomato and Meat Sauce	Salsa Bolognese
Tomato Sauce	Salsa Napoletana	Garlic	Aglio
Oil	Olio	Pepper	Pepe
Salt	Sale	Fruit	Frutta
Orange	Arancia	Cherries	Ciliege
Strawberry	Fragola	Lemon	Limone
Apple	Mela	Melon	Melone
Beer	Birra	Mineral Water	Aqua Minerale
Orange Soda	Aranciata	7 Up-like	Gassatta
Lemon Soda	Limonata	Juice (of)	Succo (di)

Wine — Vino

Red	Roso	White	Bianco
House wine	Vino di Casa	Dry	Secco
Slightly Sweet	Amabile	Sweet	Dolce

Local Wine	Vino del Paese	Liter	Litro
Half Liter	Mezzo Litro	Quarter Liter	Un Quarto
A Glass	Un Bicchiere		

In all restaurants in Italy there used to be a universal cover charge, pane e coperto (literally "bread and cover"), which was different restaurant to restaurant, and in some cases was quite expensive. **Pane e coperto** was tacked on to your bill above and beyond any tip you decided to leave; but in msot cases, many places in Italy has decided that foreigners would not understand what pane e coperto is so they have eliminated it. Butm if your bill has an extra E5 or so, that is the pane e coperto, which covers the cost of the basket of bread at your table and gives you the right to sit there.

There will also be a statement about whether service is included, **servizio incluso**, or not, **servizio non incluso**. If service is included it is usually 15% of the bill. If you felt the service was good, it is customary to leave between 5-10% more for the waiter. Another feature on most menus are **piatti di giorno** (daily specials) and **prezzo fisso** (fixed price offerings.) The latter can be a good buy if you like the choices and is usually a better deal than ordering a la carte. If you have trouble reading the menu, ask your waiter for assistance. Usually they will speak enough English to to help. And in many restaurants there are menus in different languages to help you choose the food you want.

Chapter 10

best places to stay

Florence

HOTEL TORRE DI BELLOSGUARDO, *Via Roti Michelozzi 2, Tel. 055/229-8145, Fax 055/229-008. E-mail: torredibellosguardo@dada.it. Web: www.torrebellosguardo.com/ . 16 room all with bath. Single E195; Double E265; Suites E275-325. All credit cards accepted.* ****

If you have the means, this is definitely the most memorable place to stay while in Florence. With stunning views over all of Florence, a swimming pool with a bar at which to relax, olive gardens in which to take an evening stroll, the Bellosguardo is like no other hotel in Florence. Housed in a huge old castle that has been separated into only 16 luxury rooms, it goes without saying that the size of accommodations are quite impressive. The interior common areas with their vaulted stone ceilings and arches, as well as staircases leading off into hidden passages, all make you feel as if you've stepped back in time.

The hotel is a short distance outside of the old city walls in the middle of pristine farmland. You will find pure romance, complete peace, and soothing tranquillity all with stunning views of the city of Florence. In fact the hotel is so well thought of that they are booked solid year round, so you have to reserve well in advance. I can't say enough about the Bellosguardo, it is simply something you have to experience. Also, and most importantly, if you aren't already in love, you'll find it or rekindle it in this wonderfully majestic hideaway.

LOGGIATO DEI SERVITI, *Piazza SS. Annunziata 3, Tel. 055/289-593/4, Fax 055/289-595. E-mail: info@loggiatodeiservitihotel.it. Web: www.loggiatodeiservitihotel.it/. All credit cards accepted. 29 rooms all with private bath. Single E139; Double E201; Suite E268-382. Breakfast included. E40 for an extra bed.* ***

Located in a 16th century *loggia* facing the quiet, quaint and colorful Piazza della SS Annunziata, this hotel is filled with charm, character and is a three star of the highest quality. The interior common areas consist of polished terra-cotta floors, gray stone columns and high white ceilings.

The rooms are pleasant and comfortable and are filled with elegant antique furnishings. All are designed to make you feel like you just walked into the 17th century, and it works. But they do have the modern amenities necessary to keep us weary travelers happy, especially the air conditioning in August.

The best room possible would definitely be #30. From here you have unobstructed views of the Duomo, the spire of the Palazzo Vecchio, and Fort Belvedere beyond the Arno. Out the side windows of this unique room, you can look down into the Accademia and the skylight under which the David stands! A special treat for any traveler.

Some rooms face what many believe is one of the most beautiful piazzas in Italy (no cars allowed), while many of the rest face onto a lush interior garden. They are finished renovation on five additional rooms on the third floor, which will be top of the line accommodations. This place only gets better and better. All the bathrooms come with every modern comfort. The service, the accommodations, everything is at the top of the three star category. So, if you want to have a wonderful stay and also to feel as if you've stepped back in time, book a room here. They also have facilities for weddings and business functions.

LA SCALETTA, *Via Guicciardini 13, Tel. 055/283-028, Fax 055/289-562. E-mail: lascaletta@italyhotel.com. Web: www.venere.com/it/firenze/lascaletta/. Mastercard and Visa accepted. 12 rooms, 11 with private bath. Single without E75; Single E85-95; Double without E100; Double E110-130. Breakfast included.* **

Looking for a great place to stay for a lot less money? No ifs, ands, or buts about it, this is the best place to stay in the Oltrarno ... and maybe all of Florence for the value. But you have to reserve months in advance to guarantee a room overlooking the garden! There's no air conditioningexcept in three rooms, but it's not needed. This ancient building seems to soak up the cold air in the summer and retain the warm in the winter.

The rooms are large, clean and comfortable. The location is ideal and quiet. And best of all there are two incomparable terraces overlooking all the best sights of Florence. Relaxing on these terraces after a day on the town makes a stay here sublime.

The furnishings are eclectic and simple, but comfortable; and the layout is scattered throughout the building, with everything connected by staircases. The prices are superb but they won't last forever.

Elsewhere in Tuscany

VILLA SAN MICHELLE, *Via Doccia 4, 50014 Fiesole. Tel. 055/59-451, Fax 055/598-734. 36 rooms all with bath. American Express, Diners Club, Mastercard and Visa accepted. Single E350; Double E500-650. Jr. Suite E950-1,000. Suite E1,200. Breakfast included.* *****

Located in a converted 15th century monastery that has a facade attributed to Michelangelo, this hotel in Fiesole will allow you to bring home stories of beautiful views, ancient habitations, and opulent surroundings. There's a private park and beautiful gardens on-site. The reception area of the hotel is an old chapel, and in the dining room, the bar is made from an ancient Etruscan sarcophagus.

Each room has a four poster bed and everything else is rustically luxurious. The best rooms overlook the gardens that surround the hotel. You can enjoy an outdoor pool (with waterfall) during the day, a wonderfully scenic view from the restaurant in the evening (you can dine indoor or out), and a boisterous piano bar at night.

Note: the hotel is only open March through November.

Umbria

RESIDENZA DELL'OSCANA, *06134 Locanda Cenerente, Perugia. Tel. 075/690-125, Fax 075/690-666, Email: oscano@krenet.it, Web: www.oscano-castle.com & www.assind.krenet.it/oscano/welcome.htm. 100 rooms all with bath. All credit cards accepted. Breakfast included.* **Castle**: *Suite or junior suite on the top floor of the castle is E220; three rooms elsewhere in the castle E170.* **Villa Ada**: *Double E120 per room per night.* **La Macina**: *Weekly rates E320 to E700. Buffet breakfast included and is served in the dining room of the castle.*

Stunning. Incredibly beautiful. Amazing. Like something out of a fairy tale. Simply unbelievable. By far the best place to stay in all of Umbria. If you have a car, and you have the means, this is definitely the place to stay in Umbria. Near Perugia but set deep in the surrounding verdant forested hills, this amazing medieval castle offers an atmosphere of unparalleled charm and ambiance.

There are three locations to choose from: the Castle (a medieval structure complete with towers and turrets that is simply but elegantly decorated and equipped with every comfort); the Villa Ada (a 19th century residence adjoining the castle that is more modern but no less accommodating); and La Macina (a country house down the hill from the other two structures, which comes with complete apartments and an adjacent pool). All three offer the setting for an ideal vacation, but the castle is the place to stay because of its unique, one of a kind, medieval ambiance and charm. A perfect place to spend a honeymoon or simply have the vacation of a lifetime.

Besides the excellent accommodations, you will also find the finest quality cuisine served nightly in the grand hall in the castle. World class chefs cater to your every need as they creatively concoct regional and international dishes from fresh locally grown produce and game. This is a residence and not a hotel, so it does not carry a star rating, but it would easily receive four stars if it decides to allow itself to be regulated by the tourist industry.

LA BADIA, *1a Cat., 05019 Orvieto. Tel 0763/301-959 or 305-455, Fax 0763/305-396. All credit cards accepted. Single E140; Double E320.* ****

An unbelievably beautiful 12th century abbey at the foot of Orvieto is now an incredibly beautiful hotel and restaurant. Located only an hour from Rome, you will find one of the most unique and memorable experiences in the entire world. This historic abbey became a holiday resort for Cardinals in the 15th century, and today, through painstakingly detailed renovations, you can stay or dine in incomparable ambiance and charm.

The rooms are immense, the accommodations exemplary, the service impeccable, and the atmosphere like something out of the Middle Ages. For a fairy tale vacation stay here, and make sure that you eat at least once at their soon to be world renowned restaurant that offers refined local dishes — many ingredients culled from owner Count Fiumi's farms and vineyards — in an incredibly historic and romantic atmosphere.

Chapter 11

florence

A visit to Italy is not complete without a trip to **Firenze** (**Florence**), which is one of the most awe-inspiring cities in all of Europe. The Renaissance reached its full heights of artistic expression here, and it was in Florence that countless master artists, writers, inventors, political theorists and artisans lived and learned their craft, then excelled at filling the world with the glow of their brilliance. Michelangelo and Leonardo da Vinci may be the best known outside of Italy, but I'll wager you've also heard of Dante, Petrarch, Machiavelli, Giotto, Raphael and many other learned and talented Florentines.

Strolling through the cobblestone streets of Florence is like being in an art history book come to life. The sights, smells, and sounds of this wonderful medieval city must be experienced first-hand to appreciate and understand the magical atmosphere. So read on, and I'll guide you through the amazingly lovely city of Florence!

Alive with History – Beautiful Firenze!

Florence started out simply, as the market square for the ancient Etruscan town of **Fiesole**, which is located on a hill about three miles (five kilometers) to the northeast. Farmers displayed their fruits and vegetables on the clearing along the **Arno**, and the Fiesole people came down to buy. About 187 BCE, the Romans built a road through the marketplace, and later a military garrison was established here.

As the Roman roads extended through central and northern Italy, Florence grew and prospered, and it became a trade center for goods brought down from the north. Because of its significance invaders sought its spoils; and in 401 CE a horde of Ostrogoths besieged the city; then in 542 the Goths made an unsuccessful attack. Soon after, the Lombard conquest swept over Florence, and the city became the capital of a Lombard dukedom. In time, the Holy Roman Empire led by Charlemagne drove the Lombards out and in 799 ordered new fortifications built. Charlemagne's death in 814 ended the Holy Roman Empire's hold on Florence, at which time it became an independent city-state.

With its new-found freedom, Florence expanded rapidly. The Florentines became energetic merchants and bankers, expert workmen, brave soldiers, and shrewd statesmen. By the 1100s their guilds were among the most powerful in Europe, and Florentine textiles were sold throughout the continent. Florentine bankers financed enterprises in many countries, and in 1252 the city coined its first gold pieces, called **florins**, which became the accepted currency for all of Europe.

Although Florence was largely self-governing, for a long time the city was the property of German princes. The last to hold it was Countess Matilda of Tuscany. At her death in 1115, the countess bequeathed Florence to the papacy. In the early 1200s, the papal power was supported by a political group called the **Guelfa**, while the claims of the German emperor were backed by another group, the **Ghibellines**. This conflict lasted almost a hundred years and was formally initiated in 1215 when the rival factions each tried to seize control of the city.

Aided by several popes, the Guelfa held power in the city until 1260 when their army was almost wiped out at a battle near Siena. The Ghibellines held the reins for six years, until in 1266, Charles of Anjou, the champion of Pope Clement IV, marched down from France and smashed the forces of the German emperor at the battle of Benevento – at which point the Guelfa exiles were able to return to Florence.

In 1293, the **Ordinances of Justice** were passed. These laws excluded from public office anyone who was a member of a Florentine guild. As a result many powerful people were barred from holding public positions, and the strength of the merchant-nobles was thus reduced for a time. Because of these laws, Florence remained a republic for about 150 years; but the control of the city, however, soon passed back into the hands of the wealthy.

The **Medici** family gradually took possession of Florence, installing their puppets throughout city government. Giovanni de' Medici was the first of this family to gain real wealth and influence. His son Cosimo was the real ruler of Florence for many years; it was he who brought exiled Greek scholars to the city. Under Cosimo's grandson **Lorenzo the Magnificent**, Florence ascended to its greatest heights as a cultural center.

After Lorenzo died in 1492, the city's excesses brought on a reform movement headed by **Girolamo Savonarola**, a Dominican friar. The Medici family was expelled in 1494 and Savonarola then ruled Florence himself until 1498, when a popular reaction to his rule erupted and he was put to death.

In 1512 'la familgia Medici' were restored to the city, and in 1537 it became part of the Grand Duchy of Tuscany. Upon the death of the last Medici in 1737, Tuscany passed to the Austrian Hapsburgs. In 1861 it was formally annexed to the newly formed Kingdom of Italy, of which Florence was the capital from 1865 to 1870.

In World War II, Florence was a battleground, as was the entire country. Italy entered the war on the German side in 1940, and soon after German troops occupied Florence. When the Allies advanced in 1944, the Germans declared Florence an open city, yet in retreating they destroyed all the bridges except the Ponte Vecchio, and they demolished many medieval dwellings as well. Later the Allied Military Government restored the less seriously damaged structures helping to maintain the old charm the city retains today.

In 1966, Florence's many masterpieces were lost when the Arno River overflowed its banks, rising as high as 20 feet

An Incredible Statue, a Fabulous Inn!

If this is your first visit to la bella Italia, you must visit Florence. The small Renaissance streets, the countless art galleries, the friendly people, and the fine food all make this city a joy to visit. But not in high season. Florence in the summer is a zoo of tourists (not quite as bad as Venice, but close) all crammed together or queued for blocks to see the main sights. Florence definitely should be visited in the off-season, not only to save on your hotel bills (hotels drop their rates dramatically in the off-season) but also to make your entire stay more enjoyable and relaxing.

It is one thing to savor the excellence of Michelangelo's **David** virtually alone, and almost believe that you saw it move, but quite another to have to fight your way through a crowd just to get close enough to try and see that majestic statue. But no matter when you visit, if you're looking for some peace and tranquillity, try the unmatched **Torre Di Bellosguardo**, one of my favorite hotels anywhere.

A medieval castle perched prominently above the city, here you'll find some of the best views of Florence. It is a supremely romantic spot filled with gardens, olive trees where horses graze, an open lawn in front, and a pool with a bar all overlooking this magnificent city. But there are only 16 rooms here, so if you want to experience the best accommodations Florence has to offer you must plan far enough in advance.

Rebirth of Art & Science in Florence

Florence, rather than Rome, was the cradle of the Italian **Renaissance**. This rebirth of classical knowledge soon gave way to new creativity in art and literature, and Florentines led the procession. **Dante's** magnificent poetry made the Tuscan dialect the official language of Italy. **Francesco Petrarch** composed his lovely sonnets here, and **Giovanni Boccaccio's** Decameron was penned here as well. **Niccolo Machiavelli**, another Florentine, set down his brilliant, cynical observations on politics based on the intrigue intrinsic to Florentine politics.

Giotto was the first of many immortal Florentine painters and sculptors. **Michelangelo** worked by day on the city's fortifications and by night on his paintings and statues. **Ghiberti** labored almost a lifetime on the doors for the Florentine Baptistery. Many other great artists studied or worked in Florence, among them **Leonardo da Vinci, Donatello**, and **Raphael**.

(6 meters) in some places. Many of the more important damaged works have since been restored, but thousands of irreplaceable treasures were lost to ruin brought by the mud and water.

Four Day Itinerary In & Around Florence

These itineraries include day trips elsewhere in Tuscany; see chapter 12, *Elsewhere in Tuscany*, for more details.

DAY ONE
Morning

To begin, let's walk to the **Accademia** and see Michelangelo's *David*. Make sure that you have made reservations already by going to *www.firenze.net* and booking specific entry times. Take in all the other works by the master which are located here.

Lunch

Walk back to the **Piazza San Lorenzo** where there is a daily market. Go to **Nerbone's** in the **Mercato Centrale** for lunch. Try one of their amazing Panini (boiled beef or pork) served on a Panino bread roll. They'll ask whether you want some juice (sugo) placed on the roll. Tell them si (yes); it makes it much tastier. Order a beverage and sit at one of the tables directly in front of the quaint little place.

After your meal, wander through the market. Check out all the different cuts of meat the Italians use in their recipes. Upstairs is the vegetable and fruit market. A good place to buy some healthy snacks for later.

Afternoon

After you're done shopping head to the nearby **Piazza Duomo**. Admire the bronze doors on the belfry, the simplicity of the baptistery, and the expanse of the church. Take the time to go all the way up top of the dome.

If needed, take a little siesta. If it's not needed head to the **Piazza della Signoria** and admire the statues in the Loggia. Also go into the **Palazzo della Signoria** and admire the staircase that leads to their museum. This was the residence of the Medici until the Palazzo Pitti was made available. If you're interested go upstairs and pay the fee to see the inside.

Just outside of the Piazza dell Signoria is the **Uffizi Gallery**, which you'll be going to tomorrow. Remember to have made your reservations well in advance using *www.firenze.net.*

Now make your way to the **Ponte Vecchio** over the river **Arno**. Shop for jewelry in the many little stores if you want, but make sure you stop in the middle of the bridge and take each other's photo with the river as a background. Follow the bridge over to the other side of the Arno.

From here we're going to the **Pitti Palace** and the **Boboli Gardens**. Each museum has beautiful artwork in the building, and the gardens offer peace and tranquillity are filled with many wonderful statues. If you bought some snacks at the **Mercato Centrale** you may want to take the time to have a brief picnic in the gardens. When you leave, check out the store **Firenze Papier Mache** in the piazza across from the palace.

Evening

Return to your room to freshen up and get ready for dinner. Tonight we're going to a wonderful local place called **La Bussola**, Via Porta Rossa 58, *Tel. 055/293-376*. You can either sit at the counter and have a simple meal of pizza or sit in the back and soak up all the ambiance and romance of Florence. Try their spaghetti alla Bolognese (with a meat and tomato sauce) or their tortellini alla panna (cheese or meat stuffed tortellini in a cream sauce).

After dinner wander over to the Piazza Santa Maria Novella and stop at the **Fiddler's Elbow** for a pint. This place has an authentic Irish Pub atmosphere, great Italian people and fun times. If dancing is your desire, try the **Space Electronic** nearby at Via Palazzuolo 37, *Tel. 055/292-082*.

DAY TWO
Morning

Get to the **Uffizi Gallery** a half an hour before your reservations indicate you should and pick up your tickets. You'll probably spend all morning here.

Lunch

For lunch try a quaint basement restaurant between the **Duomo** and the train station and near Piazza Santa Maria Novella, **Buca Lapi,** Via del Trebbio 1, *Tel. 055/213-768*. There are old travel posters plastered all over the walls and ceiling, and the tables surround the cooking area so you can view quite a display while you wait for your food. Depending on the season, it may be closed for lunch. Try their cinghiale con patate fritte (roasted wild boar with fried potatoes) or their pollo al cacciatore con spinacio (chicken 'hunter style' which is made with tomatoes, spices and brandy and comes with spinach)

Afternoon

Remember the church in the piazza where the **Fiddler's Elbow** was last night? We're going there now (**Chiesa di Santa Maria Novella**) to check out the overall ambiance and to admire the frescoes painted by Michelangelo. While we're in this area of town, check out the store **Il Tricolore**, Via della Scala 25, just off the piazza. This is the official outlet for the police and military in Florence where you can buy a variety of items like pins, hats, shirts, badges, that you can take home as gifts. Some items they won't sell to you, like guns, knives, and uniforms.

Next we're walking slightly across town to get to the place where Michelangelo is buried, **Chiesa di Santa Croce**. Inside the church you will also find many other graves of prominent Florentines including Dante Aligheri. There is a leather shop attached to the church where you can find some of the best hand-made leather goods anywhere. It is also a treat to watch them work the leather. A great place to visit and/or shop.

Late Afternoon

From here, we're going up to the **Piazzale Michelangelo** to watch the sun set. This is really a hike. If you do not want to walk, the cab ride will be quite dear, but the view is worth it. Remember to take your camera and high speed film to catch all the light possible. You'll get some of the best shots of Florence from up here. If you want to splurge on a fantastic meal, try **La Loggia**, Piazzale Michelangelo 1, once you get up here. It's very expensive but well worth it. Or, on the way back down the hill into town, stop at **Il Rifrullo**, Via San Niccolo 55, to get a pint of beer or glass of wine. At night this is an isolated and relaxing place to come and savor the Florentine evenings.

From here take the long walk across the river to the train station to establish your itinerary for tomorrow. You may have to wait a little while in the information office, but it's worth it so you won't have to do it in the morning.

Evening

For dinner tonight we're going to the **Tredici Gobbi** (which means "13 hunchbacks") located on Via Porcellana. Situated down a small side street near the Arno, here you can enjoy a combination of Italian and Hungarian cuisine. For an after-diner drink wander over to the nearby **Excelsior Hotel** and go up to their roof deck. Enjoy a sambuca con tre mosce, literally translated it means "sambuca (a liquorice drink) with three flies," but in actuality the flies are coffee beans. When you bite into the beans as you sip the Sambuca the combination of tastes is phenomenal. Here you have a view over all of Florence as it lines the Arno.

DAY THREE

Since you've now seen virtually everything that a traveler is supposed to see in Florence, let's take a day trip outside of the city to **Pisa** and **Lucca**. We'll first go to Pisa to admire the leaning tower, and its cute little market near the Arno. Next we'll go to Lucca to walk around the romantic walls and see a virtually perfectly preserved old medieval town.

Pisa

Once you arrive in Pisa, stop in the tourist office just outside the station to the left and pick up a map of the city. Then if you're tired take the No. I bus directly to the **Piazza dei Miracoli** which has the church, baptistery and leaning tower. Admire them all and take plenty of pictures. If you decide to walk (it only takes about 15 minutes to get to the Piazza dei Miracoli) you must pass by the colorful market of **Piazza Vettovaglie** near the river and just off of the **Borgo Stretto**, the street with the famous covered sidewalk. It's well worth the visit.

For lunch we'll stop at the **Il Cavallino**, Via San Lorenzo 66, *Tel. 0577/ 432-290*. It's off the beaten tourist path and that's one reason why the food is so great. Try the Roman specialty, penne all' arrabiata ('literally translated it means 'angry pasta' and is a tomato-based sauce with garlic, hot peppers, and parsley). Or sample the sogliola alla griglia (grilled sole) or the petto di pollo alla griglia (grilled chicken breast).

Lucca

Now it's back to the train station and onto Lucca. Once you arrive simply walk out of the station towards the old walls of the city. Follow the path leading to the walls where you will find an entrance into the walls themselves. Follow the stairs inside up to the top. Now you're on the old battlements and ramparts. Walk around them to your left about 400 meters until you get to the **Piazza Verdi/Vecchia Porto San Donato** where the tourist office is located. You'll know you're there by the size of the piazza inside the walls and the fact that this is where tour buses park. Descend and pick up a map of the city from the tourist office, you'll need it.

Now it's time to go to the **Torre del Guinigio**. This tower has trees and bushes growing on its top. Go up here to get great views of the city and the surrounding area. Use the map to explore the old Roman amphitheater, Puccini's museum, the cathedral, and more. And of course, take some more walks along the romantic tree-lined battlements.

For dinner, we'll be going to **Da Leo Fratelli Buralli**, Via Tegrini, *Tel. 0583/492-236*. This is the best, most authentic restaurant in Lucca. It caters to the locals, the food is stupendous and the atmosphere festive. Try the fettucine all rucola e gamberi (pasta with a cheese and shrimp sauce), the pollo arrosto con patate (exquisite roasted chicken and potatoes flavored with rosemary and olive oil), or the pollo fritto e zucchini (chicken and zucchini fried in olive oil). If you miss the last train back to Florence, which leaves at 9:00pm, get a room at the **Piccolo Hotel Puccini**, Via di Poggio 9, *Tel. 0583/55-421*.

DAY FOUR
Siena

Located about an hour and a half from Florence, Siena is a perfect day trip. Here you have the famous **Campo**, a tower that rises above the city for great photos, quaint medieval streets and plenty of ambiance to spare. The cathedral seems out of place since it is so large in a relatively small square. If the Florentines hadn't conquered the city when they did, the locals would have made the tower almost twice as large. Did you know that in its hey-day Siena was larger than either London or Paris?

Once you arrive at the station you can easily walk up the hill, then descend into the old town. Or take bus number 1 or 8 to get dropped off near the tourist office (ask at the information desk inside which bus takes you to the tourist office; I was told they may be changing).

Despite its past prominence, you can wander around Siena quite easily. In your walking make sure you stop in **Pizzigheria** at 95 Via della Citta just off the Campo. Here you'll find the most savory aromas emanating from their meats and cheeses hanging haphazardly all over the store. A perfect place to get a snack. You'll recognize the store from afar by the stuffed boar's head hanging outside with sunglasses on.

If you want a sit-down meal on the quaint Campo with actual waiters serving you, try the **Spada Forte**. Their specialty is all types of pizza and the succulent Cinghiale alle Senese (wild boar).

Arrivals & Departures
By Bus

There are many different bus companies in Italy, each serving a different set of cities and sometimes the same ones. Buses should be used only if the train does not go to your destination since traffic is becoming more and more of a problem in Italy.

The most convenient bus company in Florence is located directly next to the train station in **Piazza Adua**, called **Autolinee Lazzi**, *Tel. 055/215-154*

If You Miss These Places, You Haven't Been to Florence

After spending all your time and money to come to this Renaissance paradise, there are a few sights that if you don't see you can't really say you've been to Florence. The first of which, the **Duomo** with its campanile and baptistery, is hard to miss. The next, the **Ponte Vecchio**, is a gem of medieval and Renaissance architecture and is filled with gold and jewelry shops. And if you miss Michelangelo's **David** in the Accademia you shouldn't show your face back in your home town. That work of art is as close to sculpted perfection as any artist will ever achieve.

Last but not least is the art collection in the **Uffizzi Gallery**. To actually do this museum justice you may need to spend close to one day wandering through its many rooms. And don't forget to shop at the **San Lorenzo Market** or browse through the local **Mercato Centrale**.

There are countless other wonderful sights to see and places to go in Florence. Walking the streets is like walking through a fairy tale. But if you haven't seen the items above, you haven't been to Florence.

. They have over 50 arrivals and departures a day to and from a variety of different locations like Pisa, Lucca, Prato, and Pistoia. Two other bus companies are: **Autolinee Sita**, *Tel. 055/214721 or 284661*, and **Autolinee CAP**, *Tel. 055/218603*.

By Car

If arriving in Florence from the south, for speed you will be on the **A1 (E35)**. If you were looking for a more scenic adventure, you would be on the **Via Cassia** which you can take all the way from Rome. If arriving from the north in a hurry, you would also take the **A1 (E35)**, but if in no rush you would probably take the **SS 65**.

If you need to rent a car while in Florence, please refer to the *Getting Around Town* section of this chapter, below.

Sample trip lengths on the main roads:
• **Rome**: 3 1/2 hours
• **Venice**: 4 hours
• **Bologna**: 1 1/2 hours

By Train

The station, **Stazione Santa Maria Novella**, is located near the center of town and is easily accessible on foot to and from most hotels. The **tourist**

information office in the station, *Tel. 055/278-785,* is open daily from 7:00am to 10:00pm and is your first stop if you don't have a reservation at a hotel. The **railway office**, at the opposite end of the station from the tourist information office, is where you plan your train trip from Florence. To get served you need to take a number and wait your turn, a concept that is still foreign to many Italians.

The wait can be quite long, but it is entertaining watching Italians become completely confused about having to take a number, wait in a queue, and actually do something in an organized fashion. First your average Italian will attempt to assert his Latin ego to an information officer, whether they are serving someone else or not, get rebuffed, attempt to do it again with another information officer, get rebuffed again, finally look at the machine spitting out numbers and the directions associated with it, stare as would a deer trapped in an oncoming car's headlights, turn and glare at the long line formed since they first attempted their folly, then ultimately strut out of the office without getting the information they need. I've seen it happen so many times!

There are **taxis** located just outside the entrance near the tourist information office as well as **buses** that can take you all over the city.

Sample trip lengths and costs for direct *(diretto)* trains:
• **Rome**: 2 1/2 hours, E40
• **Venice**: 3 1/2 hours, E15
• **Bologna**: 1 hour, E10.

Getting Around Town
By Bus
There is no need to go by bus in Florence unless you're going up to Fiesole. But if you need to, first get information from the booth at the **Piazza della Stazione** across the piazza from the station itself. Here they can give you all the information you need to get anywhere you want to go. A ticket costs Euro 75 cents and is reusable within an hour.

At all bus stops, called **fermata**, there are signs that list all the buses that stop there. These signs also give the streets that the buses will follow along its route so you can check your map to see if this is the bus for you. Also, on the side of the bus are listed highlights of the route for your convenience. Nighttime routes (since many buses stop a midnight) are indicated by black spaces on newer signs, and are placed at the bottom of the older signs. In conjunction, the times listed on the signs indicate when the bus will pass the *fermata* during the night so you can plan accordingly.

Riding the bus during rush is very crowded, so try to avoid the rush hours of 8:00am to 9:00am, 12:30pm to 1:30pm, 3:30 to 4:30pm, and 7:30pm to 8:30pm. They have an added rush hour in the middle of the day because of their siesta time in the afternoon.

The information number for the local bus company, **ATAF-Autobus Urbani** , is *Tel. 055/5650-222*.

By Car

Renting a car is relatively simple, as things go in Italy, but it is somewhat expensive. You can rent a car from a variety of agencies all over Florence. All prices will vary by agency so please call them for an up-to-date quote.
• **Avis**, Borgo Ognissanti 128r, *Tel 055/21-36-29 or 239-8826*
• **Avis**, Lungarno Torrigiani 32/3, *Tel 055/234-66-68 or 234-66-69*
• **Budget**, Borgo Ognissanti 134r, *Tel. 055/29-30-21 or 28-71-61*
• **Euro Dollar**, Via il Prato 80r, *Tel 055/238-24-80, Fax 055/238-24-79*
• **Hertz**, Via Maso Finiguerra 33, *Tel. 055/239-8205, Fax 055/230-2011*
• **Maggiore**, Via Maso Finiguerra 11r, *Tel. 055/21-02-38*

Most companies require a deposit that amounts to the cost of the rental, as well as a 19% VAT added to the final cost, which can be reimbursed once you're home (see Chapter 6, *Basic Information*). A basic rental of a Fiat Panda costs E80 per day, but the biggest expense is gasoline. In Italy it costs more than twice as much per gallon as it does in the States. If you're adventurous enough to think of renting a car, remember that the rates become more advantageous if you rent for more than a week.

By Moped

Since Florence is so small, the areas in Tuscany I'm recommending are quite close together, and the drivers are not quite as crazy as Romans, a moped (50cc) or **vespa** (125cc) is one of the best ways to get around and see the countryside. But this isn't a simple ride in the park. Only if you feel extremely confident about your motorcycle driving abilities should you even contemplate renting a moped.

Rentals for a moped (50cc) are about E30 per day, and for a 125cc (which you'll need to transport two people) about E40 per day. From some companies you can rent even bigger bikes, but I would strongly advise against it. You can also rent the cycles for an hour or any multiples thereof.
• **Firenze Motor**, Via Guelfa 85r. *Tel 055/280-500, Fax 05/211-748*. Located in the Centro section to the right of the station and north of the Duomo.
• **Noleggio dell Fortezza** (two locations),Corner of Via Strozzi and Via del Pratello, Open 9:00am to 8:00pm, the 15th of March to 31st of October; and Via Faenza 107-109r. *Tel. 055/283-448*. **Scooter prices**: 1 hour E5/ half day E10/1 day E20. **Bicycle prices**: 1 hour E1.5/half day E5/1 day E8.
• **Motorent**, Via San Zanobi 9, *Tel. 055/490-113*. In the Centro area.
• **Sabra**, Via Artisti 8, *Tel. 055/576-256*. In the Oltrarno area.
• **Free Motor**, Via Santa Monaca 6-8, *Tel. 055/293-102*. In the Oltrarno area.

By Bicycle

Some of the moped rental places listed above also rent bicycles, but by far the best bicycle rental service and definitely the most professional is:

• **Florence By Bike**, Via San Zanobi 120/122, Tel./Fax 055/488-992, Email: ecologica@dada.it; Web: www.florencebybike.it. Open from 9:00am-7:30pm every day; Credit cards accepted. Not only do they offer bicycles for rent (1 hour E2; 5 hours E6; Day E10; Weekend E20) at great prices, but they also offer guided city tours as well as countryside tours. Located near Piazza Santa Maria Novella, this is the place to come for good quality bike rentals and fun and informative bike tours.

By Taxi

Florence is a city made for walking, but if you get tired, taxis are good but expensive way to get around. They are everywhere, except on the streets designated for foot traffic so flagging one down is not a problem. But since they are so expensive I wouldn't rely on them as your main form of transportation. Also have a map handy when a cabby is taking you somewhere. Since they are on a meter, they sometimes decide to take you on a little longer journey than necessary.

The going rate as of publication was E2.5 for the first 2/3 of a kilometer or the first minute (which usually comes first during the rush hours), then its Euro 50 cents every 1/3 of a kilometer or minute. At night you'll also pay a surcharge of E1.5, and Sundays you'll pay Euro 50 cents extra. If you bring bags aboard, say for example after you've been shopping, you'll be charged Euro 50 cents extra for each bag.

There are strategically placed cab stands all over the city. But if you cannot locate one, here are some radio taxi numbers:

• **Radio Taxi**, Tel. 055/4242 or 4798 or 4390
• **Taxi Merci**, Tel. 055/296230 or 210321 or 371334
• **Moto Taxi**, Tel. 055/4386 or 355741 or 359767

Where To Stay

Centro Storico

The **Centro Storico** is the very heart of Florence. Anywhere you stay, shop, eat, or drink will be relatively expensive, since this is the prime tourist area of Florence. In this area you have the **Duomo** dominated by Brunelleschi's huge dome; the **Baptistery** next door with its beautiful bronze doors; the **Piazza della Signoria** with its copy of Michelangelo's *David,* and under the cobblestones are Bronze age relics proving that Florence is centuries older than anyone ever thought.

There is also the unforgettable collection of art in the **Uffizi Gallery**; the **Ponte Vecchio**, built in 1345 and once home to butchers, blacksmiths, greengrocers, tanners and leather workers but now filled with gold shops; the

Florence Website

You can book museum tickets, find special events, locate quaint little stores, book hotels, and help plan all aspects of your trip with *www.firenze.net.*

Piazza della Repubblica that once was the site of a Roman Forum; the **Jewish ghetto**, which was until the end of the 19th century an open air market; the **Mercato Nuovo** or Straw Market with its many fine examples of Tuscan craftsmanship; and the Fifth Avenue of Florence, the **Via Tornabuoni**, where it seems expensive just to window shop.

1. **ALDINI**, *Via Calzaiuoli 13, Tel 055/214-752, Fax 055/216-410. Web: www.venere.com/it/firenze/aldini/. Mastercard and Visa accepted. 15 rooms all with private bath, telephone, and air conditioning. Single E60-90; Double E95-140. Breakfast Included.* **

This centrally located overpriced two star charges what it does because some of the rooms have views of the Duomo. There are no TVs in the rooms and truly limited ambiance with few amenities. What used to be a bargain is now just trying to suck tourists dry. Avoid at all cost despite the location. If they add more amenities or drop their price back down to a reasonable level I'll recommend this place again. Until then read on.

2. **BEACCI-TORNABUONI**, *Via Tornabuoni 3, Tel. 055/212-645, Fax 055/283-594. E-mail: info@bthotel.it. Web: www.bthotel.it/. All credit cards accepted. 28 rooms all with private bath. Single E130-160; Double E190-230. Extra bed E30. Buffet breakfast included.* ***

Located on the top three floors of a 14th century palazzo on the world famous and elegant shopping street, Via Tornabuoni. There is a wonderful rooftop garden terrace that will make you fall in love with Florence every evening you spend up there. I preferred the rooms overlooking the garden for the quiet, but the ones on the street make for good people watching. A much better deal with infinitely better atmosphere than La Residenza which is just down the street. This place is coordinated like an old castle, with nooks and crannies everywhere, and plenty of common space besides the terrace to sit and write your postcards home. You'll be surrounded by antiques and will feel as if you've stepped into an Agatha Christie novel.

The breakfast is an abundant buffet which can be served to you in your room at no extra charge. The rooms are all furnished differently but with the finest taste and character. All have double beds. An excellent place to stay.

3. BERNINI PALACE, *P.za di San Firenze 29, Tel. 055/288-621, Fax 055/ 268-272. Web: www.venere.com/it/firenze/berninipalace/. All credit cards accepted. 86 rooms. Single E160-260; Double E260-370. Breakfast included. Parking E25.* ****

Centrally located just behind the Palazzo Vecchio, the Bernini is an elegant and refined hotel. The breakfast room is once where the Italian Parliament met when Florence was the capital of the country. An auspicious location for an equally impressive buffet. The rooms are spacious, the windows are sound-proof, and the hotel come complete with all necessary four star amenities. The bathrooms are well appointed and also have phones. A wonderful place to stay in Florence. Professional, high end, attentive service.

4. BRUNELLESCHI, *P.za Sant'Elisabetta 3, Tel. 055/290-311. Fax 055/ 219-653. E-mail: info@hotelbrunelleschi.it. Web: www.hotelbrunelleschi.it. All credit cards accepted. 96 rooms. Single E240; Double E330. Breakfast included. Parking E25.* ****

Filled with an antique ambiance, accentuated by the 6th century Byzantine tower and the 12th century medieval church which have been absorbed into the hotel, this place is characterized by a rustic elegance and Tuscan refinement. The furnishings are a mixture of modern and antique, the structure is bathed in history accentuated by a small museum with a few Roman artifacts. The rooms are large and filled with every imaginable comfort, as are the bathrooms with their double sinks, courtesy toiletry kit and hairdryers. The breakfast buffet is abundant. From the terrace you have a wonderful view of the Duomo. Located in a tiny piazza in the heart of Florence, near all the sights, and in the middle of the best shopping in the city, this four star is a great choice.

5. CALZAIUOLI, *Via Calzaiuoli 6, Tel 055/212-456, Fax 055/268-310. Web: www.venere.com/it/firenze/calzaiuoli/. All credit cards accepted. 45 rooms all with private bath, TV, Telephone, mini-bar, and air conditioning. Breakfast included. Single E90-170; Double E110-240. Extra bed E35.* ***

Located in a recently renovated old palazzo and perfectly situated in the quiet pedestrian zone between the Duomo and Palazzo Vecchio. Some rooms have great views of the Duomo and with that view, its location, and all the amenities it offers this is a good place to stay. The rooms are spacious enough, as are the bathrooms, and have a nice floral and ribbon print motif. The rooms on the Via Calzaiuoli are perfect for people watching, but can be a little noisy on the weekend evenings. The hallways are small, so if you're there with a group of tourists getting in and out can be arduous. You can't beat the location or the service.

6. FIRENZE, *Piazza dei Donati 4 (off of Via del Corso), Tel. 055/268-301, Fax 055/212-370. No credit cards accepted. 60 rooms, 35 with private bath. Single without bath E27-33; Single E33-38; Double without bath E42-53; Double E47-63. Breakfast included.* *

This is two different hotels. One is new, the other's left in a time warp from the 1950s. My recommendation is based on the new section, so call in advance to get your reservations.

Even though this place doesn't have air conditioning, it should be higher than a one star. The lobby is all three star, as are the rooms in the new wing with their phones and TVs. Room 503 caught my fancy since it has a great view of the Duomo from the bed: when you wake up in the morning there's the most romantically picturesque scene right in front of you. Besides the beauty and comfort of the new wing, the lobby and breakfast area is of a much higher standard than any other one star I've been in. It's beautiful and quite inexpensive. They speak English, so make sure you tell them that you want to stay in the new wing.

7. GRAND HOTEL CAVOUR, *Via del Proconsolo 3, Tel. 055/282-461. Fax 055/218-955. E-mail: info@hotelcavour.com. Web: www.hotelcavour.com. American Express and Visa accepted. 89 rooms. Single E120-130; Double E180-230. Breakfast included. Parking E20.* ***

Near the Bargello and the Uffizi, this old hotel has traditional and regal common areas filled with authentic antiques. The rooms are large and very comfortable and the bathrooms come with all necessary amenities. The rooms on the top floor are the best because of the wonderful views. Make a point of requesting them. The terrace on the top floor, accessible by all guests, though less than quaint in and of itself, has panoramic views over the city. The hotel restaurant, Beatrice, has a refined and elegant atmosphere and serves exquisite food. A wonderful three star in a prime location.

8. HELVETIA & BRISTOL, *Via del Pescioni 2, Tel. 055/287-814. Fax 055/288-353. E-mail: ppanelli@charminghotels.it. Web: www.holidaycityeurope.com/helvetia-bristol-florence/index.htm. American Express and Visa accepted. 52 rooms. Single E200-250; Double E300-450. Breakfast E20. Parking E23.* *****

Located in the heart of the centro storico right by the Palazzo Strozzi, this is a refined and super elegant five star hotel. The common areas are anything but common, the bar is situated in a magnificent garden in the summer, and the restaurant is of the highest level. The rooms, each different from the other, are all furnished tastefully and the bathrooms are awash in marble. This hotel is stupendous, the staff is superb and the services offered sublime, including professional babysitting. A top of the line hotel in Florence.

9. HERMITAGE, *Vicolo Marzio 1 (Piazza del Pesce), Tel. 055/287-216, Fax 055/212-208. E-mail: florence@hermitagehotel.com. Web: www.hermitagehotel.com/. Mastercard and Visa accepted. 16 rooms all with private bath and jacuzzi. All rooms E240. Breakfast included.* ***

Only steps from the Ponte Vecchio but located above the tourist noise, this wonderful little hotel is on the top three floors of an office building and is reached by a private elevator. It has the most beautiful roof terrace, complete with greenery and flowers and a great view of the rooftops of Florence, as well

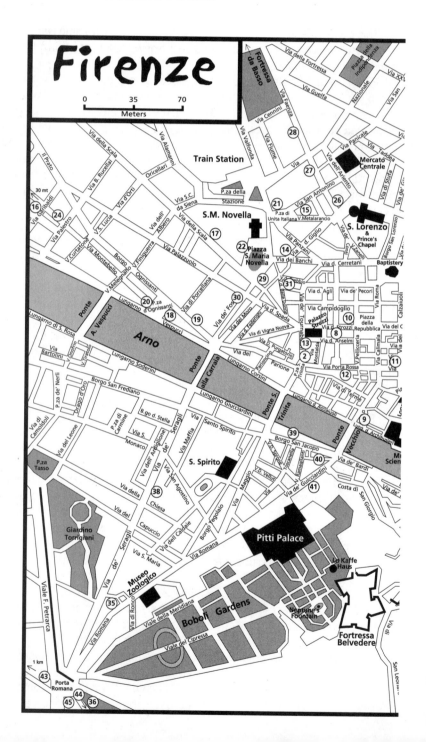

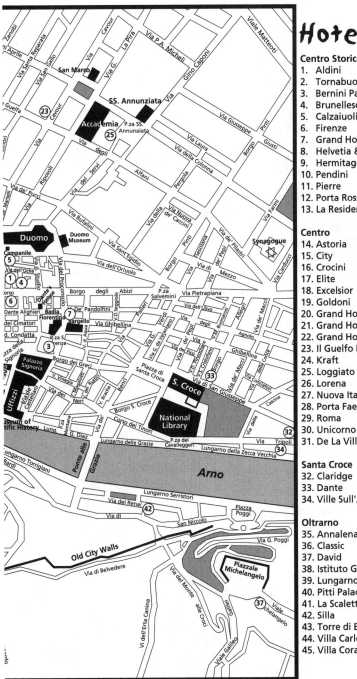

Hotels

Centro Storico
1. Aldini
2. Tornabuoni-Beacci
3. Bernini Palace
4. Brunelleschi
5. Calzaiuoli
6. Firenze
7. Grand Hotel Cavour
8. Helvetia & Bristol
9. Hermitage
10. Pendini
11. Pierre
12. Porta Rossa
13. La Residenza

Centro
14. Astoria
15. City
16. Crocini
17. Elite
18. Excelsior
19. Goldoni
20. Grand Hotel
21. Grand Hotel Bagioni
22. Grand Hotel Minerva
23. Il Guelfo Bianco
24. Kraft
25. Loggiato dei Serviti
26. Lorena
27. Nuova Italia
28. Porta Faenza
29. Roma
30. Unicorno
31. De La Ville

Santa Croce
32. Claridge
33. Dante
34. Ville Sull'Arno

Oltrarno
35. Annalena
36. Classic
37. David
38. Istituto Gould
39. Lungarno
40. Pitti Palace
41. La Scaletta
42. Silla
43. Torre di Bellosguardo
44. Villa Carlotta
45. Villa Cora

as the Arno and the Ponte Vecchio. They serve breakfast up there in good weather and it is a great place to relax in the evenings.

The rooms are not that large but the ambiance and the location make up for it, as does the spacious terrace and common areas. The staff speaks a variety of languages. For a three star the place is great. Recently updated with jacuzzi style baths in every room so you can luxuriate here at the end of the day. A great hotel in a great location.

10. **PENDINI**, *Via Strozzi 2, Tel. 055/211-170, Fax 055/-281-807. Email -pendini@dada.it. Web: www.tiac.net/users/pendini/hotel.html. All credit cards accepted. 42 rooms all with private bath. Only 25 with air conditioning. Single E90-100; Double E110-150. Breakfast included. Extra bed costs E30. ****

Ideally situated in the heart of Florence by the Piazza della Repubblica in a quaint old palazzo. The breakfast room is located in an archway between two buildings. They have twelve rooms that overlook the piazza and all are well appointed and quite large, perfect for family stays. Most bedrooms have brass or wooden beds, pretty floral wallpaper, and soft pastel carpeting. The furnishings are all classic antiques and exceedingly comfortable. The staff is more than accommodating, and they speak perfect English. An ideal central location for your stay in Florence. There are special rates for families.

11. PIERRE, *Viale de' Lamberti 5, Tel. 055/216-218, Fax 055/239-6573. Web: www.venere.com/it/firenze/pierre. All credit cards accepted. 39 rooms. Single E150-250; Double E190-340. Breakfast included. Parking E22.* ****

The courtesy, hospitality and professionalism of the staff helps to make a stay here wonderful. The entry hall is adjacent to a spacious bar where many guests congregate in the evenings before and after dinner. The rooms, all rather large by Italian standards, have fine furnishings and colorful carpets to complement the various amenities of this excellent four star hotel. It's located right by the Piazza della Signoria, deep in the heart of Florence's best shopping district. The continental breakfast comes complete with local Tuscan cheeses and salamis and an assortment of breakfast cereal. A good choice for a relaxing stay in Florence.

12. PORTA ROSSA, *Via Porta Rossa 19, Tel. 055/287-551, Fax 055/282-179. American Express, Diners Club, Mastercard and Visa accepted. 80 rooms all with private bath. Single E67-85; Double E100-195.* ***

Don't even think of staying here. Yes it's quaint, yes the rooms are large, yes the prices are relatively inexpensive, but the place is rather run-down and the staff is so surly and not helpful that it makes even a one night stay unbearable.

If your tour group has booked you here, make the best of it. The rooms are comfortably appointed with Liberty style antiques, and you are in the middle of everything in Florence, so the stay won't be all bad. But if you have a choice, avoid this hotel like the plague.

The Best Hotels in Florence

These are my favorite places to stay in Florence:

One Star

6. FIRENZE, *Piazza dei Donati 4 (off of Via del Corso), Tel. 055/268-301, Fax 055/212-370.*

38. ISTITUTO GOULD, *Via dei Serragli 49, Tel. 055/212-576, Fax 055/280-274.*

Two Star

16. CROCINI, *Corso Italia 28, Tel. 055/212-905, Fax 055/239-8345. E-mail: hotel.crocini@firenze.net. Web: www.hotelcrocini.com.*

41. LA SCALETTA, *Via Guicciardini 13, Tel. 055/283-028, Fax 055/289-562. E-mail: lascaletta@italyhotel.com. Web: www.venere.it/firenze lascaletta.*

Three Star

9. HERMITAGE, *Vicolo Marzio 1 (Piazza del Pesce), Tel. 055/287-216, Fax 055/212-208. E-mail: florence@hermitagehotel.com. Web: www.hermitagehotel.com/.*

36. CLASSIC, *Viale Machiavelli 25, Tel. 055/229-3512, Fax 055/229-353.*

25. LOGGIATO DEI SERVITI, *Piazza SS. Annunziata 3, Tel. 055/289-593/4, Fax 055/289-595. E-mail: info@loggiatodeiservitihotel.it. Web: www.loggiatodeiservitihotel.it/.*

Four Star

43. TORRE DI BELLOSGUARDO, *Via Roti Michelozzi 2, Tel. 055/229-8145, Fax 055/229-008. E-mail: torredibellosguardo@dada.it. Web: www.torrebellosguardo.com/.*

21. GRAND HOTEL BAGLIONI, *P.za dell'Unita Italiana 6, Tel. 055/23-580, Fax 055/235-8895. E-mail: hotel.baglioni@firenzealbergo.it. Web: www.hotelbaglioni.it.*

Five Star

20. GRAND HOTEL, *Piazza Ognissanti 1, Tel. 055/288-781, Fax 055/217-400. Toll free number in America 1-800-221-2340.*

45. VILLA CORA, *Viale Machiavelli 18-20, Tel. 055/229-8451, Fax 055/229-086. Web: www.villacora.com.*

13. LA RESIDENZA, *Via de' Tournabuoni 8, Tel. 055/218-684, Fax 055/284-197. E-mail: la.residenza@italyhotel.com. Web: www.venere.com/it/firenze/residenza/. All credit cards accepted. 24 rooms. 20 with bath. Single without bath E70-90; Single E110-130; Double without bath E110-135; Double E170-210. Breakfast included. Parking E15.* ***

A small but accommodating hotel in a central location with a clientele that is very international, many who come to have access to the world famous shopping street on which the hotel is located. The roof garden is a great place to relax in the evenings. The bar and restaurant are also located in the roof, and it is also where breakfast is served in the mornings. The rooms, many of which have some grand terraces, are simple yet comfortable, but the bathrooms are quite small. Not the best place to stay in Florence, but as it is included here, it is better than most. I can think of nothing negative, it's just that little seems to stand out about the hotel.

Centro

This section of town is north of the Duomo and west of the Via Tornabuoni, and is home to many reasonably priced hotels, restaurants, and stores. Here you'll find the **Mercato of San Lorenzo**, a huge daily outdoor clothing market, and the **Mercato Generale**, Florence's main food market where you can find everything from swordfish to buffalo-milk mozzarella.

Also located in Centro is the train station from which you'll be embarking on the terrific excursions I've planned for you in the next chapter.

14. ASTORIA, *Via del Giglio 9, Tel. 055/239-8095, Fax 055/214-632. E-mail: reception@astoria.boscolo.com. Web: www.venere.com/it/firenze/astoria/. All credit cards accepted. 103 rooms. Single E170-280; Double E220-340. Breakfast E15. Parking E20.* ****

Within walking distance of the train station, down a quaint side street, this is an elegant hotel. The communal area – bar, piano salon, and the in-house restaurant, Palazzo Gaddi - are all pleasantly refined. In the summer the hotel restaurant's garden is a wonderful place for a meal. The hotel encompasses a number of different buildings, including the 16th century structure after which the restaurant is named and where the conference facilities are located. The rooms are all soundproofed against Florence's buzzing traffic and come complete with all necessary four star amenities; and the bathrooms are more than adequate. A well situated four star, which will make your stay in Firenze a pleasant one.

15. CITY, *Via Sant'Antonino 18, Tel. 055/211-543, Fax 055/295-451. E-mail: info@hotelcity.net. Web: www.hotelcityflorence.com. All credit cards accepted. 18 rooms. Single E110-160; Double E140-195. Breakfast included. Parking E15.* ***

Located within walking distance of the train station and right by the superb San Lorenzo Market, this is a wonderful three star deep in the heart of Florence. In the hands of expert and professional service you will find your stay here more than pleasant. Filled with spacious rooms, soundproofed from Florence's city noise, each filled with wonderful furnishings and well equipped bathrooms. The common areas are nicely decorated in cathedral-like vaulted rooms. Also available is a dry cleaning service and scooter rental. This is a wonderfully intimate three-star. More of a bed and breakfast than a hotel, since there are only 18 rooms.

16. CROCINI, *Corso Italia 28, Tel. 055/212-905, Fax 055/239-8345. E-mail: hotel.crocini@firenze.net. Web: www.hotelcrocini.com. Closed December 18-26. All credit cards accepted. 1 suite, 20 rooms (17 with private bath, 2 with shared bath, 1 with private bath outside of room). Single E90; Double E110. Breakfast E8. Parking E10. ***

Situated in a tranquil residential area outside of the central tourist area, near the Teatro Comunale and the big park Le Cascine, this is a professionally run little two-star that I recommend highly. More than highly. A stay here not only does not drain your bank account, but it also liberates your soul. A member of the Family Hotels consortium, this hotel is located in a wonderful palazzo and the rooms are well, if simply appointed, and come with satellite TV. The breakfast is basic but filling. A good choice for travelers to Florence who want high quality accommodations but do not want to spend too much for it.

17. ELITE, *Via della Scala 12, Tel. and Fax 055/215-395. 10 rooms all with bath or shower. Single E50-60. Double E75. Breakfast E7. All credit cards accepted. ***

A quaint little hotel located on a great street in a perfect area for sightseeing, shopping, or dining. You'll love the wooden staircase that takes you from the lobby and breakfast salon to your quiet and spacious rooms. The prices are good for the location even though there are only a few amenities other than comfort and cleanliness, not to mention accommodating service. More of an inexpensive bed and breakfast than a hotel.

18. WESTIN EXCELSIOR, *Piazza Ognissanti 3, Tel. 055/264-201, Fax 055/210-278. Toll free number in America 1-800-221-2340. Web: www.hotelbook.com/static/welcome_05800.html. All credit cards accepted. 200 rooms all with private bath. Single E415-460; Double E520-580. Continental breakfast E15. American breakfast E22. ******

Directly across from its sister, The Grand Hotel, the prices here have really gone through the roof. Granted everything here is of the highest standard, especially the roof garden/restaurant where you can have your meal or sip an after-dinner drink, listen to the piano player, and gaze out at the splendor that is Florence, but wow, the prices have more than doubled in the past couple years. You don't have to stay here to enjoy the view; just come for dinner. Great rooms and perfect service. A superb five star luxury hotel. They have everything and more that you could want during your stay. If you can afford it, this is one of the best luxury hotels in Florence.

19. GOLDONI, *Borgo Ognissanti 8, Tel. 055/284-080, Fax 055/282-576. E-mail: info@hotelgoldoni.com. Web: www.hotelgoldoni.com. American Express and Visa accepted. 20 rooms. Single E90-140; Double E110-195. Breakfast E5. Parking E10.* ***

In a central but removed location near the Arno river, this small three star hotel is situated on the second floor of an 18th century palazzo. Most of the rooms face onto a quiet courtyard garden, and all are of different size but are comfortably furnished. The bathrooms are basic but come with all three-star amenities. The breakfast buffet is abundant. A quiet, comfortable place to stay, slightly off the beaten path.

20. GRAND HOTEL, *Piazza Ognissanti 1, Tel. 055/288-781, Fax 055/217-400. Toll free number in America 1-800-221-2340. All credit cards accepted. An ITT Sheraton hotel. 106 rooms all with private bath. Single E395; Double E615; Continental breakfast E15. American breakfast E22.* *****

Aptly named, this hotel is wonderfully grand. Located in a pale yellow and gray palazzo built in 1571, everything has been superbly restored to offer modern creature comforts while retaining the old world charm. Even though it is on a main thoroughfare, it is extremely quiet. The reception area is classically elegant. Each bedroom has beautiful neo-classic furniture and elegant decorations and frescoes; the bathrooms are a luscious oasis. Your breakfast is served on a small balcony overlooking an internal garden. More pleasant and comfortable than the Excelsior by maybe a whisker as a result of its recent renovation, but remember to go to the Excelsior for their roof-bar restaurant.

21. GRAND HOTEL BAGLIONI, *P.za dell'Unita Italiana 6, Tel. 055/23-580, Fax 055/235-8895. E-mail: info@hotelbaglioni.it. Web: www.hotelbaglioni.it. All credit cards accepted. 195 rooms. Single E210-260; Double E270-320. Breakfast included. Parking E25.* ****

Within walking distance of the train station, set in a piazza off the main road near the San Lorenzo market, this is a hotel of grand tradition situated in an austere palazzo from the 18th century. There is an elegant and spacious entry hall; and roof garden restaurant with panoramic views over the rooftops of Florence with a dramatic presentation of the Duomo. The breakfast buffet is served up here in good weather. The rooms are large and well appointed in four star style, the best of which face the piazza; the bathrooms are simply elegant. A top quality hotel in Florence.

22. GRAND HOTEL MINERVA, *P.za Santa Maria Novella 16, Tel. 055/284-555, Fax 055/268-281. E-mail: info@grandhotelminerva.com. Web: www.grandhotelminerva.it/. All credit cards accepted. 99 rooms. Single E155-185; Double E200-250. Breakfast included. Parking E22.* ****

Located in one of the best piazzas in the city, within walking distance of the train station, the Minerva is a comfortable and modern hotel. The entry hall with its garden is elegantly accommodating, off of which you will find the restaurant and breakfast room. All rooms are equipped with the necessary four star amenities and more, including video players. The bathrooms are lavish and some have hydro-massage and sauna. Available to guests for free is a pool and fitness center. And guests also receive free bicycle rentals. This is a great place to stay in a prime location.

23. IL GUELFO BIANCO, *Via Cavour 29, Tel. 055/288-330, Fax 055/295-203. E-mail: info@ilguelfobianco.it. Web: www.ilguelfobianco.it/. American Express, Mastercard and Visa accepted. 29 rooms all with private bath. Single E100; Double E170. Continental breakfast included.* ***

Not in my favorite area of Florence, even though it is close to everything important; but there is something about this hotel that catches my heart. Maybe it's Room 24, with the only terrace located on the inside courtyard. A perfect place to unwind after a day of sightseeing. Or maybe number 27 and 28, two large doubles that are basically suites with living and sleeping space. If you stay here, call well in advance to book either of these rooms. Every room has all necessary modern comforts like a mini-bar, A/C, satellite TV, and are all well appointed and comfortable. The bathrooms are modern, large and brilliantly white. There are many places to sit and relax, like two different courtyards downstairs, and little balconies and terraces strewn everywhere.

From the outside you would think this is just another hotel, but once you enter you are in another, quieter, more relaxing world.

24. KRAFT, *Via Solfernino 2, Tel 055/284-273, Fax 055/239-8267. Web: www.venere.com/it/firenze/kraft. All credit cards accepted. 80 rooms. Single E120-190; Double E150-270. Breakfast included. Parking E20.* ****

This refined hotel is out of the city center in a tranquil area, but close enough for walking access. The roof garden, where breakfast is served, offers exquisite panoramic views along the Arno. The piano bar and restaurant also have views over the rooftops of Florence, making it a wonderful place to end the day. The rooms are spacious and furnished with style and come with every imaginable four star amenity. A wonderful choice for those who want elegance outside of the main tourist area. There is also a terrace with an elongated lap pool for summer cooling and sightseeing of a different sort.

25. LOGGIATO DEI SERVITI, *Piazza SS. Annunziata 3, Tel. 055/289-593/4, Fax 055/289-595. E-mail: info@loggiatodeiservitihotel.it. Web: www.loggiatodeiservitihotel.it/. All credit cards accepted. 29 rooms all with private bath. Single E145; Double E210. Breakfast included. E40 for an extra bed.* ***

Located in a 16th century *loggia* that faces the beautiful Piazza della SS Annunziata, this hotel is filled with charm and character. The interior common areas consist of polished terra-cotta floors, gray stone columns and high white ceilings. The rooms are pleasant and comfortable and are filled with elegant antique furnishings. All are designed to make you feel like you just walked into the 17th century, and it works.

But they do have the modern amenities necessary to keep us weary travelers happy, especially the air conditioning in August. Some rooms face what many believe is one of the most beautiful piazzas in Italy (no cars allowed), while the rest face onto a lush interior garden. The bathrooms come with every modern comfort. The service, the accommodations, everything is at the top of the three star category. So, if you want to have a wonderful stay and also to feel as if you've stepped back in time, book a room here.

Selected as one of my *Best Places to Stay* – see Chapter 10.

26. LORENA, *Via Faenza 1, Tel. 055/282-785, Fax 055/288-300. E-mail: info@hotellorena.com. Web: www.hotellorena.com/. 16 rooms, 10 with bath. Single without bath E45-60; Single E60-72; Double E100. All credit cards accepted. Continental Breakfast E4. Hotel closes its doors from 2:00am to 6:00pm.* ******

A pleasantly run hotel located just off of the large San Lorenzo market. Perfectly located for shopping and sightseeing. The rooms are nondescript but comfortable and the prices are good. Not many amenities except for location, comfort and cleanliness. They have added A/C and TV in each room as a prelude to moving to three star status. There is still some work to go, but for now they are on the higher end of two stars both in quality and price.

27. NUOVA ITALIA, *Via Faenza 26, Tel. 055/287-508, Fax 055/210-941. American Express, Mastercard and Visa accepted. 21 rooms all with private bath. Single E70. Double E105. Extra person E25. Breakfast included.* ******

The fans in every room did a great job except in August. Some rooms have A/C so request those in late summer. Each room is plainly but comfortable furnished. This family-run hotel is ideally located near most of the sights and night spots, and the prices are very good. You'll just love the old Mama as she caters to you during your meals in the breakfast area, which looks just like a country *trattoria*. Not many real amenities, just a pleasant place to lay your head with friendly and accommodating service.

28. PORTA FAENZA, *Via Faenza 77, Tel 055/214-287, Fax 055/210-101. E-mail: info@hotelportafaenza.it. Web: www.hotelportafaenza.it/home.html. All credit cards accepted. 25 rooms. Single E120-180; Double E130-200. Breakfast included. Parking E12.* *******

Situated in a beautiful and completely refurbished old palazzo from the 1700s, this hotel is located near the train station, a bit removed from the centro storico. The Lelli family, including Canadian wife Rose, operates this cute little hotel, which is part of the Family Hotel consortium, and as such is well respected. A recent series of renovations have made visible some older architectural details which lends an air of history to a stay here. The rooms are spaciously spartan and filled with modern but comfortable furnishings and come with all necessary three-star amenities. There is also a babysitter service available and dry cleaning as well. Not in my favorite location in Florence, but overall a good three-star.

29. **ROMA**, *Piazza Santa Maria Novella 8, Tel. 055/210-366, Fax 055/ 215-306. E-mail: hotel.roma.fi@dada.it. Web: www.firenzealbergo.it/ hotelroma/. American Express, Diners Club, Mastercard and Visa accepted. 60 rooms all with private bath. Single E140-170; Double E170-200.* ****

The main draw of this hotel is the roof terrace which overlooks the beautiful Piazza Santa Maria Novella. All the rooms are completely modern and spartan in appearance. The common areas are decoratively appointed with marble, columns, and frescoes with an omnipresent pastel blue shade. Because of the color, when you walk into this hotel you will be instantly relaxed.

Everything about this hotel is classically elegant. The rooms are adequately spacious and are all furnished and decorated in the same style. The bathrooms come with their own phone and every other modern convenience. A good place to stay, but it is best in the off-season because the prices are much better then.

30. UNICORNO, *Via dei Fossi 27, Tel. 055/287-313, Fax 055/268-332. E-mail: hotel.unicorno@usa.net. Web: www.venere.com/it/firenze/unicorno/ . 27 rooms, all with bath. Single E130-150; Double E140-170. All credit cards accepted. Breakfast included. Parking E15.* ***

Near Piazza Santa Maria Novella, this hotel is situated in a palazzo from the 1400s. Completed renovated and complete with all modern amenities, this is a wonderfully located and comfortably accomodating three star. The rooms and bathrooms come with all necessary three star features and the staff goes out of its way to make you comfortable. The breakfast buffet is large and filling. Though not spectacular, I would definitely recommend this hotel for a stay in Florence.

31. DE LA VILLE, *P.za Antinori 1, Tel. 055/238-1805/6, Fax 055/238-1809. E-mail: delaville@firenze.net. Web: www.hoteldelaville.it. All credit cards accepted. 69 rooms. Single E190-260; Double E140-370. Breakfast included. Parking E22.* ****

An elegant hotel within walking distance of the station, in an optimal location between the Duomo, the Ponte Vecchio and the Piazza Santa Maria Novella. The rooms are very comfortable, soundproof, each uniquely furnished, and have all necessary three star amenities including satellite TV. The bathrooms are well appointed, and come complete with all amenities including a phone. The common areas are charming, especially the terrace, which is great place to relax at the end of the day. Breakfast is excellent and the staff is professional and courteous.

Santa Croce

This is the area of Florence in which Michelangelo played as a child before he was sent to the country to live with a stone carver, from whom he learned the fundamentals for his amazing ability to carve figures from huge blocks of marble. Located to the east of the Centro Storico and the Centro sections of Florence, Santa Croce is more of an authentic, residential, working class neighborhood and seems far from the maddening crowds, even though it's just around the corner from them. The church that gives this area its name, Santa Croce, contains the graves of Michelangelo, Galileo, and other Italian greats; and is the home of an excellent leather school from which you can get great products while watching them produce the wares.

This is also the area in which Florentines come to dine at regular Tuscan restaurants or some of the newer restaurants offering nouvelle cuisine. The area is also home to another food market, the **Mercato Sant'Ambrogio**, located in the Piazza Ghiberti. There is also a prime picnic location, not nearly as nice as the Boboli Gardens but still a respite from the crowds, in the Piazza Massimo d'Azeglio.

32. CLARIDGE, *P.za Piace 3, Tel 055/234-6736, Fax 055/234-1199. All credit cards accepted. 32 rooms. Single E65-90; Double E90-130. Breakfast included. Parking E15.* ***

A comfortable and functional three star hotel that has an ample entrance hall and a covered *cortile* in the center of this elegant villa. The rooms are simply decorated but come with all necessary three star comforts. What sets this hotel apart is its location. Outside of the main tourist center, here you can get away from it all while being only a short walk from everything. The highest floor has wonderful views of Santa Croce. A wonderful three-star for those who want to be in Florence but not surrounded by tourists.

33. DANTE, *Via San Cristofano 2, Tel. 055/241-772, Fax 055/234-5819. Web: www.venere.com/it/firenze/dante/. All credit cards accepted. 14 rooms. Single E80-100; Double E120-150. Breakfast E10. Parking E12.* ***

A small hotel, only 14 rooms, near the picturesque piazza of Santa Croce. The main draw of this bed and breakfast style hotel are the ten rooms with kitchenette. These are very useful for families, as are the spacious and comfortable rooms and bathrooms. The common areas are tiny but overall this is a rather pleasant place to stay in Florence, near enough to everything, but just outside the main tourist center to make your stay here authentically local.

34. VILLE SULL'ARNO, *Lungarno C. Colombo 3, Tel. 055/67-09-71, Fax 055/678-244. E-mail: info@villesullarno.it. Web: www.hotelvillesullarno.com/. 47 rooms all with bath. Single E150; Double E210-230. Breakfast included. All credit cards accepted.* ****

Located away from the center of things, about ten minutes by bus or car, which makes the hotel quiet and tranquil. They have a good-sized swimming pool and a lovely garden where breakfast is served in the summer. The rooms are large and comfortable with all the amenities of a four star, including A/C and cable TV. The ones on the river are wonderfully tranquil as are the others because in this location you are definitely away from the hustle and bustle of Florence. A good choice for those that do not like the pace of city life.

Oltrarno

Oltrarno, literally "the other side of the Arno," is home to many of Florence's artisans, leather workers, etc. It is looked upon as a city unto itself since it wasn't incorporated into the walls of Florence until the 14th century (people remember their history in Europe). Most of the beautiful architecture was destroyed during World War II, not only by the Germans but also by the Allied bombings. Thankfully both sides spared the Ponte Vecchio, The Duomo, and the other great pieces of architecture on the other side of the river.

Also spared was the **Palazzo Vecchio** (also known as the **Medici Palace**) and the **Boboli Gardens**, where Michelangelo first began his serious artistic training with the support of the Medici family. Beyond these sights and the artisans' shops, the only other place to visit is the **Piazza Santo Spirito** that boasts a 15th century church with the unfinished facade by Brunelleschi. The piazza is also home to a small fresh **produce and flower market** every morning.

35. ANNALENA, *Via Romana 34, Tel. 055/222-402, Fax 055/222-403. Email: info@hotelannalena.it. Web: www.hotelannalena.it. American Express, Diners Club, Mastercard and Visa accepted. 20 rooms, 16 doubles, four singles all with bath. Single E110; Double E145. Breakfast included.* ★★★

This place has at times been a convent, a school for young ladies, a gambling casino, a safe haven for Italian Jews during WWII, and now finally it has become the Hotel Annalena. It takes over the entire floor of a beautiful Florentine palazzo and has all the necessary amenities of a good three star hotel. The lobby area doubles as breakfast room and evening bar space. The rooms are large with high ceilings and seem to be *fresco* (cool) all year round. Located just beyond the Palazzo Pitti and near one of the entrances to the Boboli Gardens, this hotel is a little off the beaten path which makes for a wonderfully relaxing stay. The rooms all have antique style furnishings, terracotta floors and come with small terraces overlooking the garden.

36. CLASSIC, *Viale Machiavelli 25, Tel. 055/229-3512, Fax 055/229-353. All credit cards accepted. 20 rooms all with private bath. Single E100; Double E135. Breakfast included.* ★★★

Located in a quaint little palazzo from the nineteenth century situated outside the old city walls, here you can get a taste of Florentine life without the constant clamoring of mopeds riding past your bedroom window. Piazzale Machiavelli is an exclusive address and this hotel shows it. The lush garden in the rear (there's a glassed-in section for winter guests) is your breakfast location as well as your mid-afternoon slumber spot, and there's a small bar just off the garden for evening drinks.

Your rooms are palatial, with immense ceilings and clean bathrooms. Each room is furnished quite differently. Some have antique furniture, others have newer but sill attractive pieces. The diversity lends a spot of charm. I would recommend this gem to anyone who likes to tour and then escape the hectic pace of the city. One minor note, they do not have air conditioning, but when I was there on a 90 degree day each room was very cool. These old palazzi were built to keep cool in the summer and remain warm in the winter. This place really is a classic and the choice for truly discerning vacationers.

37. DAVID, *Viale Michelangelo 1, Tel. 055/681-1695, Fax 055/680-602. E-mail: info@davidhotel.com. Web: www.davidhotel.com. All credit cards accepted. 24 rooms. Single E95; Double E150-190. Breakfast included.* ***

By far one of the more pleasant little hotels in Florence. I recommend it highly. Situated in a small villa from the 19th century, the David has wonderfully accommodating and comfortable common areas. The rooms are all furnished with wonderful antiques along with safes, satellite TVs, and well appointed baths. There is a beautiful garden that is a joy to relax in during good weather. Located near the Statue of David in the Piazzale Michelangelo overlooking Florence, this wonderful hotel is in a serene setting, and is a perfect choice for the price conscious who want to see Florence, but wish to stay outside of the main town.

38. ISTITUTO GOULD, *Via dei Serragli 49, Tel. 055/212-576, Fax 055/ 280-274. No credit cards accepted. 25 rooms, 20 with private bath. Single E25; Double E35 per person.* (no stars)

If you don't have your own bathroom here you're still okay, since you only have to share two toilets and two showers with four other rooms. The office is on the ground floor of a magnificent palazzo that you will enjoy exploring. There are limited office hours (9:00am–1:00pm and 3:00pm–7:00pm) but they do give you your own key so you can go in and out as your please. (A rarity in Florence for one-stars.) The rooms, on the second and third floors scattered all over the palazzo, are quite large. In your search throughout this wonderful building you'll find immense common rooms with comfortable chairs and a quaint little terrace overlooking some rooftops in the rear, which are a great places to relax with a glass of Chianti and a meal of bread, cheese and salami.

They separate the more mature budget travelers from the younger crowd, so the late night adventures of the young'uns don't keep us older and wiser folks awake. This is a fantastic budget hotel in truly ambient surroundings. And the best part of your comfortable stay is that the proceeds benefit a home for boys and girls from eight to 18 who cannot live with their own families.

39. LUNGARNO, *Borgo S Jacopo 14, Tel. 055/264-211, Fax 055/268-437. E-mail: bookings@lungarnohotels.com. Web: www.lungarnohotels.it/ lungarno_e.shtm. All credit cards accepted. 66 rooms all with private bath. Single E230; Double E330-370; Suite E510.* ****

An excellent location right on the river, only a few meters from the Ponte Vecchio, and situated down a quaint, Florentine side street with some great restaurants and food shops. Even though most of the hotel is modern, it is a quaint, classic establishment. The lounge just off the lobby offers a relaxing view of the river and the Ponte Vecchio.

An ancient stone tower is part of the hotel, with a great penthouse suite. If you want the atmosphere of the tower, specify this upon making your reservation. Some of the rooms have terraces overlooking the river, which makes for a perfect place to relax after a tough day of sightseeing. You need to specify this too.

A great feature of the hotel is the more than 400 modern paintings that line the walls. Some by Picasso, Cocteau, Sironi, Rosai and more. Another plus is the fact that hotel has bicycles available for guests to use free of charge. This is one of the great hotels in Florence.

40. PITTI PALACE, *Via Barbadori 2, Tel. and Fax 055/239-8711. E-mail: pittipalace@vivahotels.com. Web: www.venere.com/it/firenze/pittipalace/. All credit cards accepted. 73 rooms. Single E 110-150; Double E 120-220. Breakfast included. Parking E22.* ***

A comfortable three star only a few paces from the Ponte Vecchio in the Oltrarno. The rooms are all different sizes, all furnished in a chic modern style, and some have balconies. The bathrooms are functional and complete with all necessary amenities. The two terraces on the sixth floor offer incomparable panoramic views over the Boboli gardens, Palazzo Pitti, the Duomo and the rest of the city across the river. The breakfast buffet is abundant. A well-located, nice hotel. A stay here is comfortable, quiet and accommodating.

41. LA SCALETTA, *Via Guicciardini 13, Tel. 055/283-028, Fax 055/289-562. E-mail: lascaletta@italyhotel.com. Web: www.venere.it/firenze/lascaletta. Mastercard and Visa accepted. 12 rooms, 11 with private bath. Single E90-100; Double E110-135. Breakfast included.* **

No ifs, ands, or buts about it, this is the best place to stay in the Oltrarno ... and maybe all of Florence, if you don't want to spend a lot of money. But you have to reserve your rooms well in advance. Let's say at least 4-5 months in advance, to guarantee you'll get a room overlooking the garden! Yes, there's no air conditioning, but it's not needed. This ancient building seems to soak up the cold air in the summer and retain the warm in the winter.

The rooms are large, clean and comfortable. The location is ideal and amazingly quiet and relaxing. And best of all there are two incomparable terraces overlooking all the best sights of Florence. Relaxing on these terraces after a day on the town makes a stay here sublime.

The furnishings are eclectic and simple, but comfortable; and the layout is scattered throughout the building, with everything connected by staircases. The prices are superb but they won't last forever. Management has already put air conditioning in three rooms, and when all are complete, the hotel should get its three star rating. That will send their prices through the roof, just like it did with La Scalinetta di Spagna in Rome. A great place to stay while in Florence.

Selected as one of my *Best Places to Stay* – see Chapter 10.

42. **SILLA**, *Via dei Renai 5, Tel. 055/234-2888, Fax 055/234-1437. E-mail: hotelsilla@tin.it. Web: www.hotelsilla.it/. American Express, Diners Club, Mastercard and Visa accepted. 54 rooms all with private bath. Single E120; Double E170.* ***

Located on the first floor of an old palazzo, you enter from a lightly traveled side street just off the Lungarno. The white marble stairs are covered with a red carpet that makes you feel very presidential as you ascend to the lobby. The double rooms are rather large while the singles are quite tiny, but all have high ceilings and come complete with the amenities of a good three star. The large terrace among the flowers and trees is where you have your breakfast and can enjoy a nice view of the Arno. Off the beaten path and boasting a professional staff, which makes the stay here quiet and relaxing.

43. **TORRE DI BELLOSGUARDO**, *Via Roti Michelozzi 2, Tel. 055/229-8145, Fax 055/229-008. E-mail: info@torrebellosguardo.com. Web: www.torrebellosguardo.com/. 16 room all with bath. Single E170; Double E290. All credit cards accepted.* ****

If you have the means, this is the only place to stay while in Florence. Once you walk in the gates you will love it. The ancient towered palazzo that is the hotel will make you feel like you have stepped back to the Renaissance. Besides this completely unique and accommodating building, this wonderful hotel has the best views over Florence. They are stunningly amazing. Also the grounds are filled with gardens and olive trees where horses graze; there is a huge open lawn in front flanked by fir trees; and they have a swimming pool with a bar – all of which overlook the magnificent city of Florence below.

The old palazzo used to be a small English language school, St. Michael's, that catered to 100 students (of which I was one). So you can imagine that currently, with only sixteen luxury rooms, the size of your accommodations are quite impressive. The interior common areas are like something out of a movie script, with vaulted stone ceilings and arches, as well as staircases leading off into hidden passages. You're a short distance outside of the old city walls but here you will find pure romance, complete peace, and soothing tranquillity. In fact the hotel is so magnificent that you have to reserve well in advance, since they are booked solid year round. I can't say enough about the view, it is simply something you have experience. Also, and most importantly, if you aren't already in love, you'll find it or rekindle it in this wonderfully majestic hideaway. This is one of the great, unique places to stay in all of Italy!

Selected as one of my *Best Places to Stay* – see Chapter 10.

44. **VILLA CARLOTTA**, *Via Michele di Lando 3, Tel. 055/233-6134, Fax 055/233-6147. Web: www.venere.com/it/firenze/villacarlotta/. All credit cards accepted. 27 rooms all with private bath. Five more in a gatehouse building. Single E100-185; Double E150-280. Breakfast included. A meal at their fine restaurant costs only E27.* ****

The hotel is like something out of a dream, with its sunlit tea room used for breakfast, its small garden on the side with fish swimming in the fountain, and elegant dining in the magnificent restaurant below. To top it all off you have a real bar with stools from which you can get any type of concoction your heart desires.

The location is perfect for those who like to get away from it all. Off the beaten path in a quiet and calm section of town. The rooms are all pleasantly furnished with all necessary amenities. A truly great place to stay.

45. **VILLA CORA**, *Viale Machiavelli 18-20, Tel. 055/229-8451, Fax 055/ 229-086. E-mail: reservation@villacora.it. Web: www.villacora.it. All credit cards accepted. 47 rooms all with private bath. Single E200-280; Double E280-440. A full buffet breakfast included. *****

You'll find this extravagant and ornately decorated hotel (once a nine-teenth century palazzo) on a residential street that curves up to the Florentine hills. It is truly magnificent with its chandeliers, statues, bas-relief covered walls, gilded mirrors and staff that will wait on you hand and foot. If you want to stay in the lap of luxury and are willing to pay for it, this is the place for you. There is a pool-side restaurant, Taverna Machiavelli, where you can eat and relax after a hard day's touring. Another important feature is the rooftop terrace garden, offering excellent views of Florence. And the rooms are superb, stupendous, fantavolosso – think of any adjective and the rooms will surpass it! A great place to stay if you have the money.

Where To Eat

Before I guide you to the culinary delights you'll encounter in Florence, I've prepared an augmented version of Chapter 9, *Food & Wine*, for you to better enjoy the wonders of Tuscan cuisine. Buon appetito!

TUSCAN CUISINE

During the Renaissance, Florence and Tuscany experienced a burst of elaborate cuisine, mainly the result of Catherine de Medici importing a brigade of French chefs, but today that type of cuisine has given way to more basic fare. Tuscan cooking has its roots in the frugal peasant cuisine that was the result of the region being agriculturally poor for so many centuries. The food is simple but healthy, with the emphasis on fresh ingredients which accentu-ates the individual tastes of each dish.

Grilled meats are a staple of the Florentine diet, with bistecca alla Fiorentina rivaling anything Texas could dream of producing. The Florentines tend to over-salt their vegetables and soups, but you can ask for them to be prepared senza sale, without salt, and no one will be insulted at all. You'll also find beans and olive oil prominently used in many dishes, as well as many types of game that populate the hills of Tuscany. And if you like cheese, my favorite is the full flavored pecorino made from sheep's milk.

Tuscany is not really known for its pasta dishes, but Tuscans do make an excellent pasta alla carrettiera, a pasta dish with a sauce of tomato, garlic, pepper, and parsley. If you want a simple, filling, healthy meal, you'll find one in Tuscany. Just don't expect some extravagant saucy dish. For that go to France.

You don't have to eat all the traditional courses listed below. Our constitution just isn't prepared for such mass consumption, so don't feel bad if all you order is a pasta dish or an entrée with a salad or appetizer.

ANTIPASTO - APPETIZER
- Crostini – Chicken liver pate spread on hard, crusty bread
- Pinzimonio – Raw vegetables to be dipped in rich olive oil
- Bruschetta – Sliced crusty bread roasted over a fire covered with olive oil and rubbed with garlic; sometimes comes with crushed tomatoes, or another version has an egg on top (Aqua Cotta)

PRIMO PIATTO - FIRST COURSE
Zuppa – Soup
- Ribollita – means reboiled. A hearty mushy vegetable soup with beans, cabbage, carrots, and chunks of boiled bread.
- Panzanella – A Tuscan gazpacho (cold soup) made with tomatoes, cucumbers, onions, basil, olive oil, and bread.

PASTA
- Pappardelle alla lepre – Wide homemade pasta with a wild hare sauce
- Pasta alla carrettierra –Pasta with a sauce of tomato, garlic, pepper and parsley
- Tortelli – Spinach and ricotta ravioli with either cream sauce or a meat sauce

SECONDO PIATTO - ENTRÉE
Carne – Meat
- Bistecca alla Fiorentina – T-bone steak at least two inches thick cooked over coals charred on the outside and pink in the middle. Welcome to Texas!
- Fritto misto –Usually lamb, rabbit or chicken, with peppers, zucchini, artichokes dipped in batter and deep fried
- Arista di Maiale – Pork loin chop cooked with rosemary and garlic
- Spiedini di maiale – Pork loin cubes and pork liver spiced with fennel and cooked on a skewer over open flames
- Francesina – Meat, onions, and tomatoes stewed in red wine
- Trippa alla Fiorentina – Tripe mixed with tomato sauce and served with a variety of cheeses

Pesce – Fish
- Bacca alla Fiorentina – Salted cod cooked with tomatoes and spices (usually garlic and fennel)

• Seppie in Zimino – Cuttlefish simmered with beans

Contorno – Vegetable
• Fagioli all'uccelletto – White beans with garlic and tomatoes and sometimes sage
• Insalata Mista – mixed salad. You have to prepare your own olive oil and vinegar dressing. American's lust for countless types of salad dressings hasn't hit Italy yet.

Formaggio – Cheese
• Pecorino – Cheese made from sheep's milk

TUSCAN WINES
Tuscany is known for its full bodied red wines, especially the world famous **Chianti**. A bottle of Chianti has surely graced the table of every Italian home at least once. Robust, full-bodied and zesty, the many reds produced by the Chianti vines in Tuscany have attained worldwide acclaim. To be called Chianti a wine must be made according to certain specifications and the vines must be located in certain areas. Within this production zone seven different sub-regions are recognized: Chianti Classico, Chianti Colli Aretini, Chianti Colli Fiorentini, Chianti Colli Senesi, Chianti Colline Pisane, Chianti Montalbano and Chianti Rufina.

Produced between Florence and Siena, Chianti Classico is more full-bodied than the others in its family, and comes from the oldest part of the production zone. If the wine is a Chianti Classico you'll find a black rooster label on the neck of the bottle. An austere wine, ideal when aged and served with meat dishes, it is also well suited for tomato-based pasta dishes especially those with meat in them.

Chiantis can be called *vecchio* (old) if the wine has aged two years and is given the respected and coveted *Riserva* label when aged three years and *Superiore* if aged for five years. With Chianti wines you can expect the best, especially if it is a Classico.

From the Chianti region you should try the following red wines: **Castello di Ama**, **Castello di Volpaia**, and **Vecchie Terre di Montefili**. Outside the region try some **Rosso delle Colline Luchesi** from the hills around Lucca, **Morellino di Scansano** from the hills south of Grossetto, and **Elba Rosso**, made on the island of Elba.

The hills of Tuscany are filled with vineyards large and small supplying grapes to make some of the world's best vintages. When in Tuscany you must sample at least a little of this bounty. There are plenty of wine cellars and enoteche (wine bars) in every city in this region for you to sample the regional offerings. And you can't forget a glass of wine with your meal. Some Tuscans say that their food is bland so that they can enjoy the wine with their meals more. Whatever the reason, you'll love sampling the different varieties.

Most wines are classified by the type of grape used and the district from which the wines are produced. Some of the best wines come with a DOC (Denominazione di Origine Controllata) label that indicates the wine comes from a specially defined area and was produced according to specific traditional methods. If the label reads DOCG (G stands for Garantita) the wine will be of the highest quality, guaranteed.

Some whites you might enjoy are a dry Montecarlo from the hills east of Lucca or a dry Bolgheri from the coast. The red wines mentioned above also have some excellent white wines to complement them.

Some of these wines may be a bit pricey in restaurants so you may want to buy them at a store and sample them back in your hotel room or on a picnic. At restaurants, in most cases the house wines will be locally produced and of excellent quality, so give them a try too. No need to spend a lot of money on a labeled bottle of wine, when the house wine is better than most that we get back home.

Centro Storico

1. ANTICO FATTORE, *Via Lambertesca 1-3, Tel. 055/261-225. Closed Sundays. Credit cards accepted. Dinner for two E40.*

This wonderful Tuscan restaurant was virtually destroyed when terrorists bombed the Uffizi Gallery some years ago, and now it has re-opened. A wonderful but somewhat expensive restaurant that is no worse for the wear. Everything is spotlessly clean and they have recreated their Tuscan charm. The food is as good as ever. Try their tortellini ai funghi porcini (meat or cheese stuffed tortellini with a savory mushroom sauce). It is exquisite. Then for seconds anything on the grill is great, including the lombatina di vitello (veal chop) or the bistecca di maiale (pork steak).

2. DA BENVENUTO, *Via della Mosca 16r, Tel. 055/214-833. Closed Sundats and in August. Visa accepted. Dinner for two E35.*

A little off the beaten path, behind the Uffizi gallery, this place is frequented by locals and tourists alike and is authentically Florentine. Locally know as "da Gabriella" after the hospitable owner, you'll love the atmosphere here as well as the food. Some dishes available are crostini da fegatini (baked dough stuffed with beans), spaghetti alla carrettiera (with a spicy tomato sauce), and as always meat dishes are plentiful for the main course. Tuscan cooking and character abound here. A wonderful choice while in Florence.

3. LA BUSSOLA, *Via Porta Rossa 58, Tel. 055/293-376. Visa and Mastercard accepted. Closed Mondays. Dinner for two E45.*

My favorite place in Florence. You can get superb pizza in this pizzeria/ ristorante as well as pasta. The ambiance is like something out of a movie set, especially in the back. They have a marble counter where you sit and watch the pizza master prepare the evening's fare in the wood heated brick oven. Or, if you're into the formal dining scene, try the back with tablecloths, etc. Wherever you sit the food will be excellent.

For pasta, try the quattro formaggi (four cheeses) or the tortellini alla panna (cream sauce). You can get any type of pizza you want here and can even ask to mix and match ingredients. The pizza master is more than willing to accommodate.

4. DA GANINO, *Piazza dei Cimatori 4, Tel. 055/214-125. All credit cards accepted. Closed Sundays. Dinner for two E38*

The best place to sit in the summer is at the communal wooden benches outside which are hedged in by flower pots. The two rooms inside are made to look rustic with their wooden paneling, yokes hanging from the walls and marble topped tables. The somewhat pricey food is still great, especially when eaten in the secluded piazza. Try the petto di pollo alla crema di limone (chicken breast with cream and lemon sauce) or the coniglio e verdure fritte (fried country rabbit and vegetables). You have to try rabbit at least once before you leave Tuscany, it's one of their specialties, so it might as well be here.

5. OLIVIERO, *Via delle Terme 51r, Tel. 055/287-643. All credit cards accepted. Closed Sundays and August. Dinner for two E60.*

The cuisine here is created with a little flair. The chef Francesco Altomare uses the finest fresh ingredients to prepare excellent meals that are unique every day and are based on what is available at the markets. The insalata

The Best Dining in Florence

11. BUCA LAPI, *Via del Trebbio 1, Tel. 055/213-768.*

3. LA BUSSOLA, *Via Porta Rossa 58, Tel. 055/293-376. Closed Mondays.*

27. LA CASALINGA, *Via dei Michelozzi 9r, Tel. 055/218-624.*

20. IL CIBREO, *Via dei Macci 118r, Tel. 055/234-1100. All credit cards accepted.*

12. COCO LEZZONE, *Via dei Parioncino 26, Tel. 055/287-178. No credit cards accepted.*

32. DEL GALLO NERO, *Via Santo Spirito 6r, Tel. 055/218-898.*

33. LA LOGGIA, *Piazzale Michelangelo 1, Tel. 055/234-2832, Fax 055/234-5288. American Express, Diners Club, Mastercard and Visa accepted.*

15. NERBONE, *Mercato Centrale. No telephone. No credit cards accepted.*

5. OLIVIERO, *Via delle Terme 51r, Tel. 055/287-643. All credit cards accepted.*

19. TREDICI GOBBI, *13 Hunchbacks, Via Porcellana 9R.*

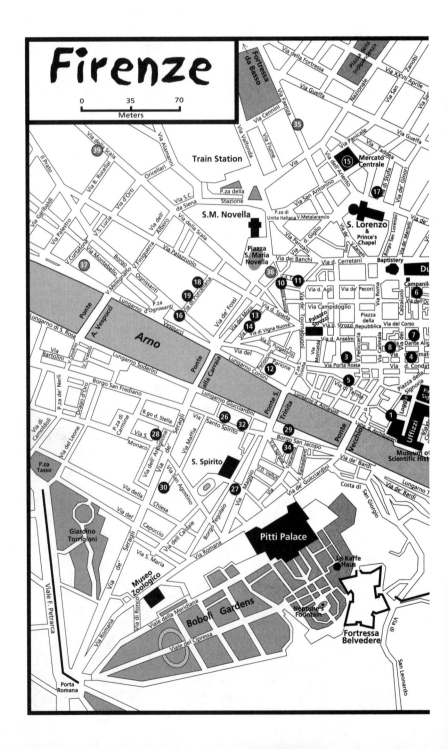

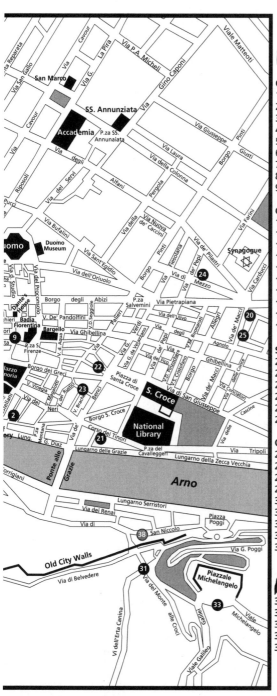

Restaurants ●

Centro Storico
1. Antico Fattore
2. Da Benvenuto
3. La Bussola
4. Da Ganino
5. Oliviero
6. Ottorino
7. Del Pennello
8. Dei Verrazzano
9. Vini Vecchi Sapore

Centro
10. Le Belle Donne
11. Buca Lapi
12. Coco Lezzone
13. Garga
14. Latini
15. Nerbone
16. Il Profeta
17. Serrolo Gozzi
18. Sostanza
19. Tredici Gobbi

Santa Croce
20. Il Cibreo
21. Del Fagioli
22. Leo in Santa Croce
23. Mossacce
24. La Pentola dell'Oro
25. Il Pizzaiuolo

Oltrarno
26. Angiolino
27. La Casalinga
28. Cavalo Nero
29. Cinghiale Bianco
30. Diladdarno
31. Fuori Porta
32. Del Gallo Nero
33. La Loggia
34. Mama Gina

Nightlife ●
35. Dublin Pub
36. Fiddler's Elbow
37. Harry's Bar
38. Il Rifrullo
39. Space Electronic

tiepida di polpo (octopus salad) is exquisite as is the tegamino di porcini gratinati al parmigiano e rosmarino (lightly fried grated porcini mushrooms with parmesan and rosemary). I am not too enamored with their pasta dishes, but their fish and meat courses make up for it. A wildly creative cotoletto di vitello farcite con cacio pecorino e pistacchi (veal cutlet cooked with pecorino cheese and pistachio) may not sound delectable, but it is. At Oliviero's you will get a wonderful meal, creatively prepared. Dine here for a culinary adventure; skip it if you want something ordinary. This is where the 'in' crowd sups.

6. OTTORINO, *Via delle Oche 12-16, Tel. 055/218-747 or 055/215-151. Visa and Mastercard accepted. Closed Sundays. Dinner for two E47.*

One of the city's oldest restaurants, Ottorino is located on the ground floor of a beautiful medieval tower, brightly lit with long pale wooden communal tables. It serves authentic Tuscan cuisine as well as some dishes that are not very Tuscan. One of my favorites is tagliatelli al coniglio (light pasta in a rabbit sauce). A place to find a great meal in a comfortable atmopshere.

7. DEL PENNELLO, *Via Dante Aligheri 4, Tel. 055/94-848. No credit cards accepted. Closed Sunday for dinner and Mondays. Dinner for two E30.*

The huge antipasto display is the perfect lunch or dinner repast. You can get as much as you want for one low price. But naturally they would rather you not eat them out of house and home. When done grazing, try the spaghetti alla carbonara (with cheese ham, peas, and an egg) or alla bolognese (tasty bologna meat sauce), followed by the petti di pollo alla mozzarella (chicken breasts smothered in mozzarella) or the bistecca di maiale (pork steak). A fine restaurant in an excellent location.

8. DEI VERRAZZANO, *Via de' Tavolini 18r, Tel. 055/268-590. Closed Sundays. American Express accepted. Dinner for two E25.*

What a wine bar. This place has excellent though simple food, incredibly refined ambiance, and all at a good price, if you can get in the door. Almost always crowded, especially at lunch, you will feel like a rather upscale native if you can get a table here. Don't expect a full menu since this is not a restaurant, but you will get great panini filled with tasty salami and cheeses, as well as salads, soups and other light fare. The wines by the glass are local Chianti from the Castello di Verrazzo region (hence the name of the place).

9. VINI VECCHI SAPORI, *Via dei Magazzini 3r, Tel. 055/293-045. Closed Mondays. No credit cards accepted. Dinner for two E20.*

A wonderful wine bar deep in the heart of the centro storico on a side street near the P.za della Signoria. An extensive wine list accompanies the simple, light traditional fare including crostini, salami, cheese, salads and soups. For those who are not wine lovers, beer is available, and everything is priced well. The atmosphere is informal, accommodating and comfortable. This place is open from 10am until the city shuts down. Despite its central location, Vini Vecchi Sapori is only lightly touristed since it is just off of the main path between the Ponte Vecchio and Duomo.

Centro

10. LE BELLE DONNE, *Via delle Belle Donne 16r, Tel. 055/2380-2609. Closed Saturdays, Sundays and in August. No credit cards accepted. Dinner for two E40.*

A bric-a-brac styled little trattoria that is always packed with locals clamoring for the excellent food they prepare here. Pasta is served in all its forms, soups are plentiful, as are the obligatory meat dishes especially the Florentine favorite – tripe. And don't forget the desserts. If you are looking for classical Tuscan cooking this is a great place to have a meal. Centrally located near the Piazza Santa Maria Novella.

11. BUCA LAPI, *Via del Trebbio 1, Tel. 055/213-768. All credit cards accepted. Closed Sunday for dinner and Mondays. Dinner for two E35.*

One of the very best restaurants Florence has to offer. On a small street, down in the basement of an old building, Buca Lapi treats you to the food of a lifetime (and the spectacle of one too). There is a small open kitchen surrounded on two sides by tables from which you can see all the food being prepared. The decor is bizarre in a fun way, with travel posters covering the walls and ceiling.

The tortelli stuffed with ricotta and spinach in a butter and sage sauce was unparalleled. Or try the spaghetti al sugo di carne e pomodoro (with meat and tomato sauce) for starters, then try either the pollo al cacciatore con spinacio (chicken cooked in tomato-based spicy sauce with spinach) or the cinghiale con patate fritte (wild boar with fried potatoes). A superbly intimate restaurant with wonderful culinary and visual experiences.

12. COCO LEZZONE, *Via dei Parioncino 26, Tel. 055/287-178. No credit cards accepted. Closed Saturdays and Sundays in the Summer and Tuesdays for dinner. In the winter closed Sundays and Tuesdays for dinner. Dinner for two E45.*

Located in what was once a dairy, Coco Lezzone's long communal tables contrast sharply with the white tiled floors. Despite the strange decor, Florentines and tourists alike pack themselves in to enjoy the authentic Tuscan cuisine and atmosphere. The portions are pleasantly large, the meats are amazingly good, especially the arista al forno (roasted pork). Also try the piccione (pigeon) cooked over the grill (don't worry, they're farm raised – they don't go out to the piazza and catch them for dinner.) Where else will you be able to eat pigeon? They also have coniglio arista (roasted rabbit), a must when in Florence since rabbit is a Tuscan specialty.

13. GARGA, *Via del Moro 9, Tel. 055/298-898. American Express, Diners Club, Visa and Mastercard accepted. Closed Sundays and Mondays. Dinner for two E45.*

If you want to get in on some of the best pasta in Florence, look no further. Try the pennette al gorgonzola e zucchine. For seconds, try the petto di pollo al pomodoro e basilico (chicken breast with tomato and basil) or the scaloppina di vitella al limone (veal with light lemon sauce). The food and the ambiance touch the edge of nouvelle cuisine, so if you're interested in trying something different in a unique atmosphere this place is great.

14. **LATINI**, *Via Palchetti 6, Tel. 055/210-916. American Express, Mastercard and Visa accepted. Closed Mondays and Tuesdays for lunch. Dinner for two E40.*

The hams hanging from the ceiling and a huge oxen yoke gives this place a wonderfully local flavor. They specialize in meat dishes (which are wonderful) but you can complement that with one of their insalata mista (mixed salad). The service is brusque in the Tuscan manner and the location down a little street makes the ambiance perfectly authentic. Try the spiedini misti (mixed meat grill) or the pollo arrosto (roasted chicken) and you won't be sorry.

15. **NERBONE**, *Mercato Centrale, 055/219-949. No credit cards accepted. Closed Sundays. Meal for two E12.*

When in Florence, you have to come here. No questions asked. This is a truly authentic Florentine eatery. In operation since 1872, this small food stand in the Mercato Centrale serves up the most incredible atmosphere. Though they offer a limited variety of food, what they do have is superb. This place is known for the best boiled meat sandwiches (pork, beef, or veal) for only E3, which are called panini. Your only choice of meats is what they have boiling in the big vats that day. The sandwich you get is just the meat, the bread, and some salt, but it is amazingly tasty. The 'chef' takes the boiled meat out of the steaming hot water, slices it right in front of you, ladles it onto the meat, pours a little juice over it for flavor (they usually ask if you want this ... say si), sprinkles it with a little salt, and presto, the best lunch you'll have in Florence. That is if you are a carnivore.

You can also order pasta, soup, and salads as well. To eat your simple but truly authentic Florentine meal, either stand at the counter and sip a glass of wine or beer, or take your meal to the small seating area just across the aisle.

16. **IL PROFETA**, *Via Borgognissanti 93, Tel. 055/212-265. American Express, Diners Club, Visa and Mastercard accepted. Closed Sundays and Mondays. Dinner for two E38.*

A cheerful unpretentious place with simple, basic food served to you by friendly waiters. The kitchen is visible at the end of the dining room so the sound of pots and pans clattering adds a rustic touch to your meal. They make good pastas, especially the penne carrettiera (garlic, tomatoes and pepper) which is a little like penne all'arrabbiata in Rome, and the house special penne profeta (with cream, ham, and mushrooms) which is really great. Next, sample the finely cooked lombatina di vitella (veal cutlet) or the ever present bistecca alla Fiorentina.

17. **SERROLO GOZZI**, *Piazza San Lorenzo 8, No telephone. No credit cards accepted. Closed Sundays. Dinner for two E22.*

This inexpensive, small, rustic trattoria is situated smack dab in the middle of the bustling San Lorenzo market. The seating is at long communal tables that line the walls with benches on one side and chairs on the other. Being just across the street from the food market, Mercato Generale, guarantees you'll have the freshest ingredients. The fare is purely Tuscan. I liked the arista di maiale al forno (pork grilled over the fire) and the vitello arrosto (roasted veal). Super inexpensive, completely authentic, and very satisfying. The service is brusque and informal. A real working man's place.

18. SOSTANZA, *Via della Porcellana 25, Tel. 055/212-691. No credit cards accepted. Closed Saturdays for dinner and Sundays. Dinner for two E50.*

Aptly named "Sustenance," this down to earth, tiny little restaurant is in itself a piece of Florentine history and is frequented by tourists, bohemian artists, the elite and more. You enter this place by pushing aside the tacky beads that line the entrance, and enter the dining area which is narrow and crowded. All around you are the noises from the kitchen in the back which adds to the charm of this place. The waiters are brusque, but that's part of their shtick; the plates land in front of you with a thud, but everyone has a great time. Try any of their meat dishes made in the perfect Tuscan manner. Other than salads that's what they do well. They have a mega-bistecca al manzo (huge beef steak) that would choke a Texan.

Come here for a taste of a non-tourist trattoria and a sampling of true Florentine cuisine. Over the years they have become a little pricey, but the meal and the simple, local, rustic atmosphere is worth it.

19. TREDICI GOBBI *(13 Hunchbacks), Via del Porcellana 9R. Tel. 055/ 284-015. Credit cards accepted. Dinner for two E35.*

Mainly Florentine cuisine, with a few Hungarian dishes added for flair. A moderately priced restaurant with some expensive meat dishes, such as the excellent bistecca Fiorentina. The pasta is average except for the exquisitely tasty rigatoni with hot sauce. They have menus in a variety of different languages so you'll always know what you ordered.

The atmosphere is simple and rustic and the back room with its brick walls is my favorite spot for dinner. Other fine dishes are the fusilli with rabbit sauce. 'Thumper' never tasted so good. For seconds they also serve wild boar and veal. After enjoying your meal, soaking up the delightful atmosphere, it's time for the dessert cart. These well-presented delicacies and a steaming cup of café will round out an excellent meal. Don't miss this place while in Florence.

Santa Croce

20. IL CIBREO, *Via dei Macci 118r, Tel. 055/234-1100. All credit cards accepted. Closed Sundays, Mondays and August. Dinner for two E65.*

They serve a combination of traditional and nouvelle cuisine and it is excellent. But, if you like pasta don't come here – there's none on the menu. Their mushroom soup is excellent as is the typically Roman buffalo-milk mozzarella. All the ingredients are basic and simple, but everything seems to be prepared in a whole new way. Their antipasti are abundant. Try the crostini di fegatini (baked dough stuffed with liver). Then for seconds sample the salsicce e fagioli (sausage and beans). If you want to try the cibreo, the restaurant's namesake, which is a tasty Tuscan chicken stew made from every conceivable part of the bird, you need to order it at least a day in advance while making reservations. If you want the same food for half the price, simply go to the vineria on the other side of the kitchen. That's where you'll find me.

21. DEL FAGIOLI, *Corso dei Tintori 47, Tel. 055/244-285. American Express, Diners Club, and Visa accepted. Closed Sundays. Dinner for two E30.*

A straightforward Tuscan trattoria with great food for a good value. The rustic appearance with the wood paneling and antlers hanging on the walls reflects the peasant cuisine served. The menu is not that extensive but you can get a good salsicce alla griglia (grilled sausage) for a dinner and some fagiole and zucchini as an appetizer. Since they are a typical Tuscan restaurant their specialty is grilled meats.

22. LEO IN SANTA CROCE, *Via Torta 7r, Tel. 055/210-829, Fax 055/239-6705. All credit cards accepted. Closed Mondays. Dinner for two E42.*

A brightly lit, trying-to-be-upscale restaurant near the church of Santa Croce that serves really good food. They prepare dishes from all over Italy so you're not confined to the normal Tuscan peasant fare. You can get the abundant antipasto di casa and sample a variety of local produce and meats. Then you can try a good rendition of the Roman favorite spaghetti all carbonara (ham, cheese, mixed with an egg). Consider also the cordon bleu or the ever tasty filetto di pepe verde (beef with green peppers).

23. MOSSACCE, *Via del Pronconsolo 55, Tel. 055/294-361. No credit cards accepted. Closed Sundays. Dinner for two E37.*

This was once a place for locals, but now the tourists have taken it over. You can still stop here for great food, but the authenticity of the atmosphere has disappeared along with the locals. The meats are especially exquisite, especially the ossobuco (stewed veal knuckle in a tomato sauce). Try some ribollita (mixed boiled meats) too. I suggest you sit all the way in the back around the "L" of a dining area so you can enjoy your meal in front of the small open kitchen and watch the cooks prepare the food. That alone makes this restaurant a lot of fun.

24. LA PENTOLA DELL 'ORA, *Via di Mezzo 24/26r, Tel. 055/241-821. Closed Sundays and August. Only open in the evenings. Visa accepted. Dinner for two E45.*

The atmosphere here is rustic as well as refined, the service is courteous, but what draws people to this lovely local place is the menu. Owner and chef supreme Giuseppe Alessi creates amazing dishes from simple ingredients. He has a number of cook books in print, and creates many notable and palate pleasing piatti. Off the beaten path so you won't find many tourists here, unless the secret is already out. An excellent choice while in Florence.

25. **IL PIZZAIUOLO**, *Via de' Macci 113r, Tel. 055/241171. Closed Sundays and in August. No credit cards accepted. Dinner for two E25.*

If you want a real Florentine experience far away from the thundering herds of tourists, this simple little pizza place is for you. In the area around Santa Croce that is fast becoming known for grand restaurants, this local joint stands out for its traditional authenticity. In some circles the pizza and calzone are considered the best in the city. There's also antipasto and salads but the reason to come here is the pizza; and to spend an authentic evening or afternoon in a typical Florentine neighborhood pizza parlor, surrounded by locals. Remember to make reservations since Il Pizzaiuolo is always packed.

Oltrarno

26. **ANGIOLINO**, *Borgo Santo Spirito 36r. Tel. 055/239-8976. Closed Mondays in summer. All credit cards accepted. Dinner for two E35.*

This is one of the best trattorie in Florence with a grand vaulted main room and aromas wafting throughout that will make your mouth water. The service if efficient, and the wine list plentiful with a distinct local flavor, a direction in which the menu also leans. You can find crostini (baked dough stuffed with meat and or vegetables), verdure all griglia (grilled vegetables), ravioli, and many other traditional Tuscan dishes. My favorites are the tortellini alla panna (meat or cheese stuffed pasta in a cream sauce) or the tagliatelli con funghi (pasta with mushrooms). The main courses are focused on meat. A wonderful place to grab either lunch or dinner while in Florence.

27. **LA CASALINGA**, *Via dei Michelozzi 9r, Tel. 055/218-624. Closed Sundays and the first 20 days in August. No credit cards accepted. Dinner for two E25.*

Here in this authentic Oltrarno-style trattoria you'll find a few tourists intermingling with the local artisans and residents. The cooking is classic Tuscan that is simple, tasty and filling. The antipasto is a mixed salad with sliced meats and cheeses thrown in. For seconds you'll find some Tuscan favorites like bolliti misti con salsa verde (mixed boiled meats in a spicy green

Learn to Cook in Florence

Since 1973, Giuliano Bugiali has been teaching Italian cooking to visitors in Florence, and it's all in English. To get information about how to spend an enjoyable culinary experience while soaking up all the glories of this great city, contact **Giuliano Bugiali's Cooking in Florence**, *PO Box 1650, Canal Street Station, New York, NY 10013-0870, Tel. 212/966-5325, Fax 212/226-0601.*

sauce), lo spezzatino (Tuscan stew), le salsicce con le rape (sausage with turnips), and il baccala alla livornese (cooked cod Livorno style – salty). Sample away and don't forget to wash it all down with some of the great house wine.

28. CAVALO NERO, *Via dell'Ardiglione 22, Tel. 055/294-744. Closed Sundays, August, Dec 25 and Jan 1. Open only in the evenings. American Express and Via accepted. Dinner for two E65.*

A high end ristorante in a local neighborhood, down a small side street, off the beaten tourist path. A mixture of traditional and creative cuisine where you can get many local favorites as well as cucina nuova concoctions. A pleasantly simple yet refined atmosphere combined with a robust cuisine makes for an excellent meal at the Cavalo Nero. And don't forget the desserts. They are exemplary. Also be aware of the automatic 10% coperto (cover charge) added on, which can act as your tip.

29. DEL CINGHIALE BIANCO, *Borgo San Jacopo 43, Tel. 055/215-706. Mastercard and Visa accepted. Closed Tuesdays and Wednesdays. Dinner for two E40.*

Wild game is the specialty here as befits a place named The White Boar, so get ready to enjoy some fine peasant dishes. I tried the wild boar cold cuts but liked the assorted salamis of Tuscany better. The chicken breast cooked with ham and cheese was not Italian, but it was great. I like the wrought-iron motif that dominates the place, especially the old cooking pot hanging from the ceiling. A simple place with good food and great atmosphere.

30. DILADDARNO, *Via de' Serragli 108r, Tel. 055/225-001. Closed Mondays, Tuesdays, and from July 16 to August 16. No credit cards accepted. Dinner for two E30.*

This trattoria offers some of the best and most authentic Florentine dishes. Try the trippa alla Fiorentina (boiled tripe), ossobuco (stew made with a veal knuckle in a tomato sauce), ribollita (boiled meats), bistecca (huge grilled steaks of beef), or the rognoncini (stewed kidneys). All can be enjoyed with some tasty house wines. There is a tiny garden inside that can be enjoyed in good weather. Off the beaten track, which is why the prices (and food!) are so good.

31. FUORI PORTA, *Via Monte alle Croci 10r, Tel. 055/234-2483. Closed Sundays and August. No credit cards accepted. Dinner for two E30.*

This lovely cantina has a rather extensive menu for a wine bar. You can get pastas – such as the tagliatelle con astice e zuchine (with onions and zucchini), crostini, soups and salads and some excellent desserts. The wine list is extensive, filled with both Italian and foreign vintages. Lovely atmosphere, with a quaint terrace, definitely off the beaten path, just outside the old walls of Florence at the foot of the hills of the Piazzaale Michelangelo. A good place to stop in for a filling snack and a relaxing glass of wine.

32. DEL GALLO NERO, *Via Santo Spirito 6r, Tel. 055/218-898. Closed Mondays and August. AMEX and Visa accepted. Dinner for two E30.*

Go down the stairs and you'll find yourself in a large vault-like room, which is the trattoria. The menu is filled with Tuscan antipasti and soups, like the minestra di pane (a tasty bread soup); but my favorites are the series of crostini (stuffed pastry baked in the oven). You can get the crostini stuffed with mozzarella, prosciutto (ham), salami, and all manner of vegetable. They are delicious and filling, especially with a wonderful bottle of Chianti. Make sure you order one with the gallo nero (black rooster) label on the stem. It's the namesake of the restaurant and indicates that the Chianti is of the finest quality.

33. LA LOGGIA, *Piazzale Michelangelo 1, Tel. 055/234-2832, Fax 055/234-5288. American Express, Diners Club, Mastercard and Visa accepted. Closed Wednesdays. Dinner for two E55.*

Come for the view of Florence, stay for the food, try to escape from the prices. This ideally located restaurant and café has a great panoramic view of Florence, which seems to make your meal that much better, until the bill arrives, then cardiac arrest sets in. Come dressed for success or the other customers will give you the once-over. Try the pollo al diavolo (chicken cooked over an open fire) after the spaghetti al frutti di mare (with seafood). The taglietelle with bacon and broccoli in olive oil is the single best pasta dish I've ever had, even at twice the price of ordinary restaurants. You can't go wrong eating here.

34. MAMMA GINA, *Borgo S Jacopo 37, Tel. 055/239-6009, Fax 055/213-908. All credit cards accepted. Closed Sundays. Dinner for two E42.*

A large place with great food. I tried their tortellini all crema with apprehension since I do not believe that Florentines know how to make good pasta, and was more than pleasantly surprised. But first I had some great bruschetta (grilled bread covered with olive oil, garlic and tomatoes). For seconds I had the petti di pollo alla griglia (chicken breasts o the grill). You might also try the penne stracciate alla Fiorentina (a meat and tomato based pasta) and the petti di pollo al cognac con funghi (chicken breast cooked in cognac with mushrooms ... it gives it kind of a cacciatore taste). This is a really great place to get great food in a wonderful atmosphere. If you do not like smoke you have to ask them to seat you away from the people who do ... and most people do.

Seeing the Sights

The sights of Florence are fascinating, incredible – add your own superlatives after you've seen them! Florence is a living breathing museum filled with inspiring open air sights, and some of the best museums in the world. The sights below are numbered and correspond to the *Florence Sights* map on the next two pages.

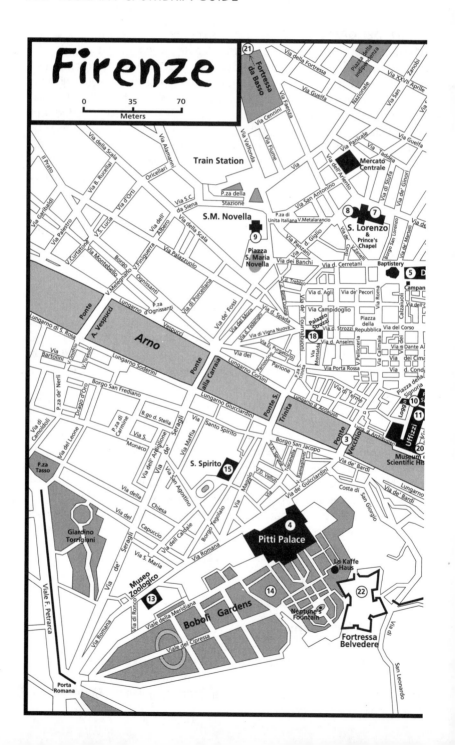

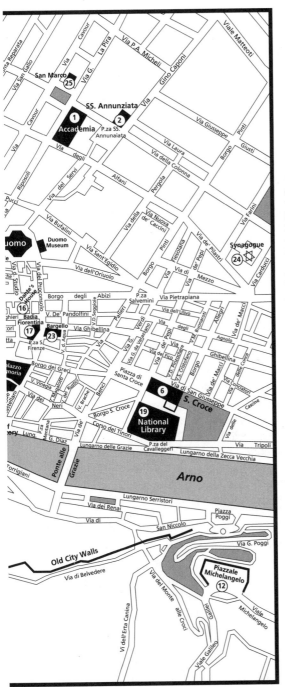

Sights

1. Academia
2. SS. Annunziata
3. Ponte Vecchio
4. Pitti Palace
5. Duomo, Baptistery, Campanile & Museum
6. Santa Croce
7. San Lorenzo
8. Prince's Chapel
9. Santa Maria Novella
10. Palazzo della Signoria
11. Uffizzi Gallery
12. Piazzale Michelangelo
13. Museo Zoologico
14. Boboli Gardens
15. Santo Spirito
16. Dante's House
17. Church of the Badia
18. Palazzo Strozzi
19. National Library
20. Museum of Scientific History
21. Fortressa da Basso
22. Fortressa Belvedere
23. Bargello
24. Tempio Israelico
25. San Marco

1. STATUE OF DAVID AT THE ACCADEMIA

Via Ricasoli 60, Tel. 055/214-375. Open 9:00am–7:00pm Tuesday–Saturday. Sundays 9:00am-1:00pm. Closed Mondays. Admission E6.

The **Accademia** is filled with a wide variety of paintings, sculptures, and plaster molds by artists from the Tuscan school of the 13th and 14th centuries; but the museum's main draw is a must-see for you in Florence. Here you will find a statue that is as close to perfection as can be achieved with a hammer and a chisel, Michelangelo's *David*. This masterpiece was started from a discarded block of marble another sculptor had initially scarred. Michelangelo bought it on his own – no one commissioned this work – since it was less expensive than a new piece of marble, and finished sculpting *David* from its confines at the age of 25 in the year 1504, after four years of labor. It was originally in front of the Palazzo della Signoria, but was replaced with a substitute in 1873 to protect the original from the elements.

Leading up to the *David* are a variety of other works by Michelangelo, most unfinished. These are called *The Prisoners,* since the figures appear to be trapped in stone. These statues were designed to hold the Tomb of Pope Giulio II on their sculpted shoulders, but Michelangelo died before he could bring the figures to life. And now they appear as if they are struggling to be freed from the marble's embrace.

Also included in this wonderful exhibit of Michelangelo's sculptures is the unfinished *Pieta*. Many art critics have spent their entire lives comparing this Pieta with the more famous one in St. Peter's in Rome. This statue looks older, sadder, more realistic, most probably since it was created by Michelangelo at the end of his life. The *Pieta* in Rome appears more vibrant, youthful, optimistic, and alive. Once again, this was probably because he sculpted the *Pieta* in Rome when he was a young man,

Also in the Accademia is the **Sala Dell'Ottocento** (The 19th Century Hall) that is a gallery of plaster model and other works by students and prospective students of the Academy. Despite the medium, plaster, these works are exquisite. The holes you see in the casts are iron markings used as guides so that when carved into marble the figure can be recreated perfectly.

2. PIAZZA & CHURCH OF SS ANNUNZIATA

Tel. 055/210-644. Open 7:00am–7:00pm.

Just around the corner from the Accademia, this piazza is relatively isolated from the hustle and bustle of Florence's tourist center, so that when you enter it you feel as if you walked back into Renaissance Florence. This is how all the piazzas must have looked and felt back then, no cars, only people milling around sharing the Florentine day.

In the center of the square sits the equestrian *Statue of the Grand Duke Ferdinando I* by **Giambologna** and **Pietro Tacca** (1608). The two bronze fountains with figures of sea monsters are also the work of Tacca (1629).

The church, like the piazza, is also a hidden jewel in Florence. Erected in 1250, reconstructed in the middle of the 15th century by **Michelozzo**, was again re-done in the 17th and 18th centuries, and remains today as it was then. Entering hte Basilica you are instantly struck by the magnificence there in, the carved and gilded ceiling, and the profusion of marble and stucco.

The church is particularly famous for a miracle which is thought to have taken place here. A certain painter named Bartlomeo was commissioned to paint a frescoe in 1252 of the Annucniation. When he was about to paint the face of Mary in the painting he fell asleep, only to find the face painted for him, supposedly by angelic hands, after he awoke. The fresco is located insie the tempietto to the left of the entrance. The frescoe became the heart of the Baslica, which was subsequently dedicated to Our Lady Annuciate. So there you have it!

3. PONTE VECCHIO

Literally meaning Old Bridge, the name came about because the bridge has been around since Etruscan times. Not in its present form, of course. The present bridge was rebuilt on the old one in the 14th century by **Neri di Fiorvanti**. Thankfully this beautiful bridge with its shops lining each side of it was spared the Allied and Axis bombardments during World War II. Today the shops on the bridge belong to silversmiths, goldsmiths, and some fine leather stores. In the middle of the bridge are two arched openings that offer wonderful views of the Arno. On the downstream side of the bridge is a bust of **Benvenuto Cellini**, a Renaissance Goldsmith and sculptor, done by Rafaele Romanelli in 1900. At night on the bridge you'll find all sorts of characters hanging out, sipping wine, and strumming guitars.

Take time to notice the **Vasarian Corridor** which spans the Ponte Vecchio and once linked the Uffizi with the Pitti Palace. It was used as a defense corridor as well as a private passageway. As you walk from the Uffizi side of the Arno to the Pitti side (the Otrarno) the corridor will be on the left above the shops. The corridor can be visited by appointment Tuesday-Saturday starting at 9:30am. Call well in advance to book a tour: *Tel. 055/23885*. Tickest are E6 and also offer entrance to the Uffizi.

On the street from the Ponte Vecchio to the Pitti Palace there used to be a series of wonderful old palazzi. Unfortunately the bombers in World War II didn't avoid these buildings as they did the Ponte Vecchio itself. Even so, today the street is filled with lovely reconstructed buildings erected just after the war which makes them older still than most buildings in North America.

4. PITTI PALACE

Piazza dei Pitti. *Tel. 055/287-096.* Building hours: Tuesday-Saturday 9:00am-7:00pm. Most museums only open until 2:00pm. Sundays and Holidays 9:00am-1:00pm. Closed on Mondays.

Built for the rich merchant **Luca Pitti** in 1440, based on a design by Filippo Brunelleschi. Due to the financial ruin of the Pitti family, the construction was interrupted until the palace was bought by **Eleonora da Toledo**, the wife of Cosimo I. It was then enlarged to its present size. And from that time until the end of the 17th century, it was the family home for the Medicis.

Currently it is divided into six different museums; and since the upkeep and security for this building is so expensive, each museum charges an entrance fee:

The **Museo degli Argenti** contains precious objects collected over time by the Medici and Lorraine families. There are works in amber, ivory, silver, crystal, precious woods and enamel work. Located in the former Summer Apartment of the grand dukes of Medici, the collection includes the *Salzburg Treasure* (gold and silver cups, vases and other articles) brought to Florence by the Archduke Ferdinand of Lorraine who was Grand Duke of Tuscany in 1790. The 1st, 3rd, and 5th Mondays and 2nd, and 4th Sundays of the month closed. Admission E6.

The **Museo delle Porcelane** is situated in the Boboli Gardens and housed in a quaint little building near the Belvedere Fortress at the top of the hill. This porcelain collection reflects the taste of the Medicis and the many families that resided in the Pitti Palace after the Medici's decline. There are pieces made in Capodimonte, Doccia, Sevres, Vienna, and Meissen and all are delicately exquisite. The 1st, 3rd, and 5th Mondays and 2nd, and 4th Sundays of the month closed. Admission E2 includes entrance to the Boboli Gardens.

The **Galleria Palatina e Apartamenti Reali**. Also known as the Pitti Gallery, this exhibit runs the length of the facade of the building and includes paintings, sculptures, frescoes and furnishings of the Medici and Lorraine families. This gallery has some fine works from the 16th and 17th centuries and the most extensive collection of works by Raphael anywhere in the world. Other artists included here are Andrea del Sarto, Fra' Bartolomeo, Titian and Tintoretto, Velasquez, Murillo, Rubens, Van Dyke and Ruisdal.

The royal apartments feature an elaborate display of furnishings, carpets, wonderful silks covering the walls, as well as some fine paintings collected and displayed by the house of Savoy – the most notable of which is a series of portraits of the family of Louis XV of France. Admission E6 includes entrance to the Museo delle Carozze.

The **Museo delle Carrozze** houses carriages used by the court of the houses of Lorraine and Savoy when they ruled Florence. This was my favorite museum in Florence when I was a child. The carriages are extremely elaborate and detailed, especially the silver decorated carriage owned by King Ferdinand II of the Two Sicilies.

The **Galleria d'Arte Moderna**. The gallery occupies thirty rooms on the second floor of the palace and offers a thorough look at Italian painting from neo-classicism to modern works covering the years up to 1945. The emphasis is on the art from Tuscany and has some works similar to French impressionists. Organized chronologically and by theme. The 1st, 3rd, and 5th Mondays and 2nd, and 4th Sundays of the month closed. Admission E4 includes entrance to the Galleria del Costume.

The **Galleria del Costume** contains clothing from the 16th century to modern day. All are exhibited in 13 rooms of the Meridiana Wind. It is an excellent way to discern the changes in fashion from the 18th century to the 1920s. Today, because of television, major fashion changes occur almost every year; but back then it could take generations before any noticeable change occurred. Also included are historical theater costumes created by the workshop of Umberto Tirelli.

5. DUOMO & BAPTISTERY, CAMPANILE, & CATHEDRAL MUSEUM

All located at the Piazza del Duomo.

Duomo – Church open Monday-Saturday 10:00am–5:00pm, Sunday 1:00pm-5:00pm. Entrance to the dome costs E3.

The Baptistery – Open everyday 2:00pm–5:30pm. Entrance E2.

The Campanile – Open 8:30am–6:50pm (9:00am -4:20pm in off season). Admission E3.

Cathedral Museum (Museo dell'Opera del Duomo) – Closed Sundays. Summer hours - Mon. through Sat. 9:00am - 7:30pm. Until 6pm in off-season. Holidays open 9:00am–1:00pm.

Tel. 055/230-2885.

Duomo

When you're in Florence the one sight you have to visit is the **Duomo**, Florence's cathedral. It was consecrated in 1436 by Pope Eugenio IV as **Santa Maria del Fiore** (Saint Mary of the Flowers), and that is still its official name, but everybody calls it "The Duomo" because of its imposing dome. It was started in 1296 by Arnolfo di Cambio on the spot where the church of Santa Reparata existed. After di Cambio's death in 1301, the famous Giotto took over the direction of the work, but he dedicated most of his attention to the development of the Bell Tower (Campanile).

When Giotto died in 1337, Andrea Pisano took over until 1349 (death didn't cause his departure, he just moved on to other projects). By 1421 everything else was finished except for the dome, which **Brunelleschi** had won a competition to design and build. It took 14 years just to construct the gigantic dome. Over the years, slight modifications and changes have been made, and in 1887, the current facade of the Duomo was finished by architect **Emilio de Fabris**.

The interior of the Duomo is 150 meters long and 38 meters wide at the nave and 94 meters at the transept. There are enormous gothic arches, supported by gothic pillars, which gives the interior a majestic quality. The dome is 90 meters high and 45.5 meters in diameter and is decorated with frescoes representing the Last Judgment done by Giorgio Vasari and Federico Zuccari at the end of the 16th century. In the niches of the pillars supporting the dome are statues of the Apostles.

The central chapel is home to the **Sarcophagus of San Zanobius** that contains the saint's relics. The bronze reliefs are the work of Lorenzo Ghiberti (1442). When you've finished wandering through the cathedral and admiring the art and stained glass windows, you can go to the top of the Duomo and get some great views of Florence. The way up is a little tiring, but the magnificent photo opportunities – both inside and out – are fabulous. Don't miss these views!

The Baptistery
Definitely considered one of the most important works in the city, the **Baptistery** was built on the remains of an early Roman structure which was transformed into a paleo-Christian monument. The Baptistery, built in the 10th and 11th centuries was dedicated to Saint John the Baptist, the patron saint of Florence. Up until 1128, it was the cathedral of Florence. This small structure just didn't reflect the growing stature of the city of Florence, so they erected the Duomo.

Its octagonal shape is covered with colored marble. On the pavement by the Baptistery you'll find the signs of the Zodiac. Inside is the tomb of Giovanni XXIII by Donatello and Michelozzo in 1427. Next to the altar, you'll see the *Angel Holding The Candlestick* by Agostino di Jacopo in 1320. To the left between the Roman sarcophagi is the wooden statue *Magdalen* by Donatello in 1560.

But the true masterpieces of the Baptistery are the bronze paneled doors by **Ghoberti** and **Andrea Pisano da Pontedera**. The public entrance is the **Southern Door**, created by Andrea Pisano da Pontedera and is of least interest. The east and north doors are far more beautiful and intricate. Michelangelo described the east door as "the door to paradise." On it you'll find stories of the Old Testament, beginning as follows from the top left hand side:
• Creation of Adam; original sin; expulsion of Adam and Eve from Paradise
• Stories of Noah and the universal deluge (coincidentally some of these panels were almost lost in the flooding of 1966)
• Jacob and Esau; Rachel and Jacob; Isaac blesses Jacob
• Moses receives the Ten Commandments on Mount Sinai
• The battle against the Philistines; David and Goliath.

From the top right hand side:
• Adam works the soil; Cain and Abel at work; Cain kills Abel
• Three angels appear to Abraham; Abraham sacrifices Isaac

• Joseph meets his brothers in Egypt; Stories of Joseph
• Joshua crosses the Jordan River; The conquering of Jericho
• Solomon receives the Queen of Sheba in the Temple.

The Campanile

Giotto died while he was attempting to complete the **Campanile**, but after his death **Andrea Pisano** and **Francesco Talenti** both scrupulously followed his designs until its completion. The only part they left out was the spire that was to go on top, which would have made the Campanile 30 meters higher than its current 84. The tower is covered in colored marble and adorned with bas-reliefs by Andrea Pisano and Luca della Robbia and Andrea Orcagna. Sculptures by Donatello, Nanni di Bartolo, and others used to be in the sixteen niches but are now in the Cathedral Museum.

Cathedral Museum (Museo dell'Opera del Duomo)

This is the place where many pieces of artwork that used to be in the Cathedral or the Campanile are now located. Their removal and placement here was mainly done to help preserve them from the environment as well as the onslaught of tourists hordes. Most of the items are statues and bas-relief work. The most famous ones to keep an eye out for are *St. John* by **Donatello**, *Habakkuh* by Donatello, *Virgin with Infant Jesus* by **Arnolfo**, and *Choir Gallery* with many scenes by Donatello.

6. SANTA CROCE

Piazza Santa Croce. Open 10:00am -12:30pm and 2:30pm - 6:30pm (3-5pm in off season). Closed Wednesdays.

The church of **Santa Croce** sits in the Piazza Santa Croce, surrounded by ancient palazzi renowned for the architecture. The one opposite the church is the **Palazzo Serristori** by Baccio D'Agnolo in the 16th century. Facing the church on the right hand side at #23 is the **Palazzo dell'Antella** built by Giulio Parigi in the 17th century. In this piazza, on any night, when all the shops are closed, you will feel as if you've stepped back into the Renaissance.

In the center of the square is a statue of **Dante Aligheri**, he of *Divine Comedy* fame, sculpted by Enrico Pazzi in 1865. This is a wonderfully ornate yet simple church belonging to the Franciscan Order. Construction was begun in 1295 but its modern facade was created in 1863 by Nicolo Matas. The frescoes on the facade were created in only 20 days by 12 painters working non-stop. It has a slim bell tower whose Gothic style doesn't seem to fit with this modern exterior. The interior, on the other hand, fits perfectly with the simple stonework of the bell tower.

Initially, the walls inside had been covered with exquisite frescoes created by Giotto but these were covered up by order of Cosimo I in the 16th century. What remains is a basic monastic church that conveys piety and beauty in its simplicity. Of the many Italian artistic, religious, and political geniuses that lie buried beneath Santa Croce, the most famous has to be that of **Michelangelo** himself. Other prominent Florentines buried here are **Niccolo Machiavelli**, **Galileo Galilei**, **Dante Aligheri** and **Lorenzo Ghiberti**.

Leather School at Santa Croce

Besides the beautiful bas-reliefs, exquisite sculptures, and other works of art in Santa Croce you can find an excellent and relatively inexpensive **leather school** (Scuola del Cuoio). To get there go through the sacristy and you'll end up in the school that was started by the monks more than three decades ago. Here you'll find all kinds of fine leather products for sale but the best part is being able to see them being manufactured right in front of you in what were once cells for the monks.

The prices and selection are good and seeing the artisans at work is something that shouldn't be missed when in Florence, *Tel. 244-533*. Hours are Tuesday-Saturday, 9:00am-12:30pm and 3:00pm-6:00pm. All credit cards accepted.

7. SAN LORENZO

Piazza San Lorenzo. *Tel. 055/213-206*. Open Tuesday-Saturday 9:00am–2:00pm, Sundays and Holidays 9:00am - 1:00pm. Closed Mondays.

One of the oldest basilicas in Florence. The architecture is the work of **Filippo Brunelleschi**, done from 1421-1446, but the church was finished by his pupil **Antonio Manetti** in 1460. The facade was never completed even though Michelangelo himself submitted a variety of designs for its completion.

The interior is made up of three naves with chapels lining the side walls. In the central nave at the far end are two pulpits that are the last two works of **Donatello** who died in 1466 after completing them. You'll find plenty of works by Donatello in this church, including:
• The stucco medallions in the Old Sacristy that represent the *Four Evangelists* that are *Stories of Saint John the Baptist*
• The terra-cotta *Bust of Saint Lawrence* in the Old Sacristy
• The bronze doors with panels representing the *Apostles and Fathers of the Church* in the Old Sacristy.

8. PRINCES' CHAPEL

Piazza San Lorenzo. *Tel. 055/213-206*. Open Tuesday-Saturday 9:00am–2:00pm, Sundays and Holidays 9:00am-1:00pm. Closed Mondays.

Attached to the church of San Lorenzo, but with the entrance just around the corner to the back of the church, this octagonal building's construction was begun in 1604 on a design by Prince Giovanni dei Medici. It houses the tombs of a variety of Medici princes ... hence the name. It is of interest to many tourists because of the tombs in the New Sacristy which were created by

Michelangelo himself. *The Tomb of Lorenzo, Duke of Urbino* (created by Michelangelo) has a statue of the duke seated and absorbed in meditation as well as two reclining figures that represent Dawn and Dusk. On the opposite wall is the *Tomb of Giuliano, Duke of Nemours* (also created by Michelangelo) which shows a seated duke replete in armor, ready for action, as well as two reclining figures that represent night and day. Another Michelangelo work in the New Sacristy is the unfinished *Madonna and Child*.

If you like Michelangelo's brilliant sculptures but want to avoid the crowds that congregate at the museum that houses the David, this is the place to come. And you can get some shopping done in the San Lorenzo market afterwards.

9. SANTA MARIA NOVELLA

Piazza Santa Maria Novella. Open 7:00am–11:30am and 3:30pm–6:00pm Monday–Saturday, and Sundays 3:30pm–5:00pm.

Built in 1278 by two Dominican friars, **Fra Ristoreo** and **Fra Sisto**, the church was created in the Gothic style with green and white marble decorations that are typically Florentine in character. The church was completed in 1470. To the left and right of the facade are tombs of illustrious Florentines all created in the same Gothic style as the church.

The interior of the church is in a "T" shape with the nave and aisles divided by clustered columns that support wide arches. Down the aisles are a variety of altars created by **Vasari** from 1565 to 1571. As a young artist, Michelangelo worked on many of the frescoes as commissioned by his teachers. This is where he got his initial training that helped him create the now famous frescoes in the Sistine Chapel in Rome.

The peaceful and expansive cloister are a rare treat. Come for a serene visit that marks back to the days of Michelangelo. Hours: weekdays 9:00am - 2:00pm. Holidays 8:00am -1:00pm. Closed Fridays. Entrance E2.

You can spend hours in here admiring these magnificent frescoes created by many Florentine artists including **Domenico Ghirlandaio** (Chapel of High Altar), **Giuliano da San Gallo** (Gondi Chapel), **Giovanni Dosio** (Gaddi Chapel), **Nardo di Cione** (Strozzi Chapel) and more. And if you're tired of sightseeing and need a little break, Florence's best pub, The Fiddler's Elbow, is in the piazza outside the church.

10. PIAZZA, PALAZZO, & LOGGIA DELLA SIGNORIA
Piazza della Signoria

This piazza, with the Palazzo, the Loggia, the fountain, the replica of the statue of David, the cafes and *palazzi* is incomparable in its beauty. Over the centuries great historical and political occurrences, as well as the lives of average Florentines, have all flowed through this piazza.

Today the square is the site of the annual sporting event, **Calcio in Costume** (soccer played in period garb), where the different sections of the city vie for dominance in a game that is a cross between soccer, rugby, martial arts and an all-out war. This annual contest used to be played in the square of Santa Croce but was moved here during modern times. If you are in Florence during June, when the event covers three of the weekends in that month, you definitely have to try and get tickets. The entire piazza is covered with sand, and stadium seats are put up all around the makeshift field, and then the fun begins. The event is a truly memorable experience.

In the small square on the left is **Ammannati's Fountain** with the giant figure of *Neptune*. The statue is commonly called *Biancone* (Whitey) by the locals because of its bland appearance. Giambologna created the equestrian statue representing *Cosimo I dei Medici* on the left of the square.

Palazzo della Signoria – Palazzo Vecchio

Piazza della Signoria. Open Monday–Friday 9:00am–7:00pm, and Sundays 8:00am–1:00pm. Closed on Saturdays. Admission E5 for upstairs galleries.

The most imposing structure in the square is the **Palazzo Signoria**. It is 94 meters past the fortified battlements to the top of **Arnolfo's Tower**. In fact I strongly encourage you to go up to top where the art conservationists work. You can walk along the turreted top, and get some terrific views of the Duomo and other aspects of the city.

The entire structure is rather severe, but at the same time elegant. Its construction began in the late 13th century and took hundreds of years to finish. It was once the home of **Cosimo de Medici** and other members of the Medici family before the Pitti Palace was completed.

In front of the building on the platform at the top of the steps, ancient orators used to harangue the crowds, and for this reason this section of the building is called *Arringhiera* (The Haranguing Area). Located here are several important sculptures including the *Marzocco* (a lion symbolizing the Florentine Republic; a stone copy of the original sits in the National Museum); *Judith and Holofernes* created by Donatello in 1460, which is a record of the victory over the Duke of Athens; the copy of Michelangelo's *David* (the original is in the Accademia), and *Hercules and Cacus* created by Baccio Bandinelli.

Above the main door is a frieze with two lions and a monogram of Christ with the inscription *Rex Regum et Dominus Dominantium* (King of Kings and Lord of Lords), which used to record the time that the Florentine republic elected Christ as their King in 1528. The inscription used to read *Jesus Christus Rex Florentinei Populi S P Decreto Electus* (Jesus Christ elected by the people King of Florence) but was changed in 1851.

The interior is mainly filled with artwork glorifying the Medici family who ruled the Florentine Republic for centuries. So if you need a break from religious art and all those paintings of the Madonna and Child, this is the respite you've been looking for. Everything is elaborate and ornate, as befitting the richest family in the world at that time.

You enter through the courtyard which was designed by Michelozzo in 1453. The elaborate stucco decorations on the columns and frescoes on the arches were added in 1565 on the occasion of the wedding between Francesco dei Medici and Joan of Austria. The fountain in the center, *Graceful Winged Cupid* was done by Verrochio in 1476. From here most of the art to see is upstairs, so either take the staircase up or use the elevator.

What follows is a description of the important works to see in each room:

Hall of the Five Hundred – Salone dei Cinquecento

This is the most splendid and artistic hall in Florence. It was designed for public meetings after the Medicis had been thrown from power. When Cosimo I regained the family's control over Florence, he had the hall enlarged and used it for his private audiences. On the wall opposite the entrance you'll find three large magnificent paintings by Baccio D'Agnolo, Baccio Bandinelli and Giorgio Vassari: *The Conquest of Siena; The Conquest of Porto Ercole; The Battle of Marciano*. On the wall across from this you'll find: *Maximilian Tries to Conquer Livorno; The Battle of Torre San Vincenzo; The Florentines Assault Pisa*. Underneath these painting you'll find sculptures by Vincenzo de Rossi representing *Hercules Labors*.

The ceiling is divided into 39 compartments with paintings by Giorgio Vasari that represent *Stories of Florence and the Medici*. The coup de grace is in the niche of the right wall at the entrance. Here you'll find Michelangelo's unfinished work, *The Genius of Victory*, which was designed for the tomb of Pope Julius II. If you only have a little time, spend it here. This room is magnificent.

Study of Francesco I de Medici

Here you'll find the work of many of Florence's finest artists crammed into as small a space as imaginable. The walls and even the barrel shaped ceiling are covered with paintings, and niches are filled with a variety of bronze statues. Elaborate, ostentatious and overwhelming. It is perpetually roped off, but you are able to view its splendor.

Hall of the Two Hundred – Salone dei Duecento

It is called thus since this is where the Council of two hundred citizens met during the time of the Republic for their important decisions. The walls are adorned with tapestry, the ceiling is ornately decorated, chandeliers hang low, and statues and busts adorn any free spot. The center of the room is occupied by the seating for the Council of 200.

Monumental Quarters – Quartieri Monumentali

These are a series of rooms that get their names from a member of the Medici family. Each are elaborate in their own right, filled with paintings, sculptures, frescoes, and more. From here you'll find many more interesting rooms and paintings as you explore, both on this floor and the one above, but this is the bulk of the beauty in the Palazzo Signoria.

The Loggia della Signoria

In the Piazza, on the right of the Palazzo as you face it, is the expansive and airy **Loggia della Signoria**, a combination of Gothic and Renaissance architecture. It was built by Benci di Cione, Simone Talenti and others during the years 1376–1382. At either end of the steps are two marble lions, one of which is very old, the other made in 1600.

Underneath the arch are some wonderful sculptures: *Persius* by Cellini in 1553 under the left hand arch; *The Rape of the Sabines* by Giambologna in 1583 under the right arch; *Hercules and the Centaur* by Giambologna in 1599 under the right arch also. There is also *Menelaus supporting Patroclus* and a few other less important works. All of them, since they are open to the elements and pollution, have been stained and discolored, but all are excellent studies in human anatomy.

11. UFFIZI GALLERY

Piazza del Uffizi. Open Tuesday to Saturday 9:00am-2:00pm, Sundays and Holidays 9:00am-1:00pm. Closed Mondays. Admission E6. *Tel. 055/218-341. Web: http://musa.uffizi.firenze.it.*

The building housing the **Uffizi Gallery** was begun in 1560 by Giorgio Vasari on the orders of the Grand-Duke Cosimo I. It was originally designed to be government offices, but today holds the most important and impressive display of art in Italy, and some would say the world. The gallery mainly contains paintings of Florentine and Tuscan artists of the 13th and 14th centuries, but you'll also find works from Venice, Emilia, and other Italian art centers as well as Flemish, French, and German studies. In conjunction there is a collection of ancient sculptures.

These fabulous works of art were collected first by the Medici family (Francesco de' Medici started it off in 1581) then later by the Lorraine family. The last of the Medici, the final inheritor of that amassed wealth, Anna Maria Luisa donated the entire Gallery to the Tuscan state in 1737 so that the rich collection gathered by her ancestors would never leave Florence. Not everything would go as planned, since in the 18th century some pieces were stolen by Napoleon's marauding forces, but most of these were later returned after a ransom was paid. Some items were damaged in the great flood of 1966, and still others were damaged in 1993 when a terrorist car bomb ripped through

Reservation Service for Uffizi & Other Museums

It is strongly recommended that you reserve tickets in advance so that you do not have to stand in the incredibly long lines which are common at the Uffizi, Accademia and other museums, especially in the summer.

Once you have ordered your tickets you will not have to wait in that incredibly long line outside the Uffizi. Simply walk up to the bookstore to the left side of the entrance, pick up your tickets, and enter at the time designated.

You can also get tickets for the Uffizi and other museums on the web through **www.firenze.net**. The site is self-explanatory and makes life so much easier for people wanting to get into Florence's wonderful museums without having to waste precious hours waiting in line.

Reservations for the Uffizi can be made for a specific day and a specific time of entry, as long as ticket availibility last: *Tel. 011/39/055/294-883, Fax 011/39/055/264-406*. Hours: Monday thru Friday 8.30am-6.30pm; Saturday 8.30am-12.30am. On Saturday and holidays an answering service is operative. Charge for reservations by phone is E2, Tickets E6.

parts of the Gallery. Even with all these occurrences, the Uffizi is still one of the finest galleries in the world.

As you enter the Uffizi, you will find the statues of Cosimo the Elder and Lorenzo the Magnificent, as well as several busts of the rest of the Medici rulers. It is ironic that they are so prominently displayed since when they ruled most Florentines despised their despotic ways. But now they are immortalized in time because of the philanthropic gesture of their last heir.

Anyway, it would be virtually impossible to list all the paintings and sculptures exhibited, so let me make a list of those that you absolutely must see if you visit the gallery. If you want a more complete listing or an audio guided tour, you can get those as you enter. Also, the museum is in the process of preparing for a move from the upper floor to the two lower floors. If that occurs, the room designations indicated below will no longer be valid.

• *Madonna of the Pomegranate*, *The Primavera*, *The Birth of Venus*, and *Annunciation* - Botticelli - Room X (This is the main Botticelli room, but there are Botticelli's strewn from Room X to XIV)
• *Self Portraits of Titian, Michelangelo, Raphael, Rubens, Rembrandt and more* - Third Corridor
• *Madonna of the Goldfinch* - Raphael - Room XXV

- *Holy Family* - Michelangelo - Room XXV
- *Venus of Urbino* - Titian - Room XXVIII
- *Young Bacchus* - Caravaggio - Room XXXVI
- *Portrait of an Old Man* - Rembrandt - Room XXXVII
- *Portrait of Isabelle Brandt* - Peter Paul Rubens - Room XLI

The most recent purchases are concerned with self-protraits of some of the world's masters including Giotto, Maasaccio, Paulo Uccello, Filippo Lipp, Botticelli, Leonardo, Michelnagelo and others. A rare peek into the past to see what these painters really looked like. Another sight to see at the Uffizi is thye view from the Cafetteria Bartolini, located on the second floor at the very end of the second hall way. The food's not that great, but the view is great for photographs.

12. PIAZZALE MICHELANGELO
From this piazza you have a wonderful view over the city of Florence being dissected by the river Arno. Remember to bring your camera since this is the best public view of the city. The best view, public or private is from the Hotel Torre di Bellosguardo, but if you desire that vista you have to spend the night since they don't allow sightseers on their grounds. At the center of the Piazzalle Michelangelo is a monument to **Michelangelo** dominated by a replica of the statue of *David*. Round the pedestal are four statues that adorn the tombs of famous Medicis which Michelangelo created. If you are up here around dinner time and want to grab something to eat, try the restaurant La Loggia on the opposite side of the piazza from the vista, across the road.

If you don't want to walk up the steep hill to the piazza, take bus number 13 from the station.

13. MUSEO ZOOLOGICO LA SPECOLA
Via Romana 17. *Tel. 055/222-451.* Closed Wednesdays. Open 9:00am–noon and until 1:00pm on Sundays.

This is an outing for the entire family. They have vast collection of stuffed animals from all over the world, some extinct, as well as bugs, fish, crustaceans, and more. You won't believe the extent of this collection, and that's just the animals. The best part of the exhibit is the collection of over 500 anatomical figures and body parts that were made in very life-like colored wax between 1175 and 1814. Every part of the body has been preserved separately as well as in whole body displays. They even put human hair on the heads of female reproductions to make them look more realistic.

One exhibit you may not want your kids to see is the part on reproduction, which gets pretty graphic. That room is at the end so you can march ahead and steer your impressionable ones into another room if you choose.

The other stuff is very tame. The last room has miniature wax scenes that are completely realistic depictions of the toll taken by the Black Death (the Plague). One particular tiny image of a rat pulling on a dead man's intestine is quite intense. Look at these pieces as art, not the anatomy tools they were used for, and you'll appreciate them immensely. The museum is used by many art students to study anatomy and you will find them discreetly sketching throughout the entire display.

14. THE BOBOLI GARDENS

Located behind the Pitti Palace. *Tel. 055/213-370.* Open 9:00am - 4:30pm (Nov-Feb), 5:30pm (Mar. & Oct.), 6:30pm (April, May & September), 7:30pm (June, July & August). Closed the first and last Mondays of each month. Admission E3 with Museo delle Porcelane.

Hidden behind the Pitti Palace is your respite from the Florentine summer heat and the hordes of tourists. Began in 1549 by Cosimo I and Eleanor of Tudor, the gardens went through many changes, additions, and alterations before they reached their present design. Among its many pathways and well-placed fields, the **Boboli Gardens** are the only true escape from the sun, humidity, and crowds that swarm through Florence in July and August. If you are inclined to walk in a calm, peaceful garden, far from the bustling crowds, or if you wish to enjoy a relaxing picnic, the Boboli is your place.

In the groves and walks of the Boboli you can find many spots to sit and enjoy a picnic lunch, or you can simply enjoy the platoons of statuary lining the walks. Some of the most famous works here include: *Pietro Barbino Riding a Tortoise*, commonly called 'Fat Baby Bacchus Riding a Turtle' (you'll find reproductions of this statue in almost every vendor's stall in Florence); a Roman amphitheater ascending in tiers from the Palazzo Pitti, designed as a miniature Roman circus to hold Medici court spectacles; and *Neptune's Fountain* at the top of the terrace, created in 1565 by Stoldo Lorenzi.

From this fountain a path leads to the adorable **Kaffeehaus**, a boat-like pavilion that offers a fine view of Florence and drinks to quench your thirst. Keep going up until you reach the **Ex Forte di Belvedere**, which offer magnificent views of all of Florence, and **Cypress Alley**, lined with statues of many different origins.

Also in the gardens is the **Museo delle Porcelane** with a delicate porcelain collection from the Medici and Lorraine families.

La Limonaia

Even if you are not looking for it, you can't miss the **Limonaia**, a room 340 feet long and 30 feet wide that became the 'hospital' for all the devastated works of art during the Flood of '66 (see story below). Originally used to house the Boboli Gardens' lemon trees during the winter months, this room, many experts felt, was the savior of the Florentine masterpieces, because of its insulation from the Florentine humidity. Most of the art treasures from the disastrous flood of '66 were brought here to be rehabilitated. I guess you could say that all art lovers can be thankful that the Medicis had a passion for lemons.

Porta Romana

This garden stretches seemingly forever, and it hides some of the best green spaces at its farthest corners, near Florence's **South Gate** (**Porta Romana**). If you exit here and take the big road to your left, Piazzale Michelangelo, you will walk through some incredibly bucolic Florentine neighborhoods.

15. SANTO SPIRITO

Piazza Santo Spirito. Open 8:00am-Noon and 4:00pm-6:00pm. Closed Wednesday afternoons.

Begun in 1444 by Brunelleschi, and continued after his death in 1446 by Antonio Manetti, Giovanni da Gaiole and Salvi d'Andrea. The last of these built the cupola that was based on Brunelleschi's design. It has a simple, plain, seemingly unfinished facade, in contrast to the interior.

Divided into three naves flanked by splendid capped Corinthian columns, this church looks very similar to San Lorenzo. There is a central cupola with two small naves in the wings of the cross that have small chapels just off of them. Lining the walls are some small chapels capped by semi-circular arches are adorned with elaborate carvings. The main altar, created by Giovanni Caccini (1599-1607), is Baroque in style and intricately displayed. In the chapels off the wings of the cross to the right and left of the main altar are many fine works of art to be enjoyed (two of which are *Madonna con Bambino* by Fillipino Lippi and *San Giovanni and Madonna with Baby Jesus and Four Saints* by Masi di Banco).

Many of these works are difficult to see since light does not find its way into this church very well.

16. DANTE'S HOUSE

Via Santa Margherita 1. *Tel. 055/219-416.* Open 10:00am-6:00pm (until 4:00pm in off season). Closed Tuesdays. Admission E3.

Dante's House and the accompanying museum of his life sits along one of the most medieval streets in Florence, tiny, cramped and evoking the conditions of his time. The house is quaintly picturesque. It was reconstructed a little haphazardly in the 19th century. The ground floor is a precursor with furnishings from Dante's time period. Upstairs is where the museum is (*entrance at Via S. Margherita 1*). It contains various manuscripts from Dante's time including many different versions of the *Divine Comedy*, Dante's most famous work. Not the greatest site in the world, but if you're a Dante fan this is a must see in Florence.

17. CHURCH OF THE BADIA

Via del Proconsolo. Open 9:00am-7:00pm.

Directly almost directly in front of the Bargello museum, this building was a Benedictine monastery founded in 978. The church is where it is rumored that Dante saw his love Beatrice for the first time. The church and accompanying buildings have gone through many changes over time. In 1285 the facade was built; in the 1400's extensive renovations were done on the cloisters, and in the sixteenth century the church was given a Baroque look and feel by Matteo Segaloni.

From the courtyard of the building you can admire the campanile of the Palazzo Vecchio, one of the characteristic structures in the skyline of Florence.

The interior of the church contains many notable paintings as well as tombs of respected Florentines, including Ugo di Toscana whose mother founded the monastery and Bernardo Giugni. The organ in the church, built by Onofrio Zeffirini da Cortona in 1558, still works and is used at every mass. Through a door on the right side of the church you enter the amazing *Chapel of the Oranges* (closed during mass) created by Bernardo Rossellino from 1432-38.

18. PALAZZO STROZZI

Piazza degli Strozzi. *Tel. 055/288342*. Hours Mon- Sat. 9:00am-1:00pm. Closed Sundays.

One of the most beautiful Renaissance palazzi in Florence built by and for one of Florence's most powerful families, the Strozzi. Construction was begun August 6th, 1489 because of astrological reasons, was stopped in 1504 for the same reasons, restarted in 1523, and suspended again in 1538 because of the death of Filippo Strozzi il Giovane. In true Italian fashion, work was never totally completed, but constant renovations and reconstructions have occurred.

The proportions of this three story building are exemplary and is something to be viewed for its Renaissance look and feel. It now houses some cultural institutes which are not open to the public, but you are allowed to enter the courtyard and look around at the archways and portals.

19. NATIONAL LIBRARY

Piazza Cavaleggeri1. *Tel. 055/249191*. Open Monday-Friday 10:00am-12.30pm; 3:00pm-6:30pm; Saturdays 10:00am-12.30pm.

The **Biblioteca Nazionale** is one of the most important libraries in Italy, located in the Santa Croce section of Florence in an eclectic building on the Piazza dei Cavaleggeri just off of the Lungarno. It was built between 1911 and 1935. The collection of books was started around 1714 by Angelo Magliabechi and was called at the time Biblioteca Magliabechiana. It was expanded in successive years by incorporating other libraries with the Magliabechi collection; then in 1861 it was renamed the National Library.

Today the library contains over 85 kilometers of shelves, 25,000-plus manuscripts and around 5 million books and 1 million letters. There are many ancient pieces in the library, including *Il Messale* (Catholic Missal) from the 10th century, *Il Codice della Commedia*, the oldest surviving Italian manuscript from before the 10th century, the *Maguntina Bible* from 1462, and *La Commedia* published in Florence in 1481 with comments by Cristoforo Landini and signed by Botticelli. Not your average titles found in libraries elsewhere. If you are a bibliophile make a pilgrimage here.

20. MUSEUM OF SCIENTIFIC HISTORY

Piazza dei Guidici 1, *Tel. 055/239-8876. Web: http://galileo.imss.firenze.it/ index.html*. Hours Monday, Wednesday, Thursday, Friday 9:30am-5:00pm. Tuesday, Saturday 9:30am-1:00pm. Closed Sundays and most holidays.

Located along the Lungarno and near the Uffizi is the **Museo di Storia della Scienza**. Situated in the severe Palazzo Castellani which was built in the 14th century, the building was first used as a civil courthouse from 1574 to 1841, and up to 1966 one part of the building was the *Accademia della Crusca*, but the massive flood of that year forced the relocation of that organization.

Since 1930 the Museo di Storia della Scienza has been housed here. The exhibit is mainly a collection of scientific instruments from the 16th and 17th centuries. There are astrolabs, solar clocks, architectural tools and more. Of great interest are the original instruments used by Galileo (rooms IV and V). Also of interest are the map-making materials and ancient geographical tools (room VII). There is also a splendid reconstruction of the map of the world made by Fra Mauro.

On the second floor you will find the precious astronomical clock from the 15th century (room XII) and many instruments created and used in the 17th century, including the amazing mechanical *mano che scrive* (hand that writes) and *l'orologia del moto perpetuo* (clock of perpetual motion). For those interested in scientific discovery, or for those who need a break from art, this is a wonderful museum to visit.

21. FORTRESSA DA BASSO

Viale Filippo Strozzi, 1. *Tel. 055/49721*. The parks inside are open 24 hours a day.

Take the Via Valfonda to the right of the train station to get here, the Fortress of San Giovanni. Also known as the Fortressa da Basso ("below") as compared to the Fortressa Belvedere ("with a good view"). This is an enormous pentagonal fortification built by the decree of Alessandro de' Medici more to eliminate internal strife through a show of force than for defense of the city. Construction was started under the guidance of Sangallo il Giovane in 1534. The outside walls were originally over 12 meters high and the walls nearest the station and the train tracks are the only ones of that height today. On the inside there is an octagonal building of note, the *corpo di guardia* (guard house).

22. FORTE BELVEDERE

Via S. Leonardo. *Tel. 055/234-2425.* Open 9:00am-8:00pm. Only the grounds are open to the public.

Also called the Fort of St. George, this fortress was constructed in the 1500s by the decree of the Grand Duke Ferdinand I on a design by Bernardo Buontalenti e Don Giovanni de' Medici. Its battlements were used in the defense of the city for centuries. From the battlements you have an amazing panorama of the city and the valley of the Arno. A great place for photo opportunities.

At the center of the structure is the Palazzina di Belvedere, built between 1560 and 1570, and only open for special exhibits.

23. MUSEO NAZIONALE DEL BARGELLO

Via del Proconsolo, *Tel 055/210-801.* Open Tuesdays - Saturdays 9:00am-2:00pm and Sundays 9:00am-1:00pm. Holidays 8:30am-1:50pm. Closed Mondays. Admission E4.

Located almost behind the Palazzo Signoria in the quaint Piazza S. Firenze, you will find one of the most important collections of art and artifacts in the world. Located in the building that was the first seat of government in Florence, and was in 1574 the seat of the justice department, police, and customs, this is a rather severe, austere palazzo that was restored from 1858 to 1865. After the great flood of 1966 most of the ground floor had to be redone.

You will find great sculptures from the Renaissance. Featured prominently are those created in Tuscany, which are some of the best ever made. After entering into the small area called Torre Volognana, you are ushered into the *Cortile* (courtyard) area complete with a fountain and six allegorical marble statues by Bartolomeo Ammannati, *Oceano* by Giambologna, *Allegoria di Fiesole* by Tribolo and *Cannone di S. Paolo* by Cosimo Cenni.

Elsewhere in the museum you will find some beautiful works by Michelangelo including *Bacco* (1496-97) *David-Apollo* (1530-32) which is the first large classical sculpture by the artist, and *Bruto* (1530), which means ugly, and is the only bust created by Michelangelo of Lorenzino di Medici. On this floor are also some beautiful bronze statues by a variety of artists.

On the second floor (which you get to by stairs constructed by Neri di Fioravante from 1345-1367) are some interesting bronze animal sculptures including the famous tacchino (turkey) made by Giambologna. The other featured artist in the museum is Donatello whose works are displayed in the Salone del Consiglio Generale, constructed by the same architect who built the stairs. Here you'll find *S. Giorgio* (1416) accompanied by two statues of *David*, one younger in marble (1408-9) and the other more famous one in bronze (circa 1440). Other works by Donatello include the *Bust of Niccolo of Uzzano* made of multi-colored terra-cotta, *Marzocco* (1418-20), a lion that symbolizes the Florentine Republic, *Atys-Amor,* a wonderful bronze, and the dramatic *Crucifixion*.

There are many other works here, too many to mention, but suffice to say that this is a museum that shouldn't be missed while in Florence, especially if you like sculpture. The Accademia and the Uffizi get all the press in Florence, but this is one of the best museums of sculpture anywhere in the world.

24. TEMPIO ISRAELICO

Via Luigi Carlo Ferini, *Tel. 055/245-252*. Open Sun.-Thurs. 10:00am - 1:00pm & 2:00pm-5:00pm. Fridays 10:00am -1:00pm. Closed Saturdays & Jewish Holidays. E3.

Built from 1874 to 1882, this eclectic synagogue with Byzantine/Moorish motifs is definitely worth seeing. There is no need to enter unless you are curious, but the building also contains the *Museo Ebraico di Firenze* (Hebrew Museum of Florence), with some ancient ceremonial objects and a sacred torah. The sight to behold is the unique architecture and facade, quite different than most buildings in Florence. Located a little ways away from everything in the Santa Croce section of town.

25. SAN MARCO

Piazza San Marco, *Tel. 055/287-628*. E7.

This place is a hidden treasure. Actually this 'place' is the church, the cloisters, the museum next to the church, and the Biblioteca de Michelozzo. The church has some incredible works by Fra Bartolemeo and Michelozzo, as well as Donatello's workshop. The museum has what could be the largest collection of Fra (Beato) Angelico paintings anywhere. The library (biblioteccha) is a spartan presentation of some ancient documents.

You can also visit the rooms on the top floor, where Fra Angelico, the accomplished artist and Dominican friar, lived and worked. Other individuals, such as Savonarola stayed for short and long periods in the little monastic cells. At the top of the main set of stairs is a beautiful Fra Angelico fresco, and the frescos in each of the cells are by Fra Angelico or his students.

THE FLOOD OF 1966

Standing at the center of the Ponte Vecchio, surveying the incomparable beauty and serenity of the sights of Florence, it seems incredible to imagine this magnificent city virtually blanketed with oily, muddy surging walls of water. But that was reality not long ago, on November 3, 1966, when Florence's last massive flood occurred and devastated many of the city's historic and artistic treasures.

On that day, the normally complacent **Arno** turned into a life threatening, destructive river, coursing through the labyrinth of Florence's many streets. On that night, and the subsequent days, despite the valiant efforts of an army of students from all over the world and the courageous Florentines, the world lost many priceless art treasures, and many irreplaceable documents and manuscripts.

Not the First

But this was not Florence's first experience with a flood's devastation. For many centuries Florentines had been ravaged by the power of nature, a power which had been enhanced by the meddlesome hand of man. What remains of these past floods are the commemorative plaques, all over the city, indicating the high water marks from each of the individual disasters.

How could such calamity occur in one of the world's most historic cities? How could it have been prevented?

Leonardo da Vinci clearly saw the cause of these periodic floods, and even made excellent recommendation for their remedy. He designed projects to develop water impoundments in the hills around Florence, to develop tributaries off the Arno, to develop chambers beneath Florence to hold excess flood waters. In conjunction, a proposal was made to initiate a government-sponsored reforestation plan, first by Gianbattista Vico del Cicerto, and later by many other visionaries.

Centuries of Deforestation

But each and every suggestion went unheeded by those in power. Why? Mainly because the trees around Florence were needed to support the growing population's demand for fuel and construction material. Couple this with the root destruction caused by grazing goats and sheep, which helped support the successful wool trade, and this left the surrounding hills, once thick with impenetrable forests, barren and desolate and open to rain water run-off that helped stimulate the devastating Florentine floods.

Since the massive flood of 1333, moderate floods have occurred in Florence every 24 years, major floods every 26 years, and massive floods (like the one in 1966) every 100 years.

Extensive Damage

The flood in 1966 was a catastrophe. Try and imagine trees and automobiles being hurled down the Arno into the living masterpiece of the **Ponte Vecchio**, destroying the gold shops in its wake. The **Uffizi Gallery**'s cellars, which were the government offices for the Medicis, were completely submerged; and many works of art, in conjunction with the State Archives containing valuable papers of the Medici family and the Florentine governments, were covered in water and fuel oil. This fuel oil was a modern addition to the Florentine floods. It was used as heating for Florentine homes, and was dredged up all over the city by the swirling waters of the Arno.

At the **Biblioteca Nazionale Centrale** the most devastation occurred, when close to one and a half million of nearly three million volumes disappeared from the miles of shelving into the brackish waters. The **Chiesa di Santa Croce** almost lost the bones of Michelangelo, Machiavelli, Galileo, and the composer Rossini to the muddy Arno water. The museum next door had its *Crucifix* by Giovanni Cimabue battered and eventually destroyed by the black tide.

The **Bargello**, a museum with sculptures comparable to the collection in the Accademia, was awash with 14 feet of oily mud and water. Many of Michelangelo's works found here were completely covered with slime, and had to be blanketed with clouds of talcum powder to extract all the potentially damaging oil.

The beautiful bronze doors of the **Baptistery** near the Duomo were almost lost to the flood. The door on the east side, containing magnificent scenes from the Old Testament, had five of its panels pried loose, luckily to be saved by a protective gate that surrounded the door. Almost every museum, library, and residence was affected in some way by the flood of 1966. But now, with better river water management, through the proper use of dams and improved communication between the two major dams above Florence, the effects of centuries of deforestation can be better controlled. And hopefully history in this case will not repeat itself.

Nightlife & Entertainment

Florence is definitely not known for its nightlife. Most Florentines usually only engage in some form of late night eating and drinking at a restaurant that stays open late. Heated dancing and wild debauchery don't seem to part of the Florentine make-up, except for a few places mentioned below.

Here are some places to go if you get that itch to be wild; you'll find each listing on the Florence restaurants map, pages 140-141.

35. **DUBLIN PUB**, *Via Faenza 27r. Tel. 055/293-049. Closed Mondays. Open from 5:00pm to 2:00am.*

A true Irish pub, dark and dingy and open only at night. They serve Kilkenny, Harp, Guinness for E3.5 a pint and E2 a half pint; as well as some Bulmers Cider. A hopping nightlife spot with true Irish ambiance. I prefer Fiddler's Elbow, but they're close enough together that you can try them both. This one is near the outdoor San Lorenzo Market and the Mercato Centrale.

36. **THE FIDDLER'S ELBOW**, *Piazza Santa Maria Novella 7R, Tel. 055/ 215-056. Open 3:00pm–1:15pm everyday. Harp, Kilkenny, Guinness, and Inch's Stonehouse Cider on draught. Pint E3.5, half-pint E2.*

If you want to enjoy a true Irish pub outside of Ireland, you've found it. Step into the air conditioned comfort, sit among the hanging musical instruments, belly up to the dark wooden bar, eye yourself in the mirror, and have a pint. For snacks (you have to pay for them), they have peanuts, salami sticks for the Italians, and four types of Highlander Scottish potato chips (they call them crisps): Roast Beef Taste, Cheddar & Onion, Caledonian Tomato, and Sea Salt.

If you want to be a part of the ex-pat community here in Florence, this is one of the places to go. But it is also one of the main nightspots for young Italians in Florence too. If you want to meet people, Italian or otherwise, this is the place to come. Whether it's sitting on the patio or inside at one of the many tables you're bound to have some fun. There is also a TV in the back room that is usually commandeered for soccer or rugby games. You can also enjoy Fiddler's Elbows in Rome, Venice and Bologna.

37. HARRY'S BAR, *Lungarno a Vespucci 22, 50123 Firenze. Tel. 055/239-6700. American Express, Mastercard and Visa accepted. Closed Sundays.*

Based on the famous Harry's Bar in Venice (see the Venice chapter in this book), but with no business connections (Italians obviously have different trademark laws than we do). This is now the place to find the best burgers in Florence. They also mix some strong drinks in the evening, so if you have nothing to do and just want to get out of the hotel room, pop in here.

38. IL RIFRULLO, *Via San Niccolo 55, Tel. 055/213-631. Large beer E2.5, small beer E1.5, Crepe E2.5. Open from 8:00am to midnight.*

Located in the Oltrarno, this is a charming and relaxing place where you can enjoy a drink in the garden in the summer, in front of the fireplace in the winter, or up at the bar whenever you please. The atmosphere in the front room is all pub, in the back room all taverna, and in the garden, all party. They have a bar set into ancient struts that hold up the building; the tables are under an overhead canopy. They serve Whitbread Pale Ale, Campbell's Scotch Ale, Stella Artois (Belgian) and Leffe (a Belgian Double Malt on tap), as well as some of the largest and most scrumptious crepes around. Come early; remember that Florence closes down early even on weekends.

39. SPACE ELECTRONIC, *Via Palazzuolo 37, 50123 Firenze. Tel. 055/292-082, Fax 055/293-457.*

The largest and loudest discotheque in the city. They've had music videos playing here before anybody knew what music videos were (I still remember seeing Mick Jagger crooning the words to Angie); and they continue to be the trendsetters when it comes to club antics. They play all sorts of music, so no one is left out. A fun place with many different levels and dance floors, where you can enjoy the company of your friends, or leave in the company of a newfound one.

Opera

If you are in Florence from December to June, the traditional opera season, and have the proper attire (suits for men, dresses for women) and a taste for something out of the ordinary, try the spectacle of the opera at **Teatro Communale**, Corso Italia 16, *Tel. 055/211-158 or 2729236, Fax 055/ 277-9410.*

Movies in English
If you need a little video fix, try **Cinema Astro**, Piazza San Simone (near Santa Croce), closed July 10–August 31 and Mondays. Tickets cost E4. There's a student discount on Wednesdays for E3. Films are in English here every night at 7:30pm and 10:00pm. Either call for the schedule or stop by and pick one up.

Sports & Recreation
Balloon Rides in Tuscany
Contact **The Bombard Society**, 6727 Curran Street, McLean VA 22101-3804. Outside Virginia, toll-free *Tel. 800/862-8537, Fax 703/883-0985. In* Virginia or outside: *Tel. 703/448-9407;* you can call collect. Call for current price and information about the most amazing way to view the most spectacular scenery in the world.

Golf
• **Circolo Golf dell'Ugolino**, Via Chiantigiano 3, 51005 Grassina, *Tel. 055/ 320-1009, Fax 055/230-1141.* Located 9 km from Florence this is a par 72, 18 hole course that is 5,728 meters long. Open all year round except on Mondays. They have tennis courts, a swimming pool, a pro shop, a nice bar and a good restaurant.
• **Poggio de Medici Golf & Country Club**, Via San Gavino 27, 50038 Scarperia. *Tel. 055/83-0436/7/8, Fax 055/843-0439.* Located 30 km from Florence this is a 9 hole, par 36 course, that is 3,430 meters long, and is open all year round except for Tuesdays. They have a driving range, putting green and a clubhouse with snacks and drinks.

Pools
If you need a break from touring and want to lounge around a pool for the day, below is a list of places that have pools that you can pay to use. Note that some of them are hotels and are conveniently located near the center of town.
• **Costoli**, Viale Paoli, *Tel. 055/678-012,* Open in the summer, 10:00am-6:00pm.
• **Bellariva**, Lungarno Colombo, 6, *Tel. 055/677-521,* Open in the summer.
• **Le Pavoniere**, Viale degli Olmi, *Tel.055/367-506,* Open in the summer.
• **Hotel Villa Medici**, Via Il Prato, 42, *Tel. 055/238-1331,* Open in the summer.
• **Hotel Villa Cora**, Viale Macchiavelli, 18, *Tel. 055/229-8451,* Open in the summer.

- **Hotel Villa La Massa**, Candeli, Bagno a Ripoli, *Tel. 055/651-0101,* Open in the summer.
- **Hotel Minerva**, Piazza S.Maria Novella, 16, *Tel. 055/284-555,* Open in the summer.
- **Hotel Kraft**, Via Solferino, 2, *Tel. 055/284-273,* Open in the summer.
- **Crest Hotel**, Viale Europa, 205, *Tel. 055/686-841,* Open in the summer.
- **Hotel Villa Le Rondini**, Via Bolognese Vecchia, 224, *Tel. 055/400-081,* Open in the summer.
- **Park Palace Hotel**, Piazzale Galileo, 5, *Tel. 055/222-431*, Open in the summer.
- **Hotel Villa Belvedere**, Via Senese, 93, *Tel. 055/222-501,* Open in the summer.

Tennis

If you have a hankering to serve and volley, here are some tennis clubs in Florence where you can rent a court.
- **Circolo Tennis alle Cascine**, Viale Visarno, 1, *Tel. 055/354-326*
- **Fiesole Tennis**, Via Pian di Mugnone, Fiesole, *Tel. 055/554-1237*
- **Circolo Tennis S. Quirichino**, Via S. Quirichino, 8, *Tel. 055/225-687*
- **Tennis Michelangelo**, V.le Michelangelo, 61, *Tel. 055/681-1880*
- **Tennis Club Rifredi**, Via Facibeni, *Tel. 055/432-552*
- **Novantanove**, Via dei Brozzi, 99, *Tel. 055/375-631*
- **Circolo di Tennis**, Via Scandicci Alto, *Tel. 055/252-696*

Shopping
Antiques

Many of the better known antique stores have been located in the **Via dei Fossi** and **Via Maggio** for years, but there are some interesting little shops in the **Borgo San Jacopo** and the **Via San Spirito**, all located in the **Oltrarno** section of Florence across the river.

When shopping for antiques in Florence, there is one important thing to remember: the Florentines are excellent crafts people and as such have taken to the art of antique fabrication and reproduction. In fact under Italian law, furniture made from old wood is considered an antique, even if it was carved yesterday. These products can be sold as antiques and usually have a price tag to match. But in terms of American understandings, they are not antiques. They only look like it.. If you find a 'real' antique by American standards, it is usually designated by a stamp indicating that it is a national treasure and as such cannot be taken out of the country.

Artisans

If you want to see some of this excellent antique fabrication and reproduction work, as well as genuine restoration in progress, you need venture no further than across the river to the Oltrarno section. In these narrow streets you'll find small workshops alive with the sounds of hammers and saws, intermingled with the odors of wood, tanning leather, and glue. When I lived in Florence this was my favorite area to come to. Watching someone creating something out of nothing has always been a relaxing adventure, and besides, not many tourists even venture into these tiny alcoves of Florentine culture.

Some of the best known shops are located in the **Via Santo Spirito**, **Viale Europa**, **Via Vellutini**, **Via Maggio** and the **Via dello Studio**. Strangely enough, on these same streets are your real antique shops. How convenient to have the fabricators and reproducers next door to the 'legitimate' antique dealers. In other words, inspect your goods carefully.

Books & Newspapers in English

BM Bookshop, Borgo Ognissanti 4r, *Tel 055/294-575.* Open Winter: Mondays 3:30pm-7:30pm, Tuesday-Saturday 9:00am-1:00pm and 3:30pm-7:30pm. Open Summer: 9:30am-1:00pm and 3:30pm-7:30pm daily. An extensive collection of English language books in both hardcover and paperback. This is also one of the meeting places for the English-speaking community in Florence. Located in the Centro area.

English Bookstore Paperback Exchange, Via Fiesolana 31r, *Tel. 055/ 247-8154.* Open Monday-Saturday 9:00am-1:00pm and 3:30pm-7:30pm. Closed in August. Closed Mondays November–February. The unofficial English-speaking bibliophile meeting place, this store has the largest and best priced selection of new and used English-language paperbacks in Florence. If you want to exchange a book you have already read they are very generous with trade-ins. The only stipulation is that the book you select as your trade-in has to be used. Located in the Santa Croce section of Florence, just around the corner from **Sbigoli Terrecotte**, which is an excellent pottery shop.

Libreria Internazionale Seeber, Via Tornabuoni 68r, *Tel. 055/215-697.* Open regular business hours. This is an extensive and old fashioned bookstore that's been around since the 1860s to serve the expatriate community. An entire room is devoted to foreign books, not all of which are in English. Even if you can't find what you want, this is a fun place to browse.

Cartolerie - Stationary Stores

L'Indice Scrive, Via della Vigna Nuova 82r. *Tel. 055/215-165.* Mastercard and Visa accepted. A wide variety of stationary products and unique pens are featured in this store. Most of the items are hand-made, including the diaries, ledgers, guest books, desk sets. etc. A great place to get a gift for someone back home.

Il Papiro, Piazza Duomo 24r, *Tel. 055/215-262.* *E-mail info@ilpapirofirenze.it, Web: www.ilpapirofirenze.it.* Credit cards accepted.

If you like marbleized paper products, this is the store for you. You can get boxes, notebooks, picture frames, pencil holders, basically anything you could imagine. The prices are a little high but that's because of the great location and high quality products. They also have three locations in Rome, all around the Pantheon.

Il Torchio, Via de Bardi 17, *Tel. 055/234-2862*. A much less expensive store than **Il Papiro**, with similar stuff, and they make it in front of you while you shop. Located 2 blocks east of the Ponte Vecchio (as you cross the bridge turn left), this place off the beaten tourist path, but well worth the slight detour.

Ceramics

If you are interested in the famous painted ceramics from Tuscany and Umbria, you don't have to go to the small towns where they are manufactured – there is a great store behind the stalls in the San Lorenzo market called **Florentina**, Via dell'Ariento 81r, *Tel. 055/239-6523*. Owned by a stereotypical friendly Irish woman and her Italian husband, this store has everything you could want at prices similar to what you would get if you traveled to Deruta in Umbria or Cortona in Tuscany.

Another ceramics store is located near Santa Croce around the corner from the English Bookstore Paperback Exchange. The **Sbigoli Terrecotte**, Via S. Egidio 4r, *Tel/Fax 055/247-9713*, has works from Deruta priced virtually the same as if you were in that town. This store also has a laboratory of its own where they make, bake and hand paint their own ceramics.

Markets

The markets in Florence are all hustle and bustle, especially in the high tourist season. But despite the crowds you can have a great time browsing and shopping. And of course, the prices are sometimes close to half what they are in stores. Remember to bargain because usually the starting price is rather

The Papier Mache Store

One store you simply cannot miss is the small studio/gallery of the artist Bijan, **Firenze of Papier Mache**, Piazza Pitti 10, *Tel. 055/230-2978, Fax 055/365-768*. He makes beautiful masks covered with intricate sketchings of famous paintings, as well as beautiful anatomical forms, all from papiermache. Even if you don't buy anything, simply browse and savor the beauty of his work. Since the shop is near the Palazzo Pitti, one of your 'must see' destinations while in Florence, there's no reason why you shouldn't take a peak in here.

high. The best bet when bargaining is to make a counter offer at half of the initial price. Then let the games begin. Bargaining is half the fun of buying something in an Italian market.

Mercato Centrale, immediately north of Piazza San Lorenzo, near the Duomo, open Monday–Friday, 7:00am–2:00pm and 4:00pm–8:00pm, Saturday 7:00am–12:15pm and 1:00pm–5:00pm. Sunday 3:00pm–5:00pm. This is Florence's main food market for wholesale and retail fish, fresh meat, vegetables, cheeses, oils, breads, and many other delicacies. The meat and fish section is on the ground floor, with a few vegetable stands thrown in, but if you're into healthy food, make your way upstairs to their fruit and vegetable market. The aroma is enough to make you want to come back every day you're in Florence. Try to find some caciotta (sheep's milk cheese) and finocchiona (salami flavored with fennel) because they are an exquisite local delicacy. This is the best place to shop for your picnic supplies as well as a must see while in Florence. The market itself is surrounded by the large clothing market of San Lorenzo.

When you visit the Mercato Centrale, don't think of leaving without getting a sandwich at Nerbone's (see review above in *Where to Eat*). In operation since 1872, this small food stand serves the absolutely best boiled pork, beef, or veal sandwiches, for only E3. They're simply called panini and your only choice of meat is what they have boiled for the day. The sandwich is just the meat, the bread, and some salt, but it is amazing. You can stand at the counter and sip a glass of wine or beer, or take your meal to the small seating area just across the aisle.

Mercato di San Lorenzo, located near the Duomo, everyday from 8:00am-dark. Closed Sundays in the winter. This is the largest and most frequented street market in Florence, and it completely dominates the church of San Lorenzo and its piazza, as well as spilling into most adjacent streets. You can find everything from shoes to pants, T-shirts, belts, and much more, most at prices close to half of what you would pay in a store. Both Florentines and tourists come here looking for bargains. Again, remember to bargain, because once a merchant marks you as a tourist the price quoted is usually higher than that quoted to Italians.

Mercato Nuovo, located in the Logge del Mercato Nuovo off the Via Por San Maria near the Piazza del Signoria, open daily 9:00am–5:00pm. This is the famous Straw Market. They sell traditional products made from straw but also exquisite leather products, ceramics, linens (like table clothes and napkins), statues, and other hand-made Florentine crafts.

Mercato dell Pulci, located in the Piazza dei Compi about four blocks north of the church of Santa Croce, open Tuesday–Saturday, 8:00am–1:00pm, 3:30pm–7:00pm, and the first Sunday of each month from 9:00am–7:00pm.This is Florence's famous flea market. If you want antiques and junk at obviously trumped up prices, come here. They think tourists will pay anything for a true Italian antique – so remember to bargain. The next market, Mercato di Sant'Ambrogio, is located just to the east of this market.

Mercato di Santo Spirito, located in the piazza in front of Santo Spirito. Open the second Sunday of every month from 8:00am-7:00pm. A great market filled with antiques, junk, clothes, imported figures from Africa, military surplus, and much more. A great place to people watch, grab a great boiled meat sandwich, pick up some cashews to snack on or buy a gift to bring home. In my book, one of the best in Florence. Come here if you happen to be in the city the second Sunday of the month. In conjunction, the only alimentari in the city open on that Sunday is in the piazza.

Picnic & Food Supplies
If you can't make it to the Mercato Centrale or the Mercato di Sant'Ambrogio for your Boboli Garden or day trip picnic supplies, here's a small list of food stores from which you can get almost everything you want. The perfect amount of meat for a sandwich would be mezzo etto (about 1/8th of a pound) and the same goes for your cheese. Also, at most bars you can order a sandwich to go if you're too lazy to make your own, and you can also get some vino or birra to take with you.

Vera, Piazza Frescobaldi 3r, *Tel. 055/215-465.* No credit cards accepted. Located in the Oltrarno section of Florence, this store is a food connoisseur's delight. It is indisputably Florence's best stocked food store, conveniently located close to the Boboli Gardens. It has the best fresh cheeses, salamis, hams, roasted meats, freshly baked breads, olive oil, soups and salads. If you want fresh fruit you're also in luck – but not here, you have to go to the store across the street.

Vino e Olio, Via dei Serragli 29r, *Tel. 055298-708.* No credit cards accepted. You can find any type of wine or olive oil you could dream of in this store. Since it is slightly expensive you may not want to get your wine for the picnic here, but it is a great place to buy gifts for friends at home. If you don't want to carry them with you on the rest of your trip, the owner will arrange to have them shipped to wherever you choose.

Alessi Paride, Via delle Oche 27-29r, *Tel. 055/214-966.* Credit cards accepted. This store is a wine lovers paradise. They have wines from every region of Italy and there's one room entirely dedicated to Chianti. This store may also be a little expensive for picnic supplies, but you can get any manner of wine imaginable here, as well as selected liquors, chocolates, marmalades, and honeys.

Superb Little Shops
Officina Profumo-Farmaceutica di Santa Maria Novella, Via della Scala 16 n, *Tel. 055/230-2883 or 2649, Fax 055/288-658.* A beautiful centuries-old establishment with the most refined soaps, shampoos, creams, bath and other

personal hygiene products. The goods were originally made from the monastery of Santa Maria Novella. Store is located nearby the same church.

Alice's Masks Art Studio, Via Faenza 72r, Tel. 055/287-370. Here you can find some great papiermache masks and other wonderful stuff.

Betty Florence, Piazza Madonna Aldobrandini 9/10r, Tel. 055/216-548. This place has great and reasonably-priced leather wallets, bags, belts, etc. Directly across the street from the entrance to the Cappelle Medici.

G. Veneziano, Via dei Fossi, 53r, Tel. 055/287-925. A lovely store with particularly nice things for the home and kitchen.

Practical Information

Airports
- **Aereoporto A.Vespucci-Firenze**, Tel. 055/3061300, www.airport.florence.it
- **Aereoporto G.Galilei -Pisa**, Tel. 050/500-707, www.pisa-airport.com/

Church & Synagogue Ceremonies in English
- **St. James**, American Episcopal Church, Via Rucellai 9, Tel. 055/294-417. Located in the Centro section of Florence.
- **St. Marks**, Church of England, Via Maggio 16, Tel. 055/294-764. Located in the Oltrarno section of Florence.
- **Synagogue**, Via L.C. Farini 4, Tel. 055/245-251/2. Located in the Santa Croce section of Florence.

Consulates
- **British Consulate**, Lungarno Corsini 2,Tel. 055/284-133
- **United States Consulate**, Lungarno Amerigo Vespucci 38, Tel. 055/239-8276

Emergencies
These are the rapid response numbers for the police, caribineiri and fire.
- **Polizia Soccorso Pubbblico** (police), Tel. 113
- **Carabinieri Pronto Intervento**, Tel. 112
- **Vigili del Fuoco** (fire), Tel. 115

Local Festivals & Holidays
- **January 1**, New Year's Day
- **April 25**, Liberation Day
- **Ascension Day**
- **May 1**, Labor Day
- **Month of May**, Iris Festivals
- **Cricket Festival**, Sunday of the Ascension, usually in May, with floats and little (mehcanical) crickets sold in cages. Live crickets were once sold, but animal rights activists convinced the city to switch to electronic crickets.

- **May and June**, Maggio Musicale Fiorentino
- **Mid-June to August**, Estate Fiesolana. Music, cinema, ballet and theater
- **Three Weekends in June**, Calcio in Costume
- **June 24**, St. John the Baptist's Day celebrated with fireworks
- **August 15**, Ferragosto
- **First Sunday in September**, Lantern Festival
- **November 1**, All Saints Day (Ognissanti)
- **December 8**, Conception of the Virgin Mary (Immacolata)
- **December 25 & 26**, Christmas

Laundry

After you're on the road for a few days, and especially if you're going to be on the road for quite a while, you're definitely going to need to do some laundry, quickly, easily, and inexpensively. If you're staying at a four star hotel don't bother reading this because you've already sent your clothes down to be starched and pressed by the in-house staff.

For the rest of us, we need to find a good coin operated laundry, and in Florence they have just the thing.

- **Wash & Dry**, four different location, all open seven days a week from 8:00am to 10:00pm. Last wash allowed in at 9:00pm. General number: *Tel. 055/436-1650.* E3 for wash, E3 for dry, E3 for detergent. E6 for large. Located at: Via dei Serragli 87/R (in the Oltrarno); Via della Scala 52/54R (by the train station and Piazza Santa Maria Novella) – has air conditioning; Via dei Servi 105/R (by the Duomo) – has air conditioning; Via Ghibellina 143r (near the Duomo).
- **Laundrette**, Via del Guelfa 33. Open seven days a week from 8:00am to 10:00pm. Wash E3, Dry E2, Detergent E3.
- **Tintoria La Serena**, Via della Scala 30r, *Tel. 055/218-183.* Open seven days a week from 8:00am - 10:00pm. Total of E7 for washing and drying one load.

On-Line Access

Internet Land, Via degli Alfani 43r, *Tel./Fax 055/263-8220, www.internetland.it.* This is the place in Florence to come to surf the web, scan a document, get one typed and printed, fax a letter home, or e-mail your friends.

Postal Services

The **central post office** in Florence, Via Pietrapiana 53-55, is in the Santa Croce section of town; but stamps can be bought at any tobacconist (store indicated by a **T** sign outside), and mailed at any mailbox, which are red and marked with the word Poste or Lettere. You can send duty free gift packages (need to be marked "gift enclosed") home to friends or relatives as long as the cost of the gift(s) in the package does not exceed $50. You will need to box them in official boxes or envelopes which can be bought at cartolerie (stationery stores).

If you need to mail a package of material which you brought with you on you trip, you need to mark the package "American goods returned." Rules, rules, rules.

Tourist Information & Maps
• **Information Office**, Via Manzoni 16, *Tel. 055/247-8141.* Located in the Santa Croce area of Florence. Provides city maps, up-to-date information about Florence and the province of Florence, which includes museum hours, events, and bus and train schedules.
• **Information Office** at the Train Station, Via Stazione 59r. Open 7:00am to 10:00pm. *Tel. 055/282-893/283-500.* They can book hotel rooms for you here; but you do have to pay the first night's stay in advance plus a fee of E5 for a deluxe hotel, E4 for a four-star, E3 for a three-star, E2 for a two star, and E1.5 for a one star. There's a form that you need to fill out prior to getting to an attendant that indicates the specific requirements you want in your room, i.e. whether there is a private bath, double bed, and how much you want to spend.
• **American Express**, Lungarno Guicciardini 49, *Tel. 055/288-751.* Located in the Oltrarno section of Florence. Via Dante Alighieri 22r, *Tel. 055/50981.* Located in the Centro Storico section of Florence. They offer a full complement of tourist information.

Tour Operators
• **American Express**, Lungarno Guicciardini 49, *Tel. 055/288-751.* Located in the Oltrarno section of Florence; Via Dante Alighieri 22r, *Tel. 055/50981.* Located in the Centro Storico section of Florence. They offer a full range of tours.
• **Wagon-Lit**, Via del Giglio 27r, *Tel 055/21-88-51.* Located in the Centro section of Florence. They offer your basic bus tours of Florence and Tuscany.
• **World Vision Travel**, Via Cavour 154/158r. *Tel 055/57-71-85, Fax 055/582-664;* and Lungarno Acciadi 4, *Tel. 055/29.52.71, Fax 055/215-666.* They offer your basic bus tours of Florence and Tuscany.
• **CIT**, Via Cavour 56-59, *Tel. 055/294-306.* Located in the Centro section of Florence. They offer your basic bus tours of Florence and Tuscany.
• **Walking Tours of Florence**, *Tel. 055/580-430. Email: holitaly@dada.it.* One of the best ways to learn all about the Roman, medieval and Renaissance history, and the architecture, people and events of Florence. Every Tuesday, Thursday, and Saturday at 10:00am and Wednesday evening at 6:00pm. Cost is only E20 per person.

Chapter 12

elsewhere in tuscany

If you have the time, there are a number of great day trips and longer excursions in Tuscany. For many, a trip to Italy is not complete without visiting one of the most famous sights in the world – the **Leaning Tower of Pisa**, – here in Tuscany.

Lucca

Florence

Pisa

San Gimignano

Cortona

Siena

Montepulciano

Isola del Giglio

There's also the charming walled city of Lucca with its romantic walkway on the ramparts of the old walls; the winding medieval streets and expansive Campo of **Siena**, with one of the most impressive clock towers in Italy; the ancient town of **Fiesole**, once the Roman Empire's dominant town in Tuscany; the romantic towers and simple beauty of the small hill town of **San Gimignano**; the wonderful churches and market of **Cortona**; the Renaissance palazzi and churches of **Montepulciano**; and the seaside splendor of the **Isola del Giglio**, the mostly undeveloped and little-touristed islands just off the Tuscan coast in the Mediterranean Sea.

Pisa

Located 56 miles west of Florence, with a population of a little over 100,000 people, **Pisa** is mainly known for its leaning tower; but it is alive with history and filled with many beautiful architectural landmarks that are decorated with intricate ornamentation.

The famous **Campo dei Miracoli** is in the northwestern part of the city. In this square are the **baptistery**, a circular church building used for baptisms; the **cathedral**, built from 1063 to 1160; and the marble bell tower, known to the world as the **Leaning Tower of Pisa**. It is thought that in the cathedral the astronomer **Galileo** first made the observation that later became known as the principle of the motion of a pendulum. But the bell tower is why people come to Pisa.

At 179 feet (55 meters) high and 50 feet (15 meters) wide, it was built on unstable ground and as a result it began to tip during its construction and is now 15 feet (4.6 meters) out of perpendicular. Other monuments include a cemetery, the Church of Santa Caterina, several museums, and many libraries. The city suffered considerable damage during World War II, but its art treasures and architectural purity still attract a large number of tourists from all over the world.

A naval base under Roman control, Pisa became a Roman colony after 180 BCE. The town had a Christian bishop by 313 CE. Pisa's greatest time was back in the 12th century, when its population was greater than 300,000. Pisa was considered a city of marvels because its merchants and its strong navy had traveled all over the Mediterranean, bringing back not only new products but new ideas and styles in art. The famous **Pisan Romanesque** architecture, with its stripes and blind arcades, had its origins in the Moorish architecture of Andalucia in Spain, whose ideas and styles were brought back by Pisa's world travelers.

During this successful time, the **Duomo** was built and the Baptistery and Campanile were begun. But these weren't the only glory of Pisa. It has been described as being a city of ten thousand towers, most of which do not exist today. How unfortunate that the one which has survived is about to fall. Most of the other Pisan monuments no longer with us today were destroyed in the bombings at the end of World War II.

Pisa historically aligned itself with the rulers of Tuscany, mainly in Florence, if only for expediency. Their navy was vast and fierce and they were constantly at war somewhere in the Mediterranean, usually against the Muslim world, even if they did adapt their science and architecture to their own uses.

Pisa's decline began in 1284, when the mercantile port of Genoa devastated the Pisan navy at the **Battle of Meloria** near Livorno. But the final blow to Pisa's Mediterranean dominance was delivered by nature. The silt from the Arno gradually filled in the Pisan port and the cost of dredging was too great for the city to bear. From that point on Pisa became a pawn that the other Italian city states traded back and forth. Eventually coming under the control of Florence, the Medici dukes gave Pisa a lasting gift, Florence's own university. This institution helped Pisa stay alive and vital, and in touch with the changes going on in the world.

For more information about Pisa, check out their well organized website at *www.pisaonline.it.*

Arrivals & Departures

By car, take the A11 directly to Pisa from Florence. Trains from Florence arrive at the Stazione Centrale, which is a pleasant 10-15 minute walk to the leaning tower and the other tourist sights. Or if you are a little tired, take the No. 1 bus from the station to the sights.

Where to Stay

I'm suggesting that you take a day trip up this way from Florence, spend the day, see the sights, explore the old city by the Arno, have lunch and maybe dinner, then catch one of the frequent trains home. But if you happen to tarry a little longer than expected, here's a concise list of hotels in a variety of price ranges that are worthy of your attention.

1. ARISTON, *Via Cardinale Maffi 42, Tel. 050/561-834, Fax 050/561-891. E-mail: hotelariston@csinfo.it, Web: www.pisaonline.it/hotelariston/. 35 rooms all with bath and radio. Single E26-44; Double E35-57. Breakfast E5. All credit cards accepted.* ***

Located right by the Leaning Tower and the other main sights in Pisa. You'll have the tower to keep you company, but this is so far away from the real center of the city located around the river. But even so, this is a good inexpensive option for a short stay in Pisa.

2. JOLLY CAVALIERI, *Piazza della Stazione 2, 56125 Pisa. Tel. 050/43290, Fax 050/502-242. E-mail: pisa@jollyhotels.it, Web: www.jollyhotels.it. Toll free in Italy 167-017703. Toll free in US and NYC 800/221-2626. Toll free in NY State 800/247-1277. 100 rooms. Single E145-170; Double E170-220.*

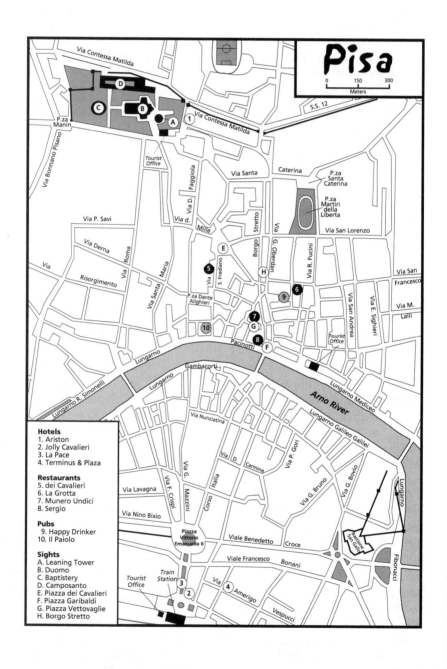

Pisa

0   150   300
Meters

Hotels
1. Ariston
2. Jolly Cavalieri
3. La Pace
4. Terminus & Plaza

Restaurants
5. dei Cavalieri
6. La Grotta
7. Munero Undici
8. Sergio

Pubs
9. Happy Drinker
10. Il Paiolo

Sights
A. Leaning Tower
B. Duomo
C. Baptistery
D. Camposanto
E. Piazza dei Cavalieri
F. Piazza Garibaldi
G. Piazza Vettovaglie
H. Borgo Stretto

Located near the train station and away from the main sights, this could be an option if you've lingered too long over dinner and don't want to take the train back to Florence or have missed the last one. All the amenities of afour star including air conditioning, cable TV, piano bar and more. Its location is not so hot in terms of tourist sights, but this is the place to stay in Pisa.

3. LA PACE, *Viale Gramsci 14, Tel. 050/29351. Fax 050/502266. E-mail: info@HotelLaPace.it, Web: www.hotellapace.it/. 70 rooms all with bath. Single E70; Double E90. Breakfast included. All credit cards accepted.* ***

Just your basic, run of the mill, three star hotel located near the train station in Pisa. Located in a commercial gallery that is a little bland. Here you will find peace and quiet but not much else. The rooms are clean and comfortable, but the atmosphere is not too electric. Let's be honest. Pisa is not known as a hot bed for hotels.

4. TERMINUS & PLAZA, *Via Colombo 45, Tel. and Fax 050/500-303. 55 rooms all with bath. Single E65; Double E85. Breakfast E6. Diner's Club, American Express and Visa accepted.* ***

A hospitable hotel in an austere building, which is well kept up and finely decorated. The rooms have functionally furnished, nothing special, and the bathrooms are sufficient. The common areas are ambiant and the staff personal and professional. A good option while in Pisa.

Where to Eat

5. DEI CAVALIERI, *Via San Frediano 16, Pisa. Tel. 050/49-008. Closed Saturdays for lunch and Sundays. Credit cards accepted. Dinner for two E32.*

A small place near a public high school (right around lunch the place empties out to the sounds of excited kids and their motorbikes). They have good pasta dishes here, such as con funghi porcini (with mushrooms), coniglio e asparagi (rabbit and asparagus) or vongole verace (clams in a garlic and oil sauce). For secondo, try either the coniglio al origano (rabbit made with oregano) or the fileto di pesce fresco can patate e pomodoro (fresh fillet of the catch of the day with roasted potatoes and tomatoes).

6. LA GROTTA, *Via San Francesco 103, Tel. 050/578-105. No credit cards accepted. Closed Sundays and in August. Dinner for two E35.*

An old Pisan restaurant built in 1947 that has the look and feel of a cave, hence the name. As such the atmosphere is unique and compliments the rustic Pisan cuisine. Try the risotto ai fiori di zucchini (rice with zucchini flowers), the spaghetti alla vongole (with clam sauce), then for later sample either the coniglio (rabbit) or the vitello (veal). If you're up late, this place stays open until 1 or 2:00am and becomes a wine bar serving drinks and cold plates after 11:00pm. It's one of Pisa's hip hangouts.

7. NUMERO UNDICI, *Via Cavalca 11. Tel. 050/544-294. No credit cards accepted. Closed Saturdays at dinner and Sundays. Dinner for two E23.*

A small, down to earth, local place situated by the University that has a nice outside patio. Located near the old market in Pisa this is the perfect place to sample Pisan home cooking. They make great lasagnas, crepes, and foccace (a crepe-like concoction with meats, cheeses, and vegetables baked inside the crisp doughy exterior), but my favorite was a dish of assorted salamis. Centrally located, good atmosphere and great food.

8. SERGIO AMERICAN BAR, *Lungarno Pacinotti 1 Tel. 050/48-245. American Express, Diners Club, Visa and Mastercard accepted. Closed Sundays and Mondays for lunch. An expensive place. Dinner for two E75.*

Why this place is called an American Bar I will never understand since they serve traditional Pisan fare. Great fresh food prepared in exquisite Pisan style in an environment that looks like something out of an old castle. They have large keys and porcelain dishes hanging on the walls interspersed among the haphazardly placed paintings. If you try any of the antipasti that can be enough for a meal. Two such dishes are the salumi tipici toscani con crostini (Tuscan salami with crostini) or the pesce spada con insalata di stagione (swordfish with salad). If you sample any of their meats or seafood dishes your price will easily meet the anticipated E75, if not your bill will be dramatically less.

9. HAPPY DRINKER, *Vicolo del Poshi 5-7. Open from 4:00pm to 12 midnight.*

An authentic Irish atmosphere serving up great pints of Guinness, Harp, or Caffreys for E3. On a side street off the main Borgo Stretto. Inside seating only but what a wonderful place it is. Frequented by locals and tourists alike.

Graveyard of Ancient Ships

Just a short stroll from the Leaning Tower, archaeologists are unearthing at least ten Roman ships, many complete with cargoes, that sank some 2,000 years ago in a recently rediscovered harbor in Pisa. Merchant vessels, a warship, and a ceremonial boat are all being excavated, along with boxes and boxes of artifacts, from coins and lamps to amphorae that are still full. These artifacts, and the boats themselves, are being readied for removal to the nearby Arsenali Mediciei, a large warehouse structure which is being transformed into a temporary laboratory and museum where the final phases of restoration will occur.

This important find will be open to the public soon, but if you want a sneak preview , visit their website at *www.navipisa.it*. When in Pisa, take some time to visit this historic find.

10. IL PAIOLO, *Via Cortatone e Montanara 9. Open for lunch and dinner.*
The interior has the look and feel of a German beer garden complete with the communal wooden tables. Outside it's just another café on a quiet street. They serve the German beer Weininger for E3 a pint. They also have a limited trattoria type menu for those desiring to have some food with their ale. A wonderfully rustic, medieval atmosphere.

Seeing the Sights
Much of the main tourist area centers around the **Campo dei Miracoli** (Square of Miracles) and its famous **Leaning Tower**, but Pisa has other attractions that you should explore as well. The sights below are lettered and correspond to the letters on the map of Pisa.

PIAZZA DEL MIRACOLI
It is called the **Square of Miracles** because of the stupendous architectural masterpieces filling the square. These are living testimony to the greatness that the city of Pisa reached at the height of its glory. The square is surrounded by imposing walls begun in 1154, which in turn are surrounded by countless vendors selling a wide variety of trinkets for the tourists.

The following sights are on display in the piazza:

A. THE CAMPANILE, OR THE LEANING TOWER
Tickets E15. You will need to make reservations in advance at *www.duomo.pisa.it.*

It's open once more. You can climb the leaning tower of Pisa again. So get ye to Pisa. The 293 steps of the tower can once again be traversed.

The most unique tower in the world because of the fact that it leans, and the degree to which it does. There are other towers in Italy, but none has the beauty and charm of this one, nor are any others on the verge of falling over as is this one.

The lean in the tower was not planned, but it was noticed when the tower reached a height of 11 meters. The builders continued to build even though they realized that the foundation was unstable. The tower was begun in 1174 by Bonanno Pisano and finished in 1350 by Tomaso Pisano, so the family spent many years trying to discover ways to eliminate the list, unsuccessfully. The tower is 55 meters, 22 centimeters high, and its steepest angle is almost 5 meters. This angle has been increasing at almost a millimeter a year.

It was getting so bad that serious measures were undertaken to reduce the list of the tower. Cables were attached around the outside to keep the tower from leaning any further. And a drilling rig removed soil from underneath the side of the foundation opposite the list. Pressure was exerted on the cable to pull the tower into the space vacated by the drilled soil, and the tower's lean has been corrected one-half a degree, or about 16 inches. The authorities could have corrected the entire lop-sided structure, but that would eliminate it as a unique tourist attraction, now wouldn't it?

Anyway, during its useful days the tower was employed by **Galileo Galilei** when he conducted experiments with the laws of gravity. Today the tower, with its six galleries each surrounded by arches and columns, as well as the bell cell located at the top, is only used for drawing the tourist trade to Pisa.

B. THE DUOMO

Open 8:00am–12:30pm and 3:00pm–6:30pm. In January only open until 4:30pm.

Started in 1063 by Buschetto, it was finally consecrated in 1118 after Rainaldo finished the work. The bronze doors are reproductions, by 16th century Florentine artists, of the originals that were lost in the fire of 1569. The facade is covered with many columns and arches as was the Pisan style at the time.

The interior contains numerous sculptures and mosaics, among which is the famous mosaic *Christ and the Madonna* started by Francesco of Pisa and continued by Cimabue. The celebrated pulpit is the work of Giovanni Pisano, of the same family that built the Campanile. There is also the famous lamp that hangs in the center of the nave that was created by Stolto Lorenzi. It is called the **Lamp of Galileo**, who, as rumor has it, discovered through observation and experimentation the oscillation of pendulum movements. Last but not least is the statuette in ivory by Giovanni Pisano of the *Madonna and Child*.

C. BAPTISTERY

Open 9:00am–1:00pm and 3:00pm–6:30pm. In January only open until 4:30pm.

Begun in 1153 by the architect Diotisalvi, it is circular in form with a conical covering. Later the facade was adapted by Nicola Pisan and his son Giovanni to fit the other works in the square. The interior has five baptismal fonts created by Guido Bigarelli of Como in 1246 and the masterpiece of a pulpit created by Nicola Pisano in 1260.

D. CAMPOSANTO

Open 8:00am–6:30pm. In January open from 9:00am–4:30pm. Admission E3.

A rather serene and unpretentious cemetery, very unlike the foreboding "city of the dead" found in Genoa. This one was started in 1278 by Giovanni di Simone. It was enlarged in the 14th century and stands today like an open air basilica with three aisles. The center soil is rumored to have been brought from the Holy Land. The corridor around the earth is formed by 62 arches in a Gothic style of white and blue marble.

You'll also find some beautiful frescoes along the walls and floors that were partially destroyed during World War II but have since been restored.

E. PIAZZA DEI CAVALIERI

This is the most harmonious piazza in the city after the famous Piazza dei Miracoli with its leaning tower. Literally translated the name means square of the knights, and it is named for the Knights of St. Stephen, an order established by Cosimo I de Medici to defend Florence and her holdings from pirates. The statue above the fountain by Francavilla in 1596 that is opposite the **Palazzo dei Cavalieri** (Knights Palace) is dedicated to this order. On its facade you'll find floral displays, symbols, coats of arms as well as sacred and profane images which are described as graffito style decorations. In niches above the second row of windows you'll find six busts of Tuscan grand dukes, from Cosimo I to Cosimo III de Medici.

The other buildings in this irregularly shaped piazza were built in the 16th and 17th centuries and include the **Church of St. Stephen's**, next to the Palazzo dei Cavalieri on the eastern side. On the western sides is the **Palazzo del Collegio Puteano** built in 1605. The southern side is occupied by the **Palazzo del Consiglio** (Council Chambers) of the order of the Knights of St. Stephen. On the northern side is the **Palazzo dell'Orologio** (Clock Palace). In the same piazza, next to the Palazzo dell'Orologio, the infamous **Muda Tower** (Tower of Hunger) used to sit. This was where Count Ugolino della Gherardesca was imprisoned with his sons and nephews in 1288 and left to starve to death. This situation was recorded for all to remember in Dante's *Inferno*.

If you're walking from the train station to the Leaning Tower walk through this piazza. It's a nice place to sit and watch Pisan life pass you by.

F. PIAZZA GARIBALDI

This piazza is at the end of the Borgo Stretto with its covered walkways, and is brimming with real Pisan life – not the tourist trap situation like at the Piazza dei Miracoli. From here you are mere meters away from the Piazza Vettovaglie with its outdoor market, and are near the Ponte de Mezzo, from which you can see the beautiful palazzi lining the Arno as it meanders towards the sea. If you are walking from the train station you will most probably pass over this bridge and through this piazza to get to the Piazza dei Miracoli. The area around the Piazza Garibaldi will give you a genuine feel for the real life in Pisa.

G. PIAZZA VETTOVAGLIE

There's a market in this square every morning from 7:00am to 1:30pm. Just off the Via Stretto, here you'll find the hustle and bustle of a small Italian market, with vendors hawking their wares rather vocally. You'll find everything from produce to used clothes in the stalls and around the piazza are little shops that compliment the food being sold outdoors. There are butchers, alimentari, and bakers so that the Pisan housewife can get all she needs here to make her family's daily meals.

The market spills out onto the Via Domenico Cavalca and around the corner. Great sights, sounds, and smells to remember Pisa by. Also, the street just mentioned has a variety of different little restaurants to sample if the market's wares have tempted your appetite.

H. BORGO STRETTO

If you can't get to Bologna to see their famous covered streets, this little street has a taste of it for you. The sidewalks are covered so this street is always filled with people whatever the weather. Just look out for the motor scooters and bicycles that find their way up on the sidewalk at those times. You'll also find street performers and mimes entertaining the bustling crowds. You can either people-watch or shop at the many delightful stores. The market in the Piazza Vettoglie is just off this street.

Practical Information

Car Rental
• **Avis**, Airport, *Tel. 050/42028*
• **Hertz**, Airport, *Tel. 050/49187*

Tourist Information
• **Piazza Duomo**, to the right of the Camposanto, *Tel. 050/560-464.*
• **Piazza Stazione**, just as you exit the doors of the station the office is located directly on the left, *Tel. 050/42-291*. They can give you a map to guide your way through the streets to the sights.

Lucca

Try not to miss this city. Instead of making this a one-day adventure, I highly recommend staying at least one or two days to savor its beauty and charm. Located 46 miles west of Florence and 14 miles northeast of Pisa, **Lucca** is closer to Pisa than to Florence and it is still one of the least visited cities in Tuscany, but we guidebook writers are starting to change that.

Most motorists coming from the north drive past in their haste to get to Pisa, and most people arriving from Florence fail to take the hour ride further north because Lucca doesn't have an architectural anomaly like the Leaning Tower of Pisa. But what Lucca has, even with a slowly growing tourist trade, is charm, and lots of it.

Lucca's Walls

Lucca is surrounded by walled fortifications, which were designed to keep marauding Florentines at bay, and which are now the site of a flowering

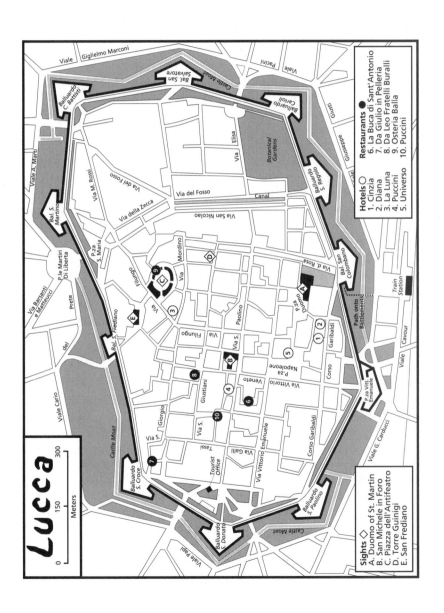

Lucca

0 150 300
Meters

Sights ◇
A. Duomo of St. Martin
B. San Michele in Foro
C. Piazza dell'Antifeatro
D. Torre Guinigi
E. San Frediano

Hotels ○
1. Cinzia
2. Diana
3. La Luna
4. Puccini
5. Universo

Restaurants ●
6. La Buca di Sant'Antonio
7. Da Giulio in Pelleria
8. Da Leo Fratelli Buralli
9. Osteria Balla
10. Puccini

greenbelt around the city. A tree-lined garden boulevard on top of the walls and encompassing the ramparts of the old fortifications extends clear around the city and is perfect for a passegiatta (slow stroll). A peaceful and enchanting activity any time of the day. The garden walkway has a thin sliver of asphalt which bicyclists and roller bladers share with strolling pedestrians. But on either side of the walkway is grass, countless trees and shrubs that make this city a wonderfully romantic paradise.

At the battlements, of which there are 10, each coincidentally shaped like a heart, there are plenty of places to cuddle with your loved one, or sit at a wooden table and have a calming afternoon picnic. If you're with a family, the kids can roam free, exploring the nooks and crannies of the walls, while you and your spouse enjoy brief interludes of intimacy.

Besides the walls, which with Ferrarra's are the best preserved in Italy, Lucca offers a tight grid road system, a remnant of its Roman occupation, which now gives it the feel of a compact Renaissance town. I love exploring the many tiny little streets and reveling in the enjoyment of making new discoveries in the maze. In this labyrinth of a city is **San Michel in Foro**, which is located on what used to be Lucca's Forum. Every column on this church is different, some are intertwined like corkscrews, some doubled, and some carved with medieval looking monsters.

Often confused with San Michel is Lucca's **Cathedral**. The Duomo rests at the end of the Via Duomo in Piazza San Martino. This structure is perhaps the most outstanding example of the Pisan style of architecture outside of Pisa. Its porch with three arches, and three levels of colonnades, give it an unusual facade, but typically Pisan.

Explore Lucca!

Besides these sights, Lucca is a city to explore. You can walk its labyrinth of tiny streets and feel a part of the Renaissance. Through your exploration you will find the busy shopping area around Via Fillungo, the 12th century church of **San Frediano**, the Roman **amphitheater** (a must-see so you can compare the different centuries and cultures combined into modern day life), the **Torre Giungi**, which is the tower that overlooks the city. It has one special feature, a garden complete with full-grown trees on the top. Here you can take fine panoramic pictures of the area. Besides these there are plenty of other discoveries waiting for you in Lucca.

Arrivals & Departures

Car is quickest, about one hour away from Florence on the A11 past Prato and Pistoia, two excellent destinations on their own. So if you stop at them, the trip will take somehwat longer. When driving in Italy always remember "Fare il Pieno" (fill 'er up) whenever you stop for gas, because sometimes gas stations are few and far between.

Trains from Florence take between an hour and an hour and a half depending on how many stops the train has to make. As of press time the trains that depart Florence for Lucca are at 9:42am, 1:42pm, 3:42pm, 4:42pm, 5:13pm, 5:42pm, 6:45pm, and 8:35pm. Returning to Florence you'll find many trains in the evening, also usually leaving every two hours: 3:00pm, 5:00pm, 7:00pm, and 9:00pm. Make sure you check all this information prior to your departure if you're going for a one-day adventure.

To get inside the city walls when you arrive by train you can either take the adventurous/native route or the more mundane. The native route from the station is to walk straight out of the station and keep going straight on the left hand side of the Piazza Ricasoli. Cross the road avoiding the maniacal drivers and follow the path to a passageway that leads into the walls. At night it's very well lit and safe. When you enter the stairs inside the ancient walls, if you can ignore the graffiti covering them, you'll feel as if you've walked back into the Middle Ages. Follow the stairs up to the wooded walkways on top of the walls. The perfect way to introduce yourself to the city, up on the picturesque and romantic walkway of the old walls. From here descend to the walled city below and you're on your way to exploring.

The more mundane way to enter the city would be to go through the elaborate and imposing **Porta San Pietro**, which was built around 1566, just a short distance left down the main road from the station. The gate still has Lucca's proud motto of independence, *Libertas*, etched over the top.

Where to Stay

The hotels listed here are inside the walls of the old city. If you come to Lucca there is no point in staying anywhere else since all the flavor, ambiance, and romance is inside the old city walls.

1. CINZIA, *Via della Dogana 9, 55100 Lucca. Tel. 0583/491-323. No credit cards accepted. 12 rooms, 3 with bath. Single E15-20; Double E23-33.* *

On a quaint little street that has ivy covering the sign on the door, the Cinzia is a good budget hotel where you'll find quality inexpensive lodging. Everything is spic and span but there are not too many amenities. A clean and comfortable place to lay your head, but expect little else. Despite all that it lacks, this hotel is usually booked well in advance, so make reservations.

2. DIANA, *Via del Moinetto 11, 55100 Lucca. Tel. 0583/492-202, Fax 0583/47-795. E-mail: info@albergodiana.com. Web: www.albergodiana.com. Credit cards accepted. 9 rooms, 8 with bath. Single without bath E40-50; Double E60-70.* **

A nice small hotel in a great location down a cute side street deep in the heart of Medieval Lucca. If you want to stay inside the walls of Lucca at this place, it's best to book in advance, because with its location and relatively inexpensive prices, this hotel is in great demand.

3. LA LUNA, *Via Fillungo, Corte Compagni 12, 55100 Lucca. Tel. 0583/493-634, Fax 0583/490-021. E-mail: laluna@onenet.it. Web: www.hotellaluna.com/ . American Express, Diners Club, Mastercard, an Visa accepted. 30 rooms all with bath. Single E50-60; Double E80-90.* *******

This is a professionally run small hotel with beautiful rooms done up in antiques and a comfortable lobby bar area in which to relax. This hotel and the Puccini are the two best places to stay inside the old city walls. The restrurant in the tiny square, Pizzeria Italia, though not written up here, is worthy of a visit.

4. PUCCINI, *Via di Poggio 9, 55100 Lucca. Tel. 0583/55421 or 53487, Fax 0583/53487. E-mail: hotelpucciniLU@onenet.it, Web: www.hotelpuccini.com/ index0.html. 14 rooms all with bath. Single E60; Double E90. Credit cards accepted.* *******

Located right up from the *Piazza San Michelle*, this is a beautifully appointed little three star hotel that has all necessary amenities. The lobby is small but the accommodations are intimate, comfortable and cozy. The Puccini playing in the lobby is a soothing addition. This is the place to stay in Lucca despite the condescending attitude of the staff.

5. UNIVERSO, *Piazza del Giglio 1 (next to the Piazza Napoleone), 55100 Lucca. Tel. 0583/493-678, Fax 0583/954-854. Web: www.hotels-venice.com/ lucca_hotels.html. Credit cards Accepted. 72 rooms. Single E100; Double E150.* *******

Established in the 11th century and wonderfully located on the Piazza del Giglio, this is a good option while in Lucca. The rooms are not that large but have all the amenities of a good three star. It's ideally located near the station and the Duomo but its prices are a little too expensive for my taste. They have a wonderful little bar with seating on the square. A larger, less intimate place than most of the other hotels in Lucca. A close third behind Puccini and La Luna.

Where to Eat

6. LA BUCA DI SANT'ANTONIO, *Via della Cervia 1/3, Tel. 0583/55881. Closed Sunday evenings, Mondays, and in July. All credit cards accepted. Dinner for two E50.*

This is an exceptional restaurant, the most classic and traditional of all places in Lucca. In a splendid location directly behind Piazza San Michele, the atmosphere in here is 19th centruy opulence. The cooking is all local with many meat dishes to choose from, as well as tasty grilled vegetables. And the dessert cart is not to be missed. Make reservations here, and dress well when dining. Appearance is important here.

7. DA GIULIO IN PELLERIA, *Via delle Conce 45, Tel. 0583/55948. Closed Sundays and Mondays, and in August. American Expres and Visa accepted. Dinner for two E40.*

A quaint and colorful local trattoria whose menu has not changed for at least 25 years. All sorts of meat and vegetable dishes abound, as well as rustic

Best Eats in Lucca

When in Lucca there is really only one place to eat: **Da Leo Fratelli Burelli**. It has great atmosphere and is boisterously local with friends calling to each other across the crowded dining space inside. Don't sit outside at the narrow strip of terrace; only tourists bother to eat there. Inside is where the action and ambiance are. As you enter you'll pass by their kitchen where you can see two or three female chefs slaving over hot stoves preparing their scrumptious meals. Seeing how hard they work makes you appreciate even more the fantastic food they prepare. When in Lucca, don't miss this place.

pies that combine both ingredients. The prices have risen in the past few years because of this places popularity, but they are still reasonable. Come here for fine local cooking in a rustic, authentic atmosphere.

8. **DA LEO FRATELLI BURALLI**, *Via Tegrimi 1, 55100 Lucca. Tel. 0583/ 492-236. Closed Sundays. No credit cards accepted. Dinner for two E30.*

This place is perfect. If you're going to have one meal (or two, or three) have it here, but not outside in the thin sliver of seating area on a small side street. You have to come inside and truly the enjoy the vibrancy of this Luccan staple. The energy inside is electric with friends calling to each other across the room, and the food clattering down in front of you as it is served.

From the open kitchen you pass by on your way you can see the frenzied female cooks preparing the food for hundreds of people each evening. This place is the best in Lucca and the prices are inexpensive too. Try the fettucine all rucola e gamberi (with cheese and shrimp) or the pasta al pomodoro e ragu (with tomato and meat sauce). For seconds sample the pollo arrosto con patate (roasted chicken with potatoes), a cold dish of prosciutto e mozzarella (ham and mozzarella), or some pollo fritto e zucchini (fried chicken and zucchini).

9. OSTERIA BARALLA, *Via Anfiteatro 5, Tel. 0583/44-0240. Closed Sundays and in August. No credit cards accepted. Dinner for two E30.*

After ten years this place has re-opened to rave reviews, and has re-immersed itself into the social life of Lucca. A true local, hosteria that has been pain stakingly restored to offer a colorful ambiance. And under the titelage of chef Alessandro Carmassi, the food is exquisite and traditional. An excellent choice for a meal while in Lucca.

10. PUCCINI, *Corte San Lorenzo 1, 55100 Lucca. Tel. 0583/316-116, Fax 0583/316-031. Web: speweb.monrif.net/prodotti/ristorantepuccini/. Dinner for two E55.*

An expensive but pleasant restaurant that has a somewhat modern ambiance. Try the antipasto di mare (seafood antipasto) or the penne agli scampi (pasta with shrimp). For seconds, I recommend the grigliata mista (mixed grilled meats from Tuscany). A definitely high class eatery that requires proper attire.

Seeing the Sights

Lucca is a small walled city that has a few memorable sights to see, but the most important is the entire package itself. Lucca is like a medieval town come to life, with its tiny twisting streets and its converted walls and battlements. It is a great place to explore. You'll get lost without a map for sure, but since the walled city is so small you'll eventually find something you recognize, especially the walls.

If you come to Lucca, stroll and picnic along these glorious tree-lined promenades. It will be a romantic and memorable experience.

A. THE DUOMO OF ST. MARTIN

Open 7:00am–7:00pm.

This is perhaps the most outstanding example of Pisan style outside of Pisa. It was begun in the 11th century and completed in the 15th. The facade has three levels of colonnades with three different sized arches. Behind and on the arches are beautiful 12th and 13th century bas-reliefs and sculptures. If you look hard enough you can find a column carved with the tree of life with Adam and Eve crouched at the bottom and Christ at the top, as well as a variety of hunting scenes with real and fantastic animals, dancing dragons, and more, all created by anonymous artists.

The dark interior is a showcase for Lucca's most famous artist, **Matteo Civitali** whose work has not escaped beyond the walls of Lucca. Rumor has it that until his mid-thirties, a ripe old age for some at that time, he was a barber, when he then decided he'd rather be a sculptor. His most famous work is the octagonal *Tempietto* done in 1489. It is a marble tabernacle in the middle of the left aisle. It contains a cedar crucifix, The *Volto Santo* (Hol Image) which is said to have the true portrait of Jesus sculpted on it by Nicodemus, an eyewitness to the crucifixion. Every September 13th the image is removed to join a candlelight procession around town.

Further up the left aisle you can find Fra Bartolomeo's *Virgin and Child Enthroned* as well as the *Tomb of Ilaria del Caretto*, a magnificent work by the Siennese artist Jacopo della Quercia. You will also find the Madonna *Enthroned with Saints* by Domenico Ghirlandaio and a strange *Last Supper* with a nursing mother in the foreground and what looks like cherubs floating above Christ's head.

B. SAN MICHELE IN FORO

Open 7:00am – 7:00pm.

This church is so grand that most people mistake it for Lucca's cathedral.

It is located in the old Roman Forum and is a masterpiece of Pisan Gothic architecture. The huge facade rises above the level of the roof, making the church look even larger and grander. You'll notice that every column in the five levels of Pisan-style arcading is different. Some will be twisting, some doubling, some carved with relief monsters and more.

While the entire facade is quite ornate and elaborate, the interior is more austere. It is best known for the place where Puccini started his musical career as a choirboy. As a reminder of this, just down the small road directly in front of the church is a wonderfully intimate place to hang your hat, the Piccolo Hotel Puccini. Besides the memory of Puccini, the interior of San Michelle in Foro contains a glazed terra-cotta *Madonna and Child*, a 13th-century *Crucifixion* hanging over the high altar, and a memorable painting of saints that lived during the plague years.

C. PIAZZA DELL'ANFITEATRO

A remarkable relic dating from Lucca's ancient Roman past is the **Roman Amphitheater**. Today it is lined with modern shops and medieval houses, and only the barest of outlines of the ancient arches can still be seen. Any marble that was once here was used to build the Cathedral and San Michele.

This place seems like an oasis from the past filled with modern comforts where you can lounge at a café and watch the Italian children playing their never ending game of calcio.

D. TORRE GUINIGIO

Open 9:00am–7:00pm in the summer and 10:00am–4:00pm in the winter. Admission E3.

A tower rising above a neighborhood that has scarcely changed in 500 years. Here the medieval ancestors of the **Guinigi** family had their stronghold with the tower as their lookout. One of Lucca's landmarks, it is also one of the most elaborate medieval family fortresses.

From the top you have the greatest views over all of Lucca. It's just a short walk up the 230-plus steps to reach the lush garden on the top, complete with trees sprouting from the ramparts. Remember to bring your camera and take some great pictures.

E. SAN FREDIANO

Open 7:00am–7:00pm.

A rather tall church with an even taller campanile (bell tower), both built in the 12th century and

Explore Lucca By Bike!

Cicli Barbetti, Via Anfiteatro 23, *Tel. 0583/854-444,* is located near the amphitheater, and is the only place to find bicycles to rent in the city. There really isn't a need to rent one, since the city is so small, but if you like to ride, this is the place rent a bike.

completed with colorful mosaics in the 13th century. The interior contains a magnificent baptismal font which is covered with bas-reliefs. The chapels around the central nave are elaborately decorated.

Also inside is the **mummy of St. Zita**, patroness of domestic servants. She was canonized in 1696, long after her birth in 1218. She put in many years of service as a servant for a rich family in Lucca with whom she stayed until her death. She is revered for her selfless acts of charity towards the poor, and now she is pickled in a coffin in Lucca.

Practical Information
Car Rental
• **Avis**, Viale Luporini 1411, *Tel. 0583/51-36-14*
• **Hertz**, Via Catalani 59, *Tel. 0583/58585*

Tourist Information
• **APT**, Vecchia Porta San Donato/Piazzale Verdi. *Tel 0583/419-689*. Hours 9:00am–7:00pm. You can get a map, a list of hotels, or better yet, they can actually help you find the hotel you want and point you in the right direction. Very helpful, very professional (by Italian standards), and ideally located for people arriving by bus or car. For those of you arriving by train, it's a short walk from the station.

Siena

Siena is generally described as the feminine counterpart to the masculine Florence, and even its nickname, **City of the Virgin**, belies this feminine quality. Located 42 miles south of Florence, this picturesque walled city is known for its many quality buildings, narrow streets, immense churches, and quaint little restaurants; but the two reasons why I love Siena are that cars are banned from the center of the city, making for a pleasant automobile-less environment (similar to Venice but without the water); and also for the biannual event called the **Palio**.

The well-preserved walls with towers and bulwarks of Siena are seven kilometers long and were built from the 13th to the 15th centuries. The ramparts on the outskirts are now used as public gardens. They are beautiful but not nearly as romantic or inviting as those from Lucca.

Siena was once a prosperous, stable, and artistic city in its own right even before she was absorbed into the Grand Duchy of Tuscany in 1559, which was ruled by Florence, after years of siege by Cosimo de Medici. Once it became a part of Florence, Siena was not allowed to continue to pursue its previously prosperous banking activities, nor were they allowed to continue their flourishing wool trade. Because of these actions, and the general despotic rule of Florence, Siena fell into a long period of decline. But today, as other Italian cities have also, Siena has learned how to succeed by marketing its ancient charm.

For tourist information in Siena, head to the tourist office, Piazza San Domenico, *Tel 0577/940-809*; open 9:00am to 7:00pm. You can get maps and hotel reservations if needed.

Arrivals & Departures
By Car
Either take the Florence-Siena Superstrada or the slower but more scenic Route 22 that runs through the heart of the Chianti wine region. From Rome take the A1 to the Via di Chiana exit, then head west on route 326 into Siena. You'll have to leave your car at one of the many parking lots on the outskirts of the city center, since no automobiles are allowed into the city.

By Train
From Florence there are over a dozen trains a day. The trip takes 1 1/2 hours. The train station is located one mile from the center of the city, but do

Highlights of Siena
Siena is a beautifully quaint little town with winding medieval streets and charming old buildings. There's really not too much to do here except absorb the atmosphere and ambiance, and find a place to settle down for a good meal, which is enough in and of itself. Two of the best places to eat here are **Spada Forte** (#8 on the map) and **Da Vasco** (#9). You'll love them both!

Obviously if you can get to Siena while the **Palio** is in session, you simply must do it. The pageantry, the horse race, the costumes, the intensity all evoke a time long gone and will sweep you back through the centuries. Held biannually on July 2 and August 16, plan well in advance to get a place to stay and a ticket to the horse race that is held in the **Campo**.

If you only have a little while in Siena the **Campo** is where to head since it is the gathering place for the locals, young and old alike. Notice the sloped stone surface that seems to float down to the **Palazzo Pubblico**, a building regal in bearing and boasting one of the most imposing clock towers in Italy. This tower, the **Torre del Mangia**, must be scaled while you're in Siena. If you're fit enough, the 112 meters and more than 400 small confined steps can be taken easily. Once at the top you will be treated to the most amazing panoramic view over the town and the surrounding countryside.

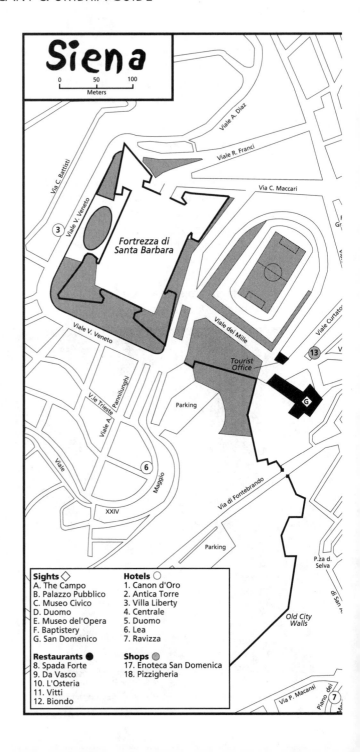

Siena

0   50   100
Meters

Via C. Battisti

Viale A. Diaz

Viale R. Franci

Via C. Maccari

Viale V. Veneto

3

Fortrezza di
Santa Barbara

Viale V. Veneto

Viale dei Mille

Viale Curtato

13

Tourist
Office

V.le Trieste

Viale A. Pannilunghi

Parking

G

Viale

Maggio

6

XXIV

Via di Fontebrando

Parking

P.za d.
Selva

Old City
Walls

di San

Via P. Macansi

Piano del

7

Sights ◇
A. The Campo
B. Palazzo Pubblico
C. Museo Civico
D. Duomo
E. Museo del'Opera
F. Baptistery
G. San Domenico

Hotels ○
1. Canon d'Oro
2. Antica Torre
3. Villa Liberty
4. Centrale
5. Duomo
6. Lea
7. Ravizza

Restaurants ●
8. Spada Forte
9. Da Vasco
10. L'Osteria
11. Vitti
12. Biondo

Shops ◉
17. Enoteca San Domenica
18. Pizzigheria

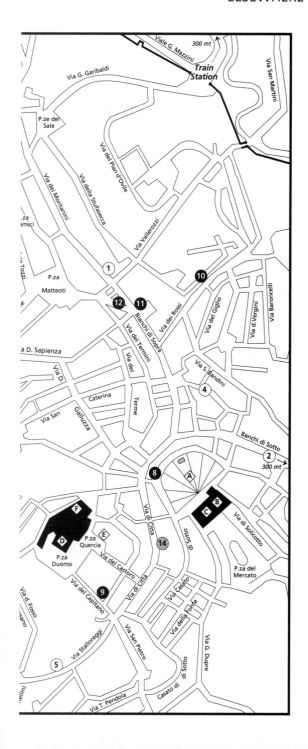

not fear. Just exit the station, stand on the curb and catch either bus 15, 2, or 6 and they will all take you to a dropping off point near the information desk in the center of town, from which you can get a map (Euro 50 cents) and hotel reservations if needed. Everything else from that point on is walking distance.

If, or should I say when, the blue bus ticket machine in the lobby of the train station is out of order, simply go to the train ticket window and purchase a bus ticket for Euro 75 cents. It's good for an hour once you punch it in the machine on the bus. I recommend buying your return fare in advance if you're not going to stay the night, so you don't have to worry about that detail on your return to the station in the evening. If you don't want to catch the bus, the old town is a short walk up the hill.

Renting a Car

If you're staying in Siena for a while and want to view the magnificent countryside, you can always rent a car, van, or moped. There's one place just outside the walled city where you can do this:

• **General Cars**, Viale Toselli 20/26, Tel. 0577/40-518, Fax 0577/47-984

Where to Stay

1. CANON D'ORO, Via Montanini 28, 53100 Siena. Tel. 0577/44-321, Fax 0577/28-08-68. Credit cards accepted. 32 rooms all with bath. Single E 40-45; Double 55-60. Breakfast E5. **

The oldest hotel in the city, located down a small white walled entrance way. Situated in two stories of a 12th century palazzo, this hotel has the feel of a three star but with better prices. The rooms are quiet since the hotel is located in part of the zona pedonale (walking area). Definitely the best inexpensive place to stay while in Siena. But you have to book well in advance for the comfort of these accommodations.

2. ANTICA TORRE, Via di Fieravecchia 7, 53100 Siena. Tel. 0577/222-255, Fax the same. 8 rooms all with bath. Single E140; Double E170. American Express, Mastercard and Visa Accepted. Breakfast E8. ***

This small hotel is located on a discrete and quiet street near Santa Maria de' Servi. The hotel itself is a tower built in the 1500s which makes the atmosphere here so unbelievably quaint. There are only two rooms per floor and to get to them you have to ascend tiny stairs so if you have a lot of bags or need an elevator don't bother staying here. And obviously the rooms are not that big since the tower itself is not gigantic, but what ambiance. From the top rooms you can look over the rooftops of the city and the green of the countryside. A very unique hotel. Stay here if you get the chance. Staying in a medieval tower is not your average run of the mill experience.

3. **VILLA LIBERTY**, *Viale Vittorio Veneto 11, 53100 Siena. Tel. 0577/449-666, Fax 0577/44770. E-mail: info@villaliberty.it. Web: www.villaliberty.it. 12 rooms all with bath. Single E130; Double E160. All credit cards accepted. Breakfast included. ★★★*

Just a little ways outside the walls of Siena near the *fortrezza* this hotel has been renovated in an eclectic Liberty style. Each room is elegantly furnished and comfortable. The best ones are in the upper area and come with more modern style furnishings. And each room has TV. Everything about this place is accommodating. More of a bed and breakfast than a Holiday Inn. Definitely not a 'cookie-cutter' hotel. A fine choice if you some to Siena.

4. **CENTRALE**, *Via Cecco Angiolieri 26, 53100 Siena. Tel. 0577/280-379, Fax 0577/42-152. Web: www.venere.it/toscana/siena/centrale. 7 rooms, 6 with bath. Double without bath E60; Double E70-80. ★★*

A small place that is clean, quiet, kept up nicely and is bucking for promotion to three star status. There are TV's, mini-bars and direct dial phones in each room, two of which are cute little terraces. To get a room here you have to book many months in advance since the location is excellent and the rooms are few. The proprietor knows he's sitting on a gold mine, but is still as pleasant as can be. A wonderful place to stay if you have the foresight to plan your trip well in advance. Not many amenities. More like a bed and breakfast (without the breakfast) than a hotel.

5. **DUOMO**, *Via Stalloreggi 34-38, 53100 Siena. Tel. 0577/289-088, Fax 0577/43-043. Web: www.sienaol.it/hduomo/indexi.htm. Credit cards accepted. 25 rooms all with bath. Single E120; Double E150. ★★★*

Comes with all the amenities of a three star, including cable TV for those in need of such entertainment. Located in part of an old palazzo just a little distance away from the Campo, this is a good place to stay within reach of all major sights. The rooms are simply furnished but clean and comfortable.

6. **LEA**, *Viale XXIV Maggio 10, 53100 Siena. Tel. 0577/283-207, Fax the same. 12 rooms all with bath. Single E50; Double E70. All credit cards accepted. Breakfast included. ★★*

Situated in a small villa from the 1800s, in a tranquil residential area near the center, surrounded by a small garden which is set with tables and chairs. From the top floors you get a magnificently unique view into the heart of Siena. This hotel offers great prices, spacious rooms, direct dial telephones, simple but comfortable furnishings and well decorated bathrooms. In the morning breakfast is a basic continental fare served in the same room that accommodates the bar and reception area. A great two star in Siena. A budget travelers paradise.

7. **PALAZZO RAVIZZA**, *Pian dei Mantellini 34, Tel. 0577/280-462, Fax 0577/221-597. E-mail: bureau@palazzoravizza.it, Web: www.palazzoravizza.it. 30 rooms all with bath. E70-170; Double E90-240. Breakfast E9. All credit cards accepted. ★★★*

A quality place to stay in Siena, right in the middle of things, this is a quaint little bed and breakfast type hotel in business since 1929. The building the hotel is located in has been owned by the same family for about two hundred years. Situated in a tranquil spot in the centro storico with good views over the city and the surrounding countryside, the furnishings are antique and the atmosphere wonderful. Buffet breakfast is served in their garden area and they are known to make a picnic lunch for you if asked. The evenings can be spent in the large tavern room.

There is a public parking area just down the Via P. Mascagni and off of Via dei Laterino near a quaint little old cemetery if you come by car. Truly a great three star in Siena and the prices show it.

Where to Eat

Since Siena is a university town, snack and fast food places abound, but there are also some excellent restaurants. Siena specialties include cioccina (a special variation on pizza) pici (thick Tuscan spaghetti with a sauce from ground pork), and pancetta (sausages and chicken breast added to tomatoes and cooked with red wine).

Siena is also known for its different varieties of salamis that you can buy at any alimentari. I recommend the alimentari **Morbidi**, Via Banchi di Sotto 27. Local food specialties include:

Soppressata, either sweet or hot, is an excellent boiled salami made from a mixture of rind and gristle with black peppercorns added. Don't let this description fool you. The sweet soppressata is the best. Buristo is a cooked salami made from the blood and fatty leftovers of sausages. It is heavily spiced.

Finocchiona is a salami made of peppered sausage meat seasoned with fennel seeds. And Salsiccioli secchi are made from lean crusts of pork or boar, spiced with garlic and black or red pepper.

8. **SPADA FORTE**, *Piazza del Campo 12. Credit cards accepted. Dinner for two E32.*

If you're at the top of the Campo looking down at the Palazzo Pubblico, this place is on your right at the end of the wall. They have scenic outside tables from which you can watch the goings-on in the Campo, as well as inside seating in a typically spartan Sienese restaurant environment. There is a huge antipasto menu which should satisfy you for lunch. If not, try one of their pizzas.

The barrocciaia (tomatoes, sausage and garlic), and the salsiccia (tomato, mozzarella and sausages) are both good. If you're into meats, try the cinghiale alle senese (wild boar cooked over the open flame) or the agnello arrosto (roasted lamb). A really good restaurant.

9. **DA VASCO**, *Via del Capitano 6/8. Tel. 0577/288-094. No credit cards accepted. Dinner for two E22.*

Small quaint little place just down from the Duomo. The atmosphere is typically austere with brick ceiling and whitewashed walls. The food is good and inexpensive. Try the penne all'arrabbiata (with a tomato, garlic, pepper sauce), the spaghetti alla carbonara (with cheese, ham, and egg), or the ravioli all quattro formaggi (thick sauce with four cheeses). For secondo, try the bistecca di maiale (pork steak) or the omelette al formaggio (cheese omelet).

10. L'OSTERIA, *Via dei Rossi 79/81. Tel. 0577/287-592. No credit cards accepted. Dinner for two E25.*

Literally translated it's "The Restaurant" and it seems to be very popular with the locals. Located down a side street past two other more touristy places making it a little ways away from the thundering crowds. Squeeze through the worn hanging beads and cram yourself in here to enjoy a wonderfully local atmosphere with superbly prepared food. Try the penne con melanzane e peperoni (eggplant and pepperoni salami) for primo, and either the pollo ai peperoni (chicken with pepperoni), the bistecca di vitello (veal steak), or the bistecca di maiale (pork steak) for secondi. You won't be disappointed.

11. VITTI, *Via Monatanini 14-16, Tel. 0577/28-92-91. No credit cards accepted. Dinner for two E22-30.*

Tranquil outside seating off the main road as well as in the zona pedonale (walking zone). Your food is passed through a window from the kitchen to the waiter. The inside is uncomfortably small with only a counter and standing room only, but the Sienese seem to enjoy the food so much they cram themselves in for lunch, leaving the outside seating to tourists. In the window of the place are some dishes that are not on the menu, so if one of them catches your eye ask to order something from the finestra (window). From the menu try some of their pasta, particularly the tortellini alla panna (cheese stuffed pasta in a rich cream sauce) or the lasagna al forno (oven baked lasagna) for primo. For secondo try the petto di tacchino arrosto (roasted turkey breast).

12. IL BIONDO, *Via del Rustichetto 10, Tel./Fax 0577/280-739. Closed Wednesdays. Dinner for two E40.*

Another place you should think of trying, since the ambiance at the outside seating is so peaceful and colorfully local and the food is great. You can get a good seat inside in a plain whitewashed Sienese-style restaurant, but try the outside. They make some good pasta here including spaghetti alla vongole (with clam sauce) and penne alla puttanesca (literally translated it means whore's pasta, made with tomatoes, garlic, black olives, olive oil and meat). For seconds, try the saltimbocca alla Romana (veal shank stewed in tomatoes and spices) or the bistecca alla griglia (beef steak cooked on the grill that would make a Texan proud).

Seeing the Sights
The Palio Race

The best time to visit because of the pageantry, and the worst time to visit because of the crowds, is during the biannual **Palio**, held on July 2 and August

16. The Palio is a festive time awash in colorful banners, historic pageantry, and a wild bareback horse race that runs three times around the **Piazza del Campo**. The race lasts all of 90 seconds but will leave you with memories to last a lifetime.

A palio literally is an embroidered banner, the prize offered for winning the race. The first official Palio was run in 1283, though many say the custom dates back farther than that. During the Middle Ages, besides the horse races, there were violent games of primeval rugby (which you can see in Florence twice a year during their **Calcio in Costume** festival) and even bullfights to settle neighborhood bragging rights.

The contestants in the horse race itself are jockeys from the seventeen neighborhood parishes or contrade in Siena. During a Palio ten horses ride in the first race and seven horses ride in the next since the square is not big enough to accommodate all the horses at once. The jockeys willingly risk life and limb for the pride of their small area of the city. At two places in the Piazza del Campo there are right angles at which the horses have to turn, and usually at these points you'll have at least one jockey lose his seat or a horse its footing.

But this is more than a horse race. It is really a sanctioned community-wide regression into the Middle Ages, with the coats-of-arms that represented each contrade at that time being displayed prominently by members of that neighborhood. The **contrade** used to be military companies, but these became outdated when the Spanish and Florentines laid siege to Siena and conquered it. At that time there were 59 contrade, but plagues and wars decimated the population until by the early 18th century there were only 23 left. Today only seventeen remain and the coats-of-arms for each contrade is as follows: Aquila (eagle), Bruco (caterpillar), Chiocciola (snail), Civetta (owl), Drago (dragon), Giraffa (giraffe), Istrice (porcupine), Leocorno (unicorn), Lupa (she-wolf), Nicchio (shell), Oca (goose), Onda (wave), Pantera (panther), Selva (wood), Tartuca (turtle), Torre (tower), and Valdimontone (ram).

Prior to the race there is a good two hour display of flag throwing by the alferi of each contrada, while the medieval **carroccio** (carriage), drawn by a white oxen, circles the Campo bearing the prized palio each neighborhood wants to claim as its own.

To witness this event, however, you have to plan way in advance since at both times of year the Palio is jam-packed. You can see the Palio in one of three ways: in the center of the Piazza where people are packed like sardines on a first come first serve basis; in the viewing stands which cost anywhere from E100 to E175; or in one of the offices or apartments that line the piazza. To get a seat in the viewing stand you'll need to plan at least 6-9 months in advance and get your tickets through your travel agent. To view the spectacle from an office or apartment you'll need to have connections. Maybe the company you work for has dealings with the banks and other companies whose offices line the square. However you witness this blast from Siena's medieval past, you will have memories for a lifetime.

A. THE CAMPO

Eleven streets lead into the square where, in the past, the people of Siena used to assemble at the sound of the **Sunto bell** to learn the latest news. Today it still is the gathering place for all the locals and tourists. You will see at most times of the day the young lounging on the stones and their elders congregating at cafés. The piazza is concave and irregular with a ring of rather austere buildings surrounding it, but even so it is a marvel of architectural harmony. On the curved side of the Campo sits the **Fonte Gaia** (Gay Fountain) made by Jacopo della Quercia. The water from this fountain comes here from 30 km away through a series of pipes and aqueducts from the 13th century. A feat of ancient engineering.

On the map the Campo looks flat, but it's actually a gradually sloping surface with bricks that seem to float down to the **Palazzo Pubblico**. A great place to grab a bite to eat at one of the many restaurants, sip a drink at one of the cafés, or to simply rest your tired tourist feet by relaxing on the cobblestone slope.

B. PALAZZO PUBBLICO

At the Campo. Tower open 10:00am–dusk. In the winter open only until 1:30pm. Admission E3.

One of the most attractive and imposing Gothic buildings in all of Tuscany. Most of it was built between 1297 and 1340, with the top story being raised in 1639. This building reflected the wealth and success of Siena, which was almost the same size as London and Paris during the fourteenth century. The little chapel underneath the tower was dedicated by the town to the Virgin Mary when the terrible plague known ever since as the Morte Nera (Black Death) came to an end. In Siena alone 65,000 people died of the plague in the summer of 1348. That was over half of their population. The intricate wrought-iron gate that covers the entrance was made in 1445.

The best part of this building is the **Torre del Mangia**. It offers the greatest sights in all of Siena. Unfortunately you have to climb up 400 small confined steps to top of the bell tower. It's 112 meters high, was built in 1334, and is still in amazing shape. The clock was made in 1360 and the huge bell was raised to its present position in 1666. Imagine having to haul a bell that weighs 6,764 kilos up a pulley system to the top of the tower? Remember to bring your camera because the views of the countryside and the city are stupendous. You can see past the old walls, look over the terra-cotta tiles of the city roofs, lush fields, and forests for as far as the eye can see. A definite must-see when in Siena.

C. MUSEO CIVICO

At the Campo. Open 9:30am–7:30pm Monday–Saturday. Open Sunday 9:30am–1:30pm.

Inside the Palazzo Pubblico is the **Museo Civico**, which is filled with many wonderful paintings, frescoes, mosaics, and tapestries. Upstairs is the famous **Sala del Mappamondo** (Hall of the Map of the World). From its large windows you can look out onto the market square. The other three walls are frescoed with scenes of the religious and civil life of the Siena Republic. In this museum you'll find many examples of the some of the finest Sienese art anywhere.

D. THE DUOMO

Piazza del Duomo. 7:30am–1:30pm and 3:00pm to dusk from December to March. From March to November open 9:00am–7:30pm. Admission E3.

The combination of Gothic and Romanesque architectural elements in the Cathedral of Siena is a result of the large amount of time spent completing it. Nonetheless it doesn't appear as if the two styles contrast too much with each other. Despite being incredibly elaborate the facade seems quite harmonious and attractive. The side walls and steeple are striped black and white like the 'Balzana' that is the standard of the town. It was started in 1200 and finished in the 1400s.

Inside the cathedral there are even more elaborate and rich decorations. It has three naves and is 90 meters long and 51 meters high, and the walls are covered with the white and black Balzana stripes also. All around the nave you'll see a row of 172 busts of Popes, from Christ to Lucius III, all made in 1400. Beneath them are 36 busts of Roman Emperors. The graffito and inlaid floor is a succession of scenes from the Old Testament, which took from 1372 to 1551 to complete. The earlier ones are done in black and white, and the later scenes have a touch of gray and red in them.

You can't miss the intricate and elaborate pulpit which was made by **Nicola Pisano** from 1265 to 1268. It is of white marble and supported by nine columns resting on nine lions. There are 300 human figures and 70 animal figures decorating this delightful work. Besides the pulpit there are countless remarkable paintings, sculptures, reliefs, and stone coffins all attributed to famous Italian masters. The statues on the Piccolo altar have been attributed to **Michelangelo**. In the **Piccolomini Library** you'll find beautiful frescoes of the life of Pope Pius II made by the master Pinturicchio. As you leave the library you'll see the monument to Archbishop Bandini's nephews made in 1570 by Michelangelo.

There were plans to have made this cathedral a small part of a much larger place of worship; but those plans were stunted for a variety of reasons, including the plague and the eventual Florentine conquest of the city. Today only a few pillars and walls remain from the plans for that grandiose church.

E. MUSEO DELL'OPERA DEL DUOMO

Piazza del Duomo. 7:30am–1:30pm and 3:00pm to dusk from December to March. From March to November open 9:00am–7:30pm. Admission E3.

In the **museum of the cathedral** is a valuable collection of the treasure of paintings, statues, and fragments the cathedral once displayed. One of the best paintings is Duccio di Buoninsegna's *Maestra* (1308-1311) that was originally on the high altar. You'll find a group of three sculptures, the *Three Graces*, which are Greek works of the 2nd century BCE that were once in the Piccolomini Library. And you can't miss the exquisitely beautiful goldsmith's work, *Rosa d'Oro* (Golden Rose) that was given to the city of Siena by Alessandro VIII in 1658. Another work of interest is the plan of the unfinished facade of the Baptistery by Giacomo di Mino del Pelliciaio.

F. BAPTISTERY OF SAN GIOVANNI

Piazza del Duomo. Open 9:00am–1:00pm and 3:00pm–5:00pm year round. In the summer open until 7:00pm.

This is really the **crypt** of the Cathedral. Here you can find the **baptismal fonts** by Jacopo della Quercia, the bronze bas-relief of Bishop Pecci by Donatello, and many bronze reliefs of the Old and New Testament. The Baptistery was begun in 1315, but its facade has never been finished.

G. CHURCH OF SAN DOMENICO & THE SANCTUARY OF SANTA CATERINA

Costa San Antonio. Church is open from 9:00am–6:00pm. The Sanctuary is closed 12:30pm–3:30pm Monday–Saturday and all day Sundays.

The Basilica is indelibly linked with the cloistered life of the local saint. It rises monumental and solitary overlooking the surrounding landscape and city. Its simple brick architecture of the 13th century was modified in the 14th and 15th centuries but still remains more like the walls of a convent than a church. You can't miss the **chapel of St. Caterina** inside where the saint's head is preserved today in the silver reliquary. In the other chapels of the church you'll find paintings by Sienese artists of the 14th through 16th centuries.

The house where St. Caterina used to live is now **Caterina Sanctuary**. The rooms she lived in as a youth have been frescoed by artists of all times with scenes from her life. It is a simple home but it is of cultural significance, since St. Caterina is one of the patron saints of Italy.

Shopping

There a a series of arts and crafts stores all over Siena, as well as the usualy internationally known boutiques. But to me, some of the best memories to take back with you are culinary in nature. As such, listed below are two stores where you can buy food products.

13. **Enoteca San Domenica**, Via del Paradiso 56. *Tel. 05/77-27-11-81.* Right near where the bus lets you off from the station you can buy gifts of great Chianti wine for only E4. They also have other wonderful gifts of local products. There are a number of these little shops all over Siena, but this one is the best and the best located.

14. **Pizzigheria**, 95 Via della Citta. There is a boar's head outside with a pair of glasses resting on his snout. Enter here and enjoy some of the most succulent food aromas. A good place to buy any picnic supplies you may need, but there's a less expensive place up the road. Just stop here for the sight and smell of the sweet salamis hanging.

Practical Information
Car Rental
• **Avis**, Via Simone Martini 36, *Tel. 0577/27-03-05*
• **Hertz**, Hotel Lea, Via XXIV Maggio, *Tel. 0577/45085*

Tourist Information
• **Piazza San Domenico**, *Tel 0577/940-809*. Get maps and hotel reservations here if needed. Open 9:00am to 7:00pm.

Fiesole

Fiesole is five miles east of Florence on a hill overlooking the city. Well before Florence existed, Fiesole dominated this part of the Arno valley. Fiesole was one of the 12 important towns of ancient **Roman Etruria** from 80 BCE on, and later was named the capital city of Roman Etruria. But in 1125 CE all this dominance came to an end, when Florence sacked and began its control of Fiesole and all of Tuscany. After the takeover, Fiesole was used by many of the Medici family as a refuge from the toil of governing, and the heat of the summer.

Even today Fiesole is a great respite from the heat or the hectic pace of Florence. Remember to bring a jacket because it is quite a bit cooler up in the hills. This is the place to stay if you want to get away from everything after you've finished your touring. It's only a 20 minute bus ride away (the buses leave from the station every 15 minutes). This is a tranquil location for a family vacation that offers access to Florence quickly and easily. If you're bothered by traffic noise or a hectic pace, I would seriously suggest staying up here and commuting to Florence every day.

Besides being a refuge, Fiesole's archaeological excavations offers visitors a small glimpse into the ancient past. There are also many fine churches and vistas to enjoy. You'll really feel above it all here, since almost every road offers a perfect panorama of Florence below.

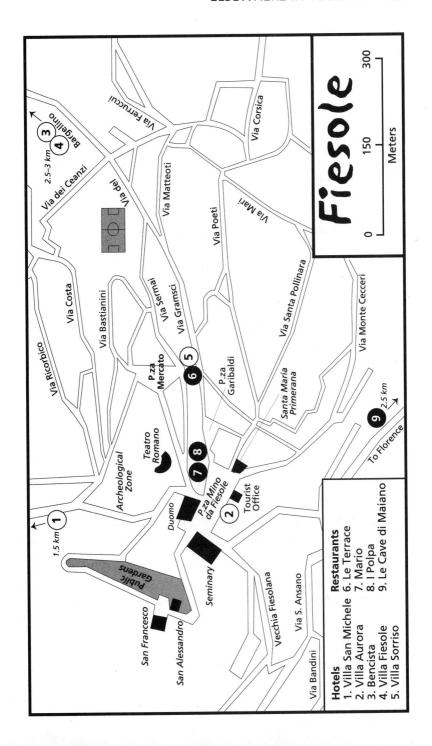

Fiesole

Meters

0 150 300

Hotels
1. Villa San Michele
2. Villa Aurora
3. Bencista
4. Villa Fiesole
5. Villa Sorriso

Restaurants
6. Le Terrace
7. Mario
8. I Polpa
9. Le Cave di Maiano

Arrivals & Departures

By Bus or Taxi

The easiest and least expensive way to get to Fiesole from Florence is to take the #7 bus from the Piazza della Stazione. The ride takes only 20 minutes (with a soundless but still intrusive advertising video playing on a TV the whole time). If you take a taxi it'll cost you about $25. Both rides will offer you glimpses of fine villas and gardens as you weave through the winding road up to Fiesole. Remember to pack yourself a picnic lunch which you can create from the ingredients you buy at one of the street markets or the *alimentari* listed in this section of the book. If you forgot, there are a number of bars, cafés, and restaurants to choose from. When in Fiesole look out for little starlings that imagine themselves cars as they sweep two feet above the road pavement on the hills surrounding the town. A beautiful sight to see.

You catch the bus at the side of the train station in Florence under the awnings. Tickets are sold at the Giornalaio inside the station or at the ticket office catty-corner to the bus stop outside. Tickets cost E2.

Where to Stay

1. VILLA SAN MICHELE, *Via Doccia 4, 50014 Fiesole. Tel. 055/59-451, Fax 055/598-734, Web: www.villasanmichele.orient-express.com. 36 rooms all with bath. American Express, Diners Club, Mastercard and Visa accepted. Single E750; Double E1,000-1,200. Jr. Suite E950-1,000. Suite E1,200. Breakfast included.* *****

Located in a converted monastery that has a facade attributed to Michelangelo. If nothing else this hotel will allow you to bring stories of beautiful views, ancient habitations, and opulent surroundings back home. The reception area of the hotel is an old chapel, and in the dining room, the bar is made from an ancient Etruscan sarcophagus (imagine if a bar in Washington, DC was made from the coffin of a Civil War soldier ... ah, the Italian culture is so laid back).

Each room has a four poster bed and everything else is rustically luxurious. The best rooms overlook the gardens that surround the hotel. This is *the* hotel for those of you with plenty of disposable income. Here you can enjoy an outdoor pool during the day, a wonderfully scenic view from the restaurant in the evening, and a boisterous piano bar at night.

2. VILLA AURORA, *Piazza Mino de Fiesole 39, 50014 Fiesole. Tel. 055/59-100 or 59-292, Fax 055/59-587, Web: www.aurorafiesole.com/. All credit cards accepted. 26 rooms all with bath. Single E100-145; Double E145-190 Breakfast costs E9.* ****

Here you've got everything a four star can offer. If you want to stay in the central square, this is the place. The rooms are large and modern and all have wonderful views. The bathrooms have every modern convenience and some have phones. Attached to a good restaurant, this hotel used to be a theater and osteria for the wealthy patrons who stayed in the villas of Fiesole.

3. BENCISTA, *Via Benedetto da Maiano 4, 50014 Fiesole. Tel. 055/ 59163, Fax is the same. 42 rooms all with bath. Single E125; Double E150. Breakfast E7. No credit cards accepted.* ***

You'll need a car to get here and get around since it is a ways away from Fiesole. You'll love the many public rooms, all of which are appointed with antique furniture. The rooms (you have to ask for one with a view) are sober but elegant. Opened in 1925, this has been a favorite for travelers ever since. Their restaurant serves up great Tuscan meals made from the freshest ingredients. Breakfast, lunch, and dinner are served in a large room dominated by two large columns. Breakfast in the summer is out on the terrace. A good place to come and relax and recharge your batteries. No TV so you have to make your own entertainment in this isolated location.

4. VILLA FIESOLE, *Via Beato Angelico 35, 50014 Fiesole. Tel. 055/597-252, E-mail: info@hotelvillafiesole.it, Web: www.villafiesole.it. 28 rooms, all with bath. Single E95-150; Double E135-180. Breakfast included. All credit cards accepted.* ***

Come here for peace and tranquillity, since this place is truly in the middle of the Tuscan hills. Located in an historic building, the Villa Fiesole is great romantic getaway that has a pool, a garden setting and relaxing ambiance. A good place to come on a second honeymoon if all you want to do is lounge around.

5. VILLA SORRISO, *Via Gramsci 21, 50014 Fiesole. Tel. 055/590-27, Fax is the same. Seven rooms, 6 with bath. Single without bath E25-35; Double without bath E40-50; Double E55-65. Breakfast included.* *

A wonderful little one star on the main road just up from the central square. Some of the rooms have great views overlooking a nearby valley, not of Florence. But that's all right, the view is superb. The rooms are all clean and comfortable and you're right next door to a good restaurant, Pizzeria Le Terrace. Another plus is that the rooms are air conditioned. A perfect low-priced getaway spot.

Where to Eat

6. LE TERRACE, *Viale Gramsci 19, 50014 Fiesole. Tel. 055/59-272. Closed Tuesdays. Credit cards accepted. Dinner for two E25.*

This is a huge place with both indoor and somewhat cramped outdoor seating, but with stupendous views of a lush green valley below. Ignore the tacky wooden life-sized waiter at the entrance and come for the view and the inexpensive food. As you enter you'll pass by the brick wood-burning oven where they make a wide variety of pizzas that will please even the most discerning eater. Besides pizza they make good pastas. Some recommendations: tortellini alla panna e prosciutto (with cream and ham), and tagliatelli della casa (house favorite made with onions, sausage, saffron in a thick cream sauce). If you're interested in meat dishes, try their pollo fritto (chicken fried in olive oil), or the coniglio fritto (rabbit fried in olive oil) and compare whether rabbit really does taste like chicken.

7. MARIO, *Piazza Mino #9, 50014 Fiesole. Credit cards accepted. Dinner for two E37.*

They have two different menus rolled into one. A traditional menu and one they call a cucina creativa (creative cooking) menu. Both are rather sparse, so check them out in the window before you stop here to see if you want anything. They have outside seating on the main square, as well as a few tables inside. Some of the more creative dishes are the ravioline salmone e vongole (little ravioli with a salmon and clam sauce), and the filetto o coniglio alle mele (thin slices of rabbit served with apples).

8. I POLPA, *Piazza Mino #21/22, 50014 Fiesole. Tel. 055/59133. Credit cards accepted. Dinner for two E30.*

Try their country style bruschetta. They brush the coarse toasted garlic bread with succulent olive oil and cover it with fresh tomatoes. Then sample their pennette all fiesolana (with cream sauce and ham). If the meat bug hits you try the scaloppini ai funghi porcini (veal with porcini mushrooms). Reservations on the weekends are recommended.

9. LE CAVE DI MAIANO, *Via delle Cave 16, 50014 Fiesole. Tel. 055/59133. Closed Thursday and Sunday nights. All credit cards accepted. Dinner for two E50.*

One of the most popular restaurants for Florentines escaping their hectic, tourist-jammed city during the summer time. You'll need a car or will have to grab a cab from Fiesole, to get here, since it is about 3-4 kilometers outside of the town of Fiesole proper. You'll be served typical Tuscan food in a truly rustic atmosphere. The restaurant is blessed with a perfect garden environment. They specialize in all types of grilled, roasted, and fried meats. A great place to try if you've come up to Fiesole and want something a little different and out of the way.

Seeing the Sights

You can see everything there is to see in Fiesole in less than a day, so you can spend the rest of your time soaking up the great panoramic views, eating wonderful food, and celebrating the tranquillity with some Chianti. But remember, you are only 20 minutes away from the center of Florence by a bus that leaves at least twice an hour. So let me reiterate: if you like the splendor of Florence but can't seem to be able to stomach the noise and congestion, stay here in Fiesole. It will make your tour that much more pleasant and rewarding.

CATHEDRAL OF SAN ROMULUS

Piazza della Cattedrale (also Piazza Mino di Fiesole). Open daily 7:30am–noon and 4:00pm–7:00pm.

Built in the 11th century, the best part of this church is the bell tower whose chimes toll the half hour and the hour. You can hear it all over the countryside informing you of your place in the universe.

THE ARCHAEOLOGICAL ZONE

Open Winter 9:00am–6:00pm, Summer 9:00am–7:00pm. Closed on Tuesdays.

The museum itself houses epics from prehistoric, Etruscan, Roman and medieval times; but the best part of this place is the **Roman Theater**, partially restored, that dates back to the 1st century BCE. It's like a mini-Pompeii or Roman Forum.

ELSEWHERE IN FIESOLE

The steep five minute climb (if you're fit) from the west end of **Piazza Mino** up to the **Church of San Francesco** will give you wonderful views of Florence and the Arno valley, especially from the benches near the **Church of San Alessandro** (open daily 7:30am–noon and 4:00pm–7:00pm.) Remember to bring your camera. The Church of San Francesca itself is relatively nondescript, but the cloisters are worth seeing as is the small museum that has a few Etruscan remains and relics collected by Franciscan missionaries in the Orient many years ago.

Below the church you can see the public gardens and the **Basilica of S Alessandro**, which is on the site of the ancient **Roman temple of Bacchus** Gardens open 7:00am – 7:00pm; Basilica open same hours).

San Gimignano

San Gimignano sits majestically on a hill overlooking the **Elsa valley**. Its earthen-colored walls contrast favorably with the surrounding green countryside. The most distinctive feature of this town are its amazing medieval towers. These structures help to create a magical atmosphere of timelessness, despite the hordes of tourists thundering through the tiny streets.

Don't get me wrong, San Gimignano is beautiful. Stunning actually. But if you come here in the summer, the peak of the high season, your experience will be tempered by a pushy polyglot ensemble of camera-toting tourists. But even then, this town is wonderful, as is Venice, Florence and other towns in Italy that also face an annual tourist inundation.

A small Etruscan village during the 3rd and the 2nd century BCE, the town's modern history started around the 10th century when it took its name from the saint himself, Bishop Gimignano. A former Bishop of Modena, he is said to have saved the village from barbarian hordes. After this magical salvation and during the Middle Ages, the town grew in importance because of its strategic location along well-traveled trade routes. This led to the commissioning of wonderful works of art that currently adorn the churches and monasteries in the area.

In 1199 the town became a free municipality, but then the depopulation caused by the Black Death in 1348 forced the town to submit to Florence's control. As the centuries slid by, and trade routes changed, San Gimignano overcame its lack of alternate economic resources by offering its beauty, charm, and cultural heritage as a tourist draw. Despite its modern success, the full time population of the town is still less than it was prior to the Black Death more than 650 years ago!

Arrivals & Departures

By Car

From the north take route 429, from the south the same road is numbered as route 2. Get off at Castel Fiorentino and follow the signs to San Gimignano. Prior to embarking on this trip, please take the time to pick up a road map. The place that has the best road maps of Italy is the **Touring Club Italiano**, Via Marsala 8, Roma, *Tel. 06/499-899, www.touringclub.it/*. Their website is in Italian. You can also get maps from the **Italian Government Tourist Office**, *www.italiantourism.com*, or any high-level travel book store.

By Train

Take the local train from Florence to Empoli. From here catch a local bus or taxi up to the town. A great web site that contains everything you need to know about rail travel in Italy is for the Italian Rail Company (**Ferrovie dello Stato** – FS), *www.fs-on-line.com*.

Where to Stay

1. L' ANTICO POZZO, *Via San Matteo 87, Tel. 0577/942-014, Fax 0577/ 942-117. E-mail: info@anticopozzo.com, Web: www.anticopozzo.com/. 18 rooms. Single E90; Double E150. All credit cards accepted. Breakfast included.* ***

Located in the center of town in a magnificent 15th century palazzo, this hotel is a wonderful place to stay. Completely restored with all modern amenities, including tasteful furnishings and accommodating restroom facilities, you will be more than comfortable here, while also being in the middle of everything the town has to offer. This place oozes with charm and ambiance. An elegant and refined boutique hotel.

2. BEL SOGGIORNO, *Via S. Giovanni 91, Tel. 0577/940-375, Fax 0577/ 940-375. E-mail: hbelsog@libero.it. Web: www.hotelbelsoggiorno.it/. 21 rooms. Single or Double E120. All credit cards accepted. Breakfast included.***

The hotel consists of two structures from the 1400s that have been completely modernized. Also included with this fine three star is a wonderful restaurant that is frequented by locals and which serves tasty local dishes (see description following). Rooms have views of either the countryside or the towers and come with tasteful furnishings and functional bath facilities. Not as charming as L'Antico Pozzo, but still a wonderful place to stay.

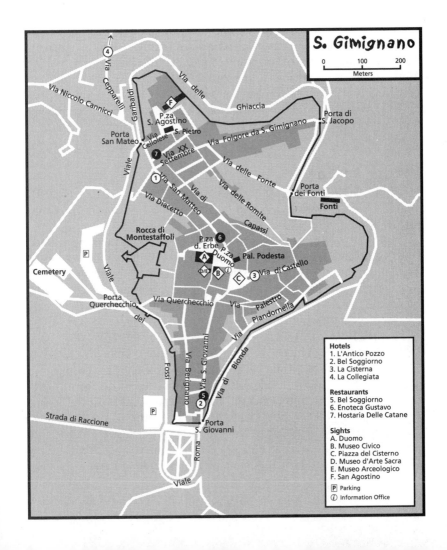

S. Gimignano

0   100   200
Meters

Hotels
1. L'Antico Pozzo
2. Bel Soggiorno
3. La Cisterna
4. La Collegiata

Restaurants
5. Bel Soggiorno
6. Enoteca Gustavo
7. Hostaria Delle Catane

Sights
A. Duomo
B. Museo Civico
C. Piazza del Cisterno
D. Museo d'Arte Sacra
E. Museo Arceologico
F. San Agostino

P Parking
ⓘ Information Office

3. LA CISTERNA, *Piazza della Cisterna 24, Tel. 0577/940-328, Fax 0577/942-080. Web: www.sangimignano.com/lacisterna/. 50 rooms. Single E70; Double E120.* ***

Set in the most charming square of this incredibly ambiant town, you will not go wrong staying here. Located in a 14th century palazzo, and containing all necessary modern three-star amenities, La Cisterna is a gem. Furnished in the Florentine style, which consists of simple yet elegant decorations, the hotel also contains a rather good restaurant of its own.

4. LA COLLEGIATA, *Località Strada 27, Tel. 0577/943-201, Fax 0577/940-566. E-mail: info@lacollegiata.it, Web: www.lacollegiata.it/. 20 luxurious rooms. Single E300; Double E450. All credit cards accepted. Breakfast included.* ****

Elegance, charm, serenity, and ambiance is what La Collegiata is all about. Nestled in the hills of Tuscany with wonderful views of San Gimignano, this hotel is a sparkling gem of luxury and comfort. Located in a building from the 16th century, and containing an excellent restaurant, an inviting pool and every imaginable four star amenity, this is the place to stay in town ... if you have the means. There is an incredible room located in the tower, on the upper floor of which is a large jacuzzi bathtub. From here the entire panorama of the valley can be admired. A truly romantic and sensual setting.

Where to Eat

5. BEL SOGGIORNO, *Via S. Giovanni 91, Tel. 0577/940-375, Fax 0577/940-375. Closed Wednesdays and between Jan 6 and March 1. All credit cards accepted. Dinner for two E60.*

Traditional Tuscan cuisine is served up with gusto in this superb eatery, which is attached to the hotel of the same name. By far the best restaurant in town, you will need to make reservations and come dressed appropriately. An elegant and refined ambiance with an extensive menu featuring local vegetables, meats, cheeses, and pasta. You will not go wrong with a meal in this excellent establishment.

6. ENOTECA GUSTAVO, *Via S. Matteo 29, Tel. 0577/940-057. Closed Mondays and in November. All credit cards accepted. Dinner for two E30.*

Despite there being a number of superb restaurants in San Gimignano, all catering to the swarm of Italophiles that make pilgrimages here, I felt it necessary to mention this wonderful little wine bar. Located in the heart of town, this small place is always packed, whether with locals or tourists. It is popular for its great wine list, as well as the fast, inexpensive and delectable food. From 10 in the morning until late at night, here you can find all manner of light and tasty sustenance. A great place to stop for a meal.

7. OSTERIA DELLE CATENE, *Via Mainardi,18, Tel.0577/941-966, Fax 0577/941-966.Closed Wednesdays. All credit cards accepted. Dinner for two E50.*

Arched brick ceilings and white walls are all the adornment this place needs, since the food is superb. Situated in the historic center of San Gimignano, the 'Tavern of the Chains' is famous for its excellent Tuscan cuisine as well as simple and elegant ambiance. All manner of excellent pasta and meat dishes are served here. Make this place one of your stops while in San Gimignano.

Seeing the Sights

A. DUOMO

Piazza del Duomo.

This church is a remarkable monument to Tuscan Romanesque architecture. It is simple, yes; plain, most assuredly; but impressive nonetheless. Though the exterior is nothing to write home about, the interior is resplendent with many fine frescos. Along the walls and in the left aisle, Bartolo di Fredi painted *Scenes from the Old Testament*. In the right aisle are displayed frescoes representing *Scenes from the New Testament*. In the central nave, on both sides of a fresco illustrating the *Martyrdom of St. Sebastiano* by Benozzo Gozzoli, there are two wooden statues by Jacopo della Quercia. On the upper part of the central nave between the two doors are Taddeo di Bartolo's frescoes showing *The Last Judgment*.

But all of this is only prelude for what we find in the right aisle, next to the transept: the famous Chapel of St. Fina built in 1468. With the elegant altar by Benedetto da Maiano and the frescoes by Domenico Ghirlandaio, this entire chapel is a wonderful work of art.

B. MUSEO CIVICO

Piazza del Duomo, *Tel. 0577/940-340*. March 1-Oct. 31: 9:30am-7:20pm; Nov 1-Feb 28: 10:00am-5:50pm. E6.

The Palazzo del Popolo (People's Palace) is home to the **Museo Civico** (Civic Museum) and is situated on the left hand side of the Piazza del Duomo. It is one of the most important monuments in San Gimignano. The museum is rich in paintings from the Florentine and Sienese schools, such as the *Crucifix* by Coppo di Marcovaldo, triptyches by Niccolò Tegliacci and Taddeo di Bartolo, and other works painted by Domenico Michelino, Pinturicchio and Filippino Lippi. On the right hand side of the Palace is the **Torre Grosso** (Great Tower) erected in 1300 from which you can take in commanding views. The hours listed above are for both the museum and the tower.

C. PIAZZA DEL CISTERNO

Just outside of the Piazza del Duomo is the **Piazza del Cisterna**, a triangular shaped plaza arrayed with brick pavement in a fish scale pattern. Constructed in 1273 and enlarged in 1346, the square is circled by medieval homes and towers, and is a wonderful place to absorb the ambiance and charm of this great town. As you pass through the passageway from the Paizza del Duomo, you will go by the **Torri Gemelle degli Ardinghello**, constructed in the 1200s.

D. MUSEO D'ARTE SACRA (Museum of Sacred Art)

Piazza Pecori, *Tel. 0577/940-316.* March 1 - March 31 & Nov. 1 - Jan. 20: 9:30am - 5:00pm; April 1 - Oct. 31: 9:30am - 7:30pm. From Jan 21 to Feb 28, the museum is closed. E6.

The museum was opened in 1915 in the sacristy of the Duomo where it remained until 1929 when it was moved to this nearby location. It has recently been reorganized and includes material from local convents, the Duomo, and artifacts donated by private citizens and the Town Council. Some of the most valuable objects include the wooden sculptures from the 14th century. *The Annunciation* is two statues, one representing *The Angel* and the other *The Madonna*, of which only the head and the shoulders still exist. Then there is *The Crucifix*, a figure of Christ which is handless.

There are also splendid psalm books as well as works by Niccolò di Ser Sozzo Tegliacci and Lippo Vanni from the 14th century. In the Silverware room, you will find intricate examples of silversmith's and goldsmith's art, most of which date back to the 17th and 18th centuries. You will also find some exceptional works in silk and satin with gold and silver braids.

E. MUSEO ARCHEOLOGICO

Jan. 1-9: 11.00am - 6pm, Closed Thursdays; Jan 10 - Feb 28: Open only Thurs, Sat, Sun, Mon 11.00am -6:00pm; March 1 - Oct 31: Open every day 11.00am - 6:00pm; Nov 1 Dec 31: 11.00am - 6:00pm, Closed Thursdays. E6.

This archaeological museum has simple but instructive exhibits of Etruscan, Roman and medieval artifacts from the city and the surrounding area. Besides the objects of more common use (plates, bowls, vases, buckles and necklaces), which help to reveal the day-to-day lives of the ancients, I found the funeral urns to be fascinating. They consist of an elongated representative figure of the deceased holding a plate containing a small offering to pay for their passage to the afterlife.

F. CHIESA DI SAN AGOSTINO

Piazza San Agostino.

Located in the northernmost quadrant of the town, near the Porta St. Matteo, the construction of this church began in 1280 and was completed in

1298. Its facade retains the simplicity of its original architectural style. As a way of protecting the door on the main façade, it is infrequently used as an entrance. Use the door on the right hand side of the church. The Cloister was built in the second half of the 15th century.

The interior of the church is in a Romanesque style with Gothic elements and consists of a single great nave with three apses. The roof is supported by a rustic wooden framework. The decorations are in a more elaborate Renaissance style.

The *Chapel of the Blessed Bartolo* contains the saint's mortal remains in a marble monument sculpted by Benedetto da Maiano in 1495. The chapel's walls and vaults were frescoed by Sebastiano Mainardi in 1500. Its terracotta floor is work of Andrea della Robbia. Above the High Altar is *The Coronation of the Madonna and the Saints* painted in 1483 by Piero del Pollaiolo. Other notable works include the frescoes in the Chancel that represent *Episodes from the life of St. Agostino*, and were painted by Benozzo Gozzoli between 1464 and 1465 with the help of two of his pupils, Pier Francesco Fiorentino and Giusto d'Andrea.

Practical Information

- **Information Office**, Piazza del Duomo 1, *Tel. 940-008, Fax 940-903.*
- **Website**, *www.sangimignano.com/*

Cortona

Cortona is commandingly situated with magnificent views over the **Val di Chiana**, the most extensive valley in the Apennine chain, which stretches to the hills of Siena. The **Sanctuary of Santa Margherita** towers above the town and is in turn overshadowed by the powerful defenses of the Medici fortress. Cortona was a sleepy little town until very recently, when *Under the Tuscan Sun* by Frances Mayes introduced the town's incredible charm and ambiance to the world. Now if you come in the high season, Cortona will be swarming with tourists, which may detract from the whole experience.

Regardless of the tourist influx, the town is a wonderful place to visit. There are also some valuable works of art preserved in the churches in and around Cortona; an estimated twenty percent of the world's greatest art treasures are housed within 80 kilometers.

In conjunction, **Lake Trasimeno**, the largest in central Italy, with lovely beaches, is just 9 kilomters away. A short drive from its shores brings you to the Umbrian capital of Perugia. And some of the most important regional towns, such as Florence, Rome and Siena, are within easy reach by either train or car.

Arrivals & Departures

By Car

Take the Autostrada del Sole (State Highway A1). Get off at the Valdichiana exit. Upon exiting the highway take the Siena - Perugia state road and continue towards Perugia. There are 3 exits for Cortona: Cortona via Manzano, Cortona via Lauretana and Cortona via Strada Statale 71.

Do yourself a favor and pick up a road map if you're driving. See page 218, *Arrivals & Departures* section for San Gimignano, for more information.

By Train

Take the train to the Terontola-Cortona station, which is 1 kilometer from the town, or the Camucia-Cortona station, which is five kilometers away. There's local bus service to Cortona from each station. Buy a ticket for the bus at the newsstand or the train ticket booth.

From Rome you will need to change trains in Chiusi. From Florence you will have a direct train. To get more information about train schedules, contact the website for the Italian Rail Company (**Ferrovie dello Stato** – FS) at *www.fs-on-line.com*.

Where to Stay

1. SAN MICHELE, *Via Guelfa 15, Tel.0575/604348, Fax 0575/630147. E-mail: info@hotelsanmichele.net, Web:www.hotelsanmichele.net/ (In Italian). 37 rooms. Single E90, Double E140. All credit cards accepted. Breakfast included. ***** ‹

Great prices for a wonderful four star deep in the heart of town. These are the prices you would pay for a two star in a big city such as Rome, but here, since we are in the country, you get the best for a reasonable price. A great place to stay for the money.

2. SAN LUCA, *Piazza Garibaldi, Tel. 0575/63-460. E-mail: info@sanlucacortona.com, Web: www.sanlucacortona.com/.60 rooms. Single E60-70, Double E90-100. All credit cards accepted. Breakfast included. ****

A simple and comfortable three star with a small roof terrace that has commanding views over the surrounding countryside. The hotel has inviting and comfortable rooms, as well as friendly professional service. A quality hotel with all three star amenities.

Where to Eat

3. DARDANO, *Via Dardano 24, Tel. 0575/601944. Closed on Mondays. No credit cards accepted. Dinner for two E30.*

In a place like Cortona that has reduced its culinary offerings to accommodate tourist palates, it is difficult to locate a place that offers authentic Tuscan food without having to spend a fortune. Dardano is one exception to

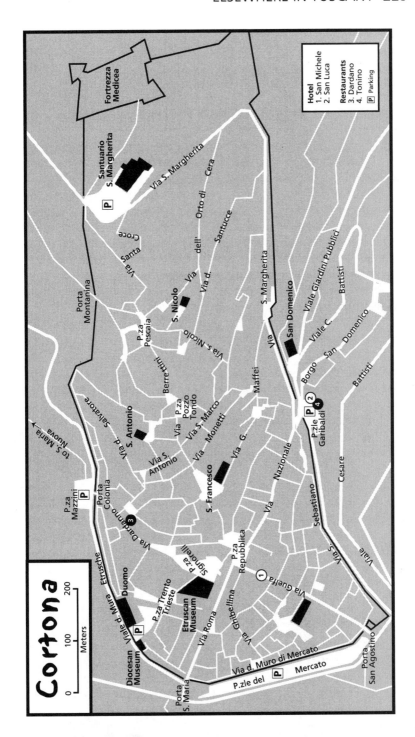

Cortona

that rule. The ambiance is all family trattoria, and the waitstaff are wonderfully courteous and friendly. The menu is simple and filled with typical local dishes. For antipasto you can have crostini (baked dough with fillings), bruschetta (Tuscan garlic bread), local prosciutto (ham) and pecorino cheese.

The specialty pasta of the house is ravioli with all sorts of fillings, including cinghiale (wild boar) and anatra (turkey). They also serve up a hearty vegetable soup. For the entree, they offer a wide array of meats on the grill. A wonderful place to eat in Cortona. Authentic and down to earth with great food.

4. TONINO, *Piazza Garibaldi 1, Tel. 0575/630-500. Closed Tuesdays and Jan 10-25. All credit cards accepted. Dinner for two E60.*

This is the place to come if you want to dine with a beautiful panoramic view over the Val di Chiano. It is also famous for what is called its antipastissimo, an abundant offering of antipasto samplings. If you are not careful you can get filled up on this alone. But please do not, because you will miss out on the rest of the fine menu. From the antipasto, you can segue into any one of their tasty pasta dishes. They were all wonderful.

As befits a quality Tuscan restaurant, their meats are first-rate, especially the filetto ai funghi porcini (filet of beef with porcini mushrooms). This restaurant is an excellent choice while in Cortona. More refined and elegant than Dardano, but no less authentic.

Seeing the Sights

Though there is not too much in the way of cultural sights in town, this being Italy there is always something to see. The **Etruscan Museum** exhibits the Etruscan chandelier known as the Lamp of Cortona, one of the most celebrated bronzes from that time period. In the **Diocesan Museum** can be found the work of such minor masters as Luca Signorelli and Fra Angelico. The most important medieval churches are those of **S. Francesco** and **S. Domenico**. Renaissance splendor is on display in the **Palazzo Casale** and in the churches of **S. Maria Nuova** and **S. Niccolò**, within which valuable works of art are preserved.

Practical Information
• **Websites**, *www.cortona.net or www.cortonaweb.net/*

Montepulciano

Montepulciano is located along a narrow limestone ridge high above the verdant plains that surround it. The town is circled by medieval walls and fortifications designed by Antonio da Sangallo the Elder in 1511. Inside the walls the tiny streets are bordered with attractive Renaissance palazzi and churches.

Today Montepulciano is nearly identical to what it was five centuries ago. Its building and streets form a historic center that appears to have been frozen in time. The beauty and majesty of the Renaissance buildings have remained intact, allowing the town to live up to its moniker as the "Pearl of the 1500s."

Many Etruscan ruins show that this town has been inhabited for some time. Despite its lengthy lineage, few Roman ruins remain today. Only after the 6th century AD, when people from Chiusi fled here with the barbarian hordes on their heals, does the historical record contain significant artifacts.

As the town grew in importance, it became a pawn in the power games between Florence, Siena, Perugia and Orvieto, with Siena holding sway most of the time because of its size and proximity. But the inhabitants of Montepulciano held no affinity for Siena and in 1202 they swore fidelity to Florence. Heady stuff for a small town. People from Montepulciano have always been known as avant-garde and renegades. This is expressed today in their annual music festival, **Cantiere Internazionale d'Arte** (see the 'Festivals & Events' section below).

Arrivals & Departures
By Car
Located almost equidistant from Orvieto in the south and Siena in the north. To reach Montepulciano take the A1 motorway to the **Val di Chiana** exit and follow the signs. You'll need a road map; see page 218, *Arrivals & Departures* section for San Gimignano, for more information.

By Train
Take the train from either Rome or Florence and get off at either **Chiusi** (south) or **Sinalunga** (north) stations. From here, take a local bus up the hill into town. You can buy a ticket at either the newsstand or the train ticket window in the station.

For train schedules, go to the Italian Rail Company (**Ferrovie dello Stato** – FS) website at *www.fs-on-line.com*.

Where to Stay
1. IL BORGHETTO, *Via Borgo Buio 7, Tel. 0578/757-535, Fax 0578/757-354. E-mail: info@ilborghetto.it, Web: www.ilborghetto.it. 15 rooms, 2 suites. Single E95; Double E105.* ***

A quaint and character-filled little hotel in the heart of Montepulciano. Situated in a 16th century building that has much more ancient foundation dug into the volcanic tufa rock, this is a wonderful place to stay. The rooms are all tastefully furnished and come complete with all three-star amenities. Request one of the rooms with views over the surrounding countryside. The vista is breathtaking.

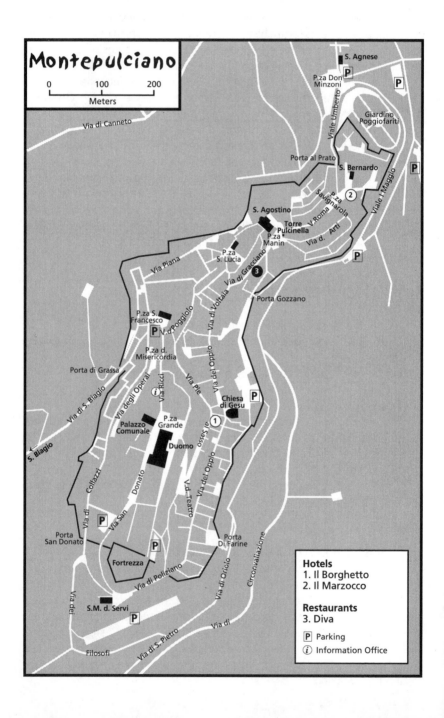

2. IL MARZOCCO, *Piazza Savonarola 18, Tel. 0578/757-262, Fax 0578/757-530 E-mail: albergomarzocco@cretedisiena.com, Web: www.cretedisiena.com/albergoilmarzocco. 16 rooms. Single E65; Double E95-125. All credit cards accepted.* ***

Though simply furnished, this hotel has incredible atmosphere. Located inside the old city walls, and situated in a 16th century palazzo, this place has been run by the same family for over 100 years. Il Marzocco is well situated with many terraces that offer stunning panoramic views of the surrounding countryside. An excellent choice for a stay in Montepulciano. Their restaurant is a good option when looking for local, rustic, and delicious food.

Where to Eat

3. DIVA, *Via di Gracciano nel Corso, Tel. 0578/716-951. Closed Tuesdays. All credit cards accepted. Dinner for two E45.*

You'll find this incredible little trattoria deep in the heart of town. The antipasto Toscano, with bruschetta, salamis, meats, and other edibles is a great way to start your meal. For your pasta course try any of their dishes with the thick Siena-style spaghetti. They are a mouthful. And to end the meal, their meat dishes are succulently tasty, especially the cotoletto di agnello (lamb cutlet). When in Montepulciano, you must have at least one meal here.

Seeing the Sights

The Church of St. Augustine is one of the most beautiful and interesting buildings in Montepulciano. Its facade was designed by Michelozzo Michelozzi (1396-1472) in the first decade of the 15th century. As Brunelleschi's disciple and collaborator in architecture, and Donatello's disciple in sculpture, Michelozzi used simple and elegant Renaissance forms in the lower level. Inside, you can admire works by Barocci, Allori, and Lorenzo di Credi. On the high altar there is a wooden crucifix attributed to Donatello. In front of the church you will see the characteristic 16th century **Pulcinella**, a bell-tower which strikes the hours sonorously.

Another interesting sight is the **Madonna di San Biagio** on the Via di San Biagio. This beautiful church is on the outskirts of Montepulciano and is built of honey and cream-colored stones. It is Sangallo's masterpiece, a Renaissance gem begun in 1518, and which occupied him until his death in 1534.

In the Piazza Grande you will find the **Palazzo Comunale**. In the 15th century, Michelozzo added a tower and facade to the original structure. On a clear day, the views that can be seen from the tower are superb.

Also in the Piazza Grande is the **Duomo**. It was designed between 1592 and 1630 by Ippolito Scalza. The facade is unfinished and plain, but the interior is elegant and tastefully adorned.

Festivals & Events

Montepulciano's festival season starts in the last week of July and the first week of August when it hosts the **Cantiere Internazionale d'Arte**, an international workshop and festival of art, music, and theater. The festival encourages artists of all ages and levels of experience to participate and collaborate. The ending result is a multicultural, international, dynamic event that is inspirational not only to participate in, but also to behold. *Tel. 0578/ 757089 or 0578/757007, Fax 0578/758307, E-mail: cantiere@bccmp.com.*

The **Bruscello** takes place on Augus 14th, 15th and 16th, when hundreds of actors reenact scenes from the town's turbulent history. A truly magical three days. Another colorful spectacle is the **Bravio delle Botti**, on the last Sunday in August. This is a race through the main town streets with 80-kilo casks. These are rolled by *spingitori* (men who push them) representing the 8 quarters of the town. Before the race there is historical procession featuring more than 200 people all wearing authentic 14th century costumes. Each of the 8 quarters is represented by drummers, flag-wavers, ensigns, ladies, knights, captain, soldiers and a magistrate. A wonderful spectacle akin to Siena's Palio but more rustic in its appeal.

Practical Information

• **Website**, *www.ctnet.it/montepulciano/*

Isola del Giglio

Situated off the coast of Tuscany this island is a hidden treasure. The Italians have been hoarding its charms successfully for years, but now the secret is out. Mild climate, quaint seaside villages, friendly locals, unspoiled natural settings, hiking, water sports, and more, all make **Isola del Giglio** a breathtakingly serene destination.

The crystal clear sea teeming with underwater life is offset by the emerald isle of which a wopping 90% is still undeveloped. The 28 kilometers of coastline alternates between cliffs of smooth granite, with coves, bays and sandy beaches, which offers a chance to find a sheltered place to spend the day. There are three main developments on the island: Giglio Porto, Castello and Campese.

Excavations show that habitation began on the island five thousand years ago. Used by the Etruscans as a military outpost, **Giglio** went through one of its most significant periods under Roman rule. The importance of the island is highlighted by the recovery of numerous Roman shipwrecks as well as several references in the literature of the time.

In 805 CE, Charlemagne donated the island to the Abby of the Tre Fontane. From 1264 onwards, the island became a possession of the town of

Pisa, which was instrumental in the foundation of the urban settlement in **Castello**. During the subsequent centuries the ownership of the island shifted many times and eventually came to rest in the hands of the Medici family from Florence. It was during their rule that Giglio underwent several Saracen raids. The last of these occurred in November 1799 and was to be the only Gigliese victory over the invaders.

Since then the island has experienced a period of peace that allowed for economic recovery, an increase in agricultural production, an upsurge in the mining of iron and hematite ores, and a renewed emphasis on quarrying stone. The closing down of the mines in 1962 refocused the island's economy on fishing, crafts and tourism.

Arrivals & Departures

By Car

Located 34 kilometers from Grosseto, and about 140 kilometers from Rome, the port of Santo Stefano, where you will catch the ferry to the island, can be reached from the SS1 Via Aurelia. In Porto S.Stefano you can leave your car in one of several parking lots for a fee, or you can bring it with you.

Parking: Piazzale Candi, Porto S.Stefano, Ticket office *Tel. 0564/810-438, Office Tel. 0564/814-237, Cell 328/455-2376 or 328/764-2151*

Ferry: Maregiglio Srl, Via Umberto I 22, *Tel. 0564/809309, Fax 0564/809-469, E-mail: info@maregiglio.it.* Fares: passengers E14, cars E26-37.

Don't forget a road map; see page 218, *Arrivals & Departures* section for San Gimignano, for more information.

By Train

Getting here by train means getting off at the Orbetello-Monte Argentario station, then taking a local bus to the port, where you catch the ferry.

To get more information about train schedules, contact the website for the Italian Rail Company (**Ferrovie dello Stato** – FS), *www.fs-on-line.com.*

Where to Stay

CASTELLO MONTICELLO, *Via Provinciale, Giglio Porto. Tel. 0564/809-252, Fax 0564/809-473, E-mail: info@hotelcastellomonticello.com, Web: www.hotelcastellomonticello.com. Single E50-60, Double E90-120.* ***

Located between Castello and Porto, this is the best three star on the island. The rooms are furnished in Tuscan Arte Povera style with wrought iron trimmings, and most have a beautiful sea view. Each room has a private bathroom, telephone, color TV, refrigerator, and air conditioning. The hotel also features a tennis court, a private parking area, a terrace and a playground surrounded by a shady garden. From the terrace, the view overlooking the sea and the cliffs is enchanting. The hotel guarantees a private free bus to shuttle guests to the beach and to the ferries. The hotel restaurant menu features local dishes and specializes in seafood.

DEMO'S, *Via Thaon de Revel, Giglio Porto. Tel. 0564/809-235, Fax 0564/809-319. E-mail: demos@hoteldemos.com, Web:www.hoteldemos.com. Single E50-60, E90-120. All credit cards accepted.* ***

Elegant, well furnished, peaceful and comfortable, this hotel in Giglio Porto has a beautiful patio as part of the bar/restaurant. The furnishings are functional and comfortable, but the ambiance is created from the hotel's scenic setting. It has a small private beach, which is beautifully framed by an enchanting panoramic scene. The small marina, with its shops and restaurants, is only a short walk away from the hotel. The restaurant features traditional cuisine and has two dining rooms, one inside and one out.

PARDINI'S HERMITAGE, *Isola del Giglio, Cala degli Alberi. Tel. 0564/809-034 Fax 0564/809-177. E-mail: hermit@ats.it, Web:www.isoladelgiglio.it/hermitage. Single or Double E105-160.* ****

This guest house hotel can only be accessed by the sea, which makes it a wonderful refuge. It's an oasis of calm, away from any village in a peaceful and serene setting. In a home-like atmosphere there are many relaxing activities to enjoy including ceramics, bocce, ping pong, and other casual leisure activities, such as seawater therapy, massages and mud baths. From here you can also go hiking, take donkey rides, go sailing, and more.

Pardini's offers you the chance to swim or to lie in the sun far away from the prying eyes of civilization. On the property is a small farm with donkeys which are bred by the owners. Fresh local goat milk is used for home-made yogurt and cheese. Easily accessible by boat in 20 minutes from Giglio Porto, this is a truly magical place to stay if you want to get away from it all.

Where to Eat

DA MARIA, *Via della Casamatta 12, Castello, Tel. 0564/806-062, Fax 0564/806-105. All credit cards accepted. Closed Wednesdays and January and February. Dinner for two E50.*

Situated in the picturesque center of Castello, in a panoramic position offering stunning views of the Gulf of Campese, this is the place to sample the local cuisine of Giglio. To start they make excellent fresh stuffed pastas such as ravioli ai gamberi (ravioli stuffed with shrimp), and the specialty of the house, fettucine di coniglio al cacciatore (pasta with rabbit sauce, wine, tomatoes and herbs). For seconds they have a large offering of fish, complemented by a full wine list. A great place to eat on Giglio.

Seeing the Sights

Giglio Porto

Giglio Porto is a small and incredibly picturesque little town. With its multicolored houses, it offers an excellent backdrop as you approach here by ferry from Porto San Stefano on the mainland. The harbor, built by the Romans, remained untouched for eighteen centuries, when it was expanded first in 1796, then again in 1979. On the left of the harbor you can see the **Tower of Saraceno**, which was built by Ferdinand I in 1596.

A short distance from the tower, the ruins of an **ancient reservoir** used by the Romans to breed moray eels can be seen just below the waterline. The reservoir was part of an extensive **Roman Villa** (1st-2nd century CE), which belonged to the family of Domizi Enobarbi, and has been incorporated into the more recent buildings.

Castello

Castello is surrounded by medieval walls, comprising ten towers, three of which have a circular base and seven of which are rectangular. The walled town, built by the commune of Pisa, was later expanded and repaired by the Grand-dukes of Tuscany. Its central core still remains almost completely intact. Castello, thanks to its narrows streets often running underneath arches to balzuoli (external stairs), has a unique and mystical charm. When out for an evening, try the strong amber local wine, the **Ansonaco**.

Campese

Campese, with its many sandy beaches, is the newest area and the most important tourist center on the island. If you are interested in medieval charm, this is not the place to stay. This is a modern beach resort, Italian-style. The charming bay features the **Faraglione** (an imposing cliff) and the **Medici Tower**. The latter, built between the end of the seventeenth and the beginning of the eighteenth centuries is on an isolated island butte and is now linked to the land by a short bridge.

The south winds, which enter the bay from behind, make Campese an ideal spot for surfing and sailing enthusiasts. At the same time its west orientation offer some stupendous sunsets.

Practical Information

• **Taxi Service on Giglio**, Antonio - Cell *Tel. 347/194-1888;* Gian Piero - Cell *Tel. 347/187-5555,* Peitro - Cell *Tel. 347/892-0411*
• **Website**, *www.isoladelgiglio.it/*

Chapter 15

Umbria

Umbria – the "Green Heart of Italy" – is a beautiful slice of mother nature's paradise, filled with stunningly beautiful fairy-tale medieval towns. Covered with lush green forest and manicured fields, Umbria is located in the center of Italy and is bordered by Tuscany and Lazio, where Florence and Rome are located. Umbria is one of the smallest regions of Italy at only 8,500 square kilometers, but what it lacks in size it makes up for in art, architecture, natural settings, outdoor sporting activities, delicious cuisine, intricate arts & crafts, welcoming people and a passionate way of life.

Even though it is one of only a few Italian provinces not bordered by the sea, Umbria's mountains offer plenty of scenic splendor. Besides the natural beauty of the rolling hills and lush valleys, Umbria is filled with stunningly beautiful medieval towns like the capital, **Perugia**. Spreading majestically over the tops of a series of hills, Perugia is interlaced with winding cobblestones streets, an aqueduct turned walkway, ancient *palazzi*, Etruscan and Roman arches, and picturesque piazzas. Besides Perugia, the main towns of interest in Umbria include, **Spoleto**, **Todi**, **Gubbio**, **Orvieto**, and **Assisi**; each of which are rewarding destinations in and of themselves. Besides all the natural scenic beauty and fairy tale-like medieval towns, one of the main attractions here is that Umbria is very lightly touristed (except for Assisi which is a major pilgrimage sight) and an incredibly inexpensive alternative to the crowding your find in the more well-known areas of Italy.

Set in the mountains, spring and fall are the best times to visit, not only because of the welcoming weather but also for the abundance of local produce turning every meal into a memory. In the summer it can be hot and muggy, and in winter cold and wet – but Umbria should not be missed because of its stunning scenic beauty.

One main attraction that this province has to offer for seasoned Italophiles is that despite being between the main tourist attractions of Rome and Florence, Umbria is off of those crowded tourist corridors. At most times of the year, when the rest of Italy is swarming with hordes of tourists, you can venture into Umbria and have it almost all to yourself. The locals still outnumber the tourists in Umbria.

In Umbria's exotic urban settings you will find some wonderful Etruscan, Roman, Romanesque and Renaissance works of art and architecture. **Perugia** has the imposing and historically significant Etruscan Arch and Roman aqueduct turned walkway. **Orvieto** has its extensive Etruscan Necropolises and an awe inspiring cathedral. In **Gubbio** there are excellent examples of an ancient Roman temple, mausoleum, and theater just outside of an incredibly beautifully, well preserved and scenic medieval hill town. **Todi** as a whole is an inspiration and a wonderful respite from the hectic pace of modern life.

But **Spoleto** is the jewel of the region. Second only to Todi in quality of medieval character, this ambient hill town is home to some of the best restaurants in Italy, a direct result of the fact that this town hosts the world-renowned **Spoleto Festival** every summer. But what sets Spoleto apart, not only from towns in Umbria, but from every place I have visited on the planet, is its immediate proximity to pristine, untouched, verdant natural settings. Just across the Ponte delle Torre — a medieval aqueduct located only a few meters from the centro storico — which spans a deep gorge over to the hillside of Monte Luco, you will find an extensive array of hiking trails through deep forest, with scenic views and the peace and calm that only untouched natural

Umbria – Land of Truffles

Truffles (tartufi) have been described by epicureans as the ultimate indulgence, and if you have ever tasted a dish flavored with them you will realize that this is not only true, but is an incredible understatement. The **tartufo nero** (black truffle) is the more abundant and has a heartier flavor of the two varieties found in Umbria. The **tartufo bianco** (white truffle) is more subtle but found in less quantities. Gathered fresh from late September through December, you would be remiss not to savor any dish flavored with these tasty tubers if you venture to Umbria during that time.

Truffles grow wild and are discovered by trained dogs whose keen sense of smell allow them to locate these aromatic morsels despite the fact that the truffles develop over a foot underground. Most truffles are not very large, and weigh very little, but are incredibly expensive. Recently a New York City restaurant bought the largest ever found, though it weighed a little under 16 oz, and paid more than $300 per ounce for it

The aroma of tartufi, or as the more upscale say, 'perfume', is indescribably luscious. The best description could be that they are pungently aromatic, since the smell is overpowering but tantalizingly delicious. Walk into any alimentari or salumeria where they are sold when in season, and the sapore (aroma) will overwhelm you.

settings can offer. Spoleto is a combination of quaint and colorful medieval setting, complete with cosmopolitan shopping and eating establishments, immediately next door to the purity of nature. A situation unique anywhere else in the world.

The Romanesque style is evident in many of the cathedrals in the region, as is the Gothic style, which is particularly exemplified by the cathedral in Orvieto. The Renaissance also flourished and spread throughout the region which has also left us with some stunning architectural wonders. Umbria also boasts some of the Renaissance period's major artists, including the most famous from the Umbrian school, **Pietro Vannucci** (better known as **Perugino**) whose works are exhibited in the National Gallery of Umbria and the Collegio del Cambio in Perugia.

The medieval towns in Umbria are so well preserved, and are as yet relatively undiscovered, that a visit to the region is truly like walking back in time. Located in every town are prime examples of floating architecture, or *casa pensili* (hanging houses) – archways connecting rooms of buildings located far above the level of the street. Something you never see in North

America. So if you want to taste all the flavor of medieval Italy without the congestion of tourists, be a true traveler and come to Umbria.

Perugia

The capital city of Umbria, the charming old medieval city of **Perugia** is a stunning place to visit. Besides being the seat of some major cultural institutions like the National Gallery of Umbria in the Prior's Palace, and the home to a number of universities including one specifically for foreigners, Perugia also has the vitality and ambiance of true Italian city.

Stretching over hilly ridges, Perugia has been the home of human development since prehistoric times. The seven bronze **Eugubine tablets** — located in Gubbio — which date from the 3rd century BCE to the 1st century BCE, give indisputable proof that the Umbrian people had their own language before they were under the dominion of the Etruscans. During the 3rd century BCE, Perugia became one of the twelve key cities of the Etruscan federation. After the Etruscans were defeated by Rome, the city was absorbed into the Roman Republic as a colony. Then when the Roman Civil War was won by Octavian, Perugia was razed because of its allegiance to Mark Anthony. Some years later it was rebuilt by Octavian, then Emperor Augustus who gave the city its name (Augustus Perusia).

Once Christianity became the religion of the Empire, Perugia followed suit and started its own diocese in the 5th century CE. Around this time the city was ruled by the Byzantine Empire since the Roman Empire had dissolved and split, until it came under ecclesiastical rule in the 8th century. From the 11th century onward Perugia became a 'free' commune (meaning the nobles ruled and the serfs served, but the city wasn't under anyone else's yoke but their own). During the 12th and 13th centuries Perugia fought a series of battles for the control of the region with Chiusi, Cortona, Assisi, Todi and Foligno; and eventually ended up victorious after defeating Assisi in 1202, allowing the city to extend its reach over much of the surrounding area.

Despite dominating the region, internally Perugia was in turmoil. Different factions of nobles fought over the right to govern, never reaching a conclusion, until finally, caught up in their own power struggles, the entire social and economic fabric of the city became frayed. Because of this weakness, in 1540, the city was conquered by the forces of Pope Farnese and came under the rule of the Papal States for three centuries.

Around 1840, a brief flirtation with freedom resulted in Napoleon's forays into the region, at which time the citizens took great pleasure in destroying the Rocca Paolina fortress (an oppressive symbol of papal control of the city) and threw the Swiss Guard out of the city. Twenty years later, on September 14, 1860, the city became part of the kingdom of Italy.

Perugia retains a quaint medieval charm with stunning old palazzi, winding streets climbing up and down the hills, with archways and buildings traversing the passageways. The main street, Corso Vannucci, and main square, Piazza IV Novembre, are the perfect place for a walk any time day or night, and is where you will find the majority of the population every night strolling along, munching on ice cream, socializing, before and after dinner.

Most of the best shops are located in this area and in the evenings the area is filled with locals taking their evening stroll. A great sense of community thrives in Perugia making the city a fun and lively place to visit when you come to Umbria. Since it is located near many of the cities of note in the region, Perugia is a perfect place from which to take day trips to the other towns mentioned in this chapter.

Arrivals & Departures

The reason that Perugia still retains much of its medieval charm is that even though it is in close proximity geographically to Rome and Florence, Italy's two main tourist centers, train schedules are not strategically coordinated between those locations. Whether coming from Florence or Rome, you will have to change trains in **Castiglione del Lago**, and most of the trains which come here are milk runs which tend to stop at every little town along the way.

If you don't rent a car — which I recommend when visiting Umbria — once here, moving around the region can be cumbersome by either bus or train. Renting a car will be more expensive, but it will also allow you to visit tiny little hill towns quickly and easily. To visit Orvieto, Todi and Gubbio from Perugia a car is best, though Gubbio can be easily accessed by bus. To visit Assisi both train and bus are good options. To visit Spoleto from Perugia the train is a good option. A bus schedule (orario) for the local line, **Autolinee Regionali**, and a train schedule (Orari Ferroviari) is available at the local tourist office in Piazza IV Novembre.

Orientation

Perugia's centro storico sits on top of the crests of five hills and looks somewhat like the claw of the city's mascot, the Griffin. At the base of the main hill surrounding the train station are more modern urban developments, which though unsightly will not detract from your visit to the quaint, colorful and character-filled old town. The centro storico is bisected by the **Corso Vanucci**, which runs from the cathedral to the **Piazza Italia**, which is where the buses from the main train station let you off. It is also where the escalator arrives — snaking through the **Papal Fortress** (Rocca Paolina) — from the **Piazza Partigiani**, where the inter-regional bus terminal is located.

Umbria Websites

For up to date information about events and activities in Perugia visit **www.perugia.com**, the official web site for the city. This site also has links for **Assisi.com**, **Gubbio.com**, **Spoleto.com**, **Todi.com** among others. Granted they are in Italian, but even so they will help you plan your trip.

Getting Around Town

Break out your hiking shoes, get a bottle of water and get ready to do some hiking. The only way to explore Perugia is on foot and since it is located on a series of hills, you are going to do some stair- and hill-climbing while here. Aware of this, the Perugini have placed escalators in key locations throughout the town making the longer climbs more manageable now, while still retaining the charm of this stunning medieval town.

One of the most interesting escalators is the one that comes from the main parking and bus area, **Piazza dei Partigiani**. These *scala mobili* (literally meaning moving stairs) are underground and surrounded first by modern concrete walls. But these walls turn to ancient brick and you find yourself in the remnants of a 16th century underground fortress with vaulted passages, parts of old rooms, pieces of ancient passageways and an odd feeling that you suddenly went back in time. This place is the **Rocca Paolina** (see **A** on map), a fortress built by Pope Paul III in 1540 on the ruins of the Palazzo Baglioni, which was destroyed when the Papal States conquered Perugia. Then when the Papal States were expelled from Perugia, the fortress the popes built was partially destroyed. This paved the way for this stunning set of *scala mobili* to be built, making an introduction to Perugia very much like an amusement park ride with one defining difference – this is real.

Interwoven with these escalators are small roads, even smaller stairways, Etruscan and Roman archways, and a pedestrian aqueduct, all of which make Perugia a perambulating paradise. At the same time much of the central core is off limits to automobiles, making Perugia a relaxing and peaceful vacation spot.

Where to Stay

1. EDEN, *Via Cesare Caporali 9, 06123 Perugia. Tel. 075/572-8102, Fax 075/572-0342. 50 rooms all with bath. Single E45. Double E60. All credit cards accepted. Breakfast E3.* ******

A wonderful little two star just off the Piazza Italia where the buses from the train station stop, and the escalator from the bus depot empties. This hotel's main lobby is on the third and fourth floor of an old building, which probably explains why they are only a two star even though and the rooms are spacious, clean and comfortable, come with televisions, and some have spectacular views. Even the rooms overlooking a quiet courtyard are great. I prefer the comfort and spaciousness of the rooms on the fourth floor. Make sure to request them. The bathrooms come with blow dryer and courtesy toiletry set. A great two star hotel, with wonderful service, in a superb location at excellent prices.

2. PRIORI, *Via del Priori, 06123 Perugia. Tel. 075/572-3378, Fax 075/572-3213, E-mail: hotelpriori@perugia.com, Web: www.perugia.com/hotelpriori. 50 rooms all with bath. No credit cards accepted. Breakfast included. Single E50-65; Double E65-85.* ******

Right in the center of town the decor here is 'old Umbrian' with antique furnishings, terra cotta tile floors and flowered drapes. The bathrooms come with blow dryer and courtesy toiletry set and are accommodating though a little cramped. The hotel has a large terrace with nice views. A great place to relax in the evenings. In the summer the terrace is used for the buffet breakfast which includes juice, fruit, cereal, pastries and coffee and tea. A quaint two star right in the middle of things with all the amenities of a three star elsewhere. Great place to stay at a good price. By far the best two star in town.

3. LOCANDA DELLA POSTA, *Corso Vannucci 97f, 06123 Perugia. Tel. 075/572-8925, Fax 075/572-2413. Web: www.venere.com/it/perugia/ locanda_della_posta/. 40 rooms all with bath. All credit cards accepted. Breakfast included. Single E115; Double E175.* ********

This is the best hotel on the best street in Perugia, Corso Vannucci, surrounded by traditional cafés, cute little shops, and old palazzi like the beautiful Priori Palace nearby. Corso Vannucci is the main promenade where all of Perugia comes out at night to parade around, young and old alike joined together in a community ritual of togetherness. Here you are ideally situated in the middle of everything. The hotel is a 17th century palazzo that once was the old post office, hence the name of the hotel. Over the centuries they've had many a celebrity stay here, including Frederick II of Prussia, Goethe, and Hans Christian Andersen. In 1990 the entire hotel was completely restored and every modern amenity was added. The hotel retains all of its charm and character, and each room is different from the next adding to the old world ambiance. The bathrooms are large and refined with all modern conveniences. By far the best place to stay in Perugia.

4. BRUNAFI PALACE, *Piazza Italia 12, 06123 Perugia. Tel. 075/573-2541, Fax 075/572-0210. Toll free in Italy 167/273-226. Toll free fax (USA) 1-888/661-0219. Email - sina@italyhotel.com, Web: www.summithotels.com. 93 rooms all with bath. All credit cards accepted. Breakfast included. Single E245; Double E300.* *********

In the centro storico right next to the Rocca Paolina, this is an over-priced yet extremely elegant and attentive hotel. Recently the Palace Hotel Bellavista

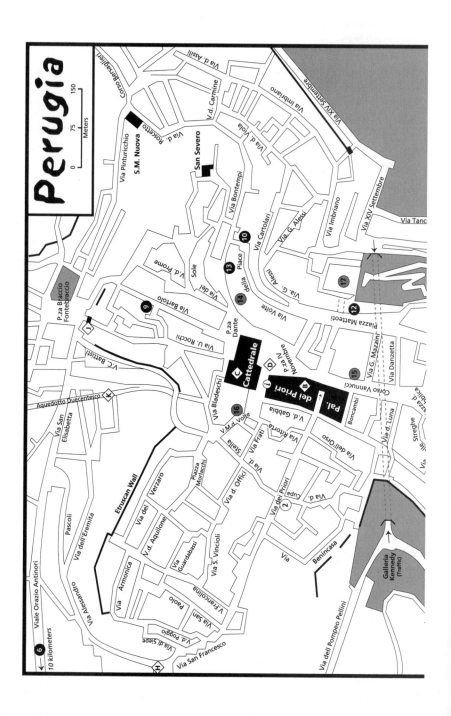

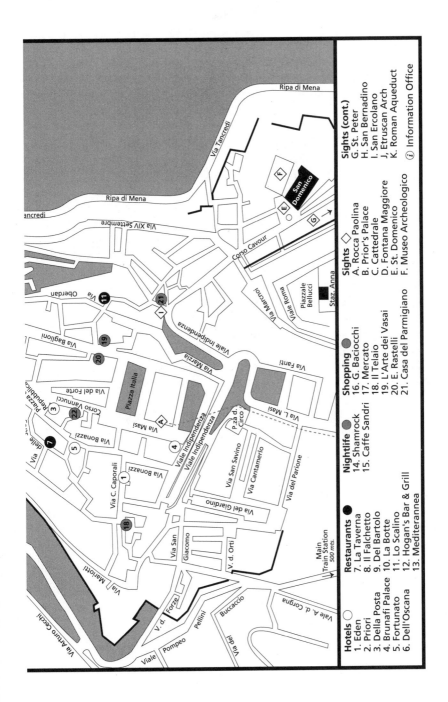

Hotels ◯
1. Eden
2. Priori
3. Della Posta
4. Brunafi Palace
5. Fortunato
6. Dell'Oscana

Restaurants ●
7. La Taverna
8. Il Falchetto
9. Del Bartolo
10. La Botte
11. Lo Scalino
12. Hogan's Bar & Grill
13. Mediterannea

Nightlife ●
14. Shamrock
15. Caffe Sandri

Shopping ●
16. G. Baciocchi
17. Mercato
18. Il Telaio
19. L'Arte dei Vasai
20. E. Rastelli
21. Casa del Parmigiano

Sights ◇
A. Rocca Paolina
B. Prior's Palace
C. Cattedrale
D. Fontana Maggiore
E. St. Domenico
F. Museo Archeologico

Sights (cont.)
G. St. Peter
H. San Bernadino
I. San Ercolano
J. Etruscan Arch
K. Roman Aqueduct
ⓘ Information Office

has been absorbed in the Brunafi, which resulted in the word 'Palace' being added to the name of the hotel. The ancient palazzo has been completely restored with all modern amenities while retaining its charm, elegance and ambiance. The entrance hall instantly transports you back in time with its elegant tapestries and antique furnishings. The rooms are all differently furnished and are all clean and comfortable. The bathrooms unfortunately are not all that big, but do have all modern necessities. A wonderful place to stay, though it is a little expensive for my taste.

5. HOTEL FORTUNA, *Via Bonazzi 19, 06123 Perugia. Tel 075/572-2845, Fax 075/573-5040. Web: www.venere.com/it/perugia/fortuna/. All credit cards accepted. Single E75-90; Double E75-120.* ***

Situated in the *centro storico*, just off of the Corso Vanucci, this place was completely restored in 1992 with air-conditioning added in 1999. Despite all the changes this hotel has maintained it charms and comes with all three star amenities. The second floor houses the breakfast room and evening bar area. The third floor has a nice sitting room with a fire place and there is a big terrace on the fifth floor overlooking the rooftops of Perugia. Wonderful little three star in an ideal location.

6. CASTELLO DELL'OSCANA, *06134 Locanda Cenerente, Perugia. 075/690-125, Fax 075/690-666. Email - info@oscano-castle.com. Web: www.oscano-castle.com. 100 rooms all with bath. All credit cards accepted. Breakfast included.* **Castle**: *Suite or jr-suite on the top floor of the castle is E200. 3 rooms elsewhere in the castle E160.* **Villa Ada**: *Double E110 per room per night.* **La Macina**: *Weekly rates E300 to 625. Buffet breakfast included and is served in the dining room of the Castle.*

Stunning. Incredibly beautiful. Amazing. Like something out of a fairy tale. Simply unbelievable. By far the best place to stay in all of Umbria. If you have a car, and you have the means, stay here. Near Perugia, but set deep in the surrounding verdant, forested hills, this amazing medieval castle presents an atmosphere of unparalleled charm and ambiance. There are three locations to choose from: the Castle (a medieval structure complete with towers and turrets that is simply but elegantly decorated and equipped with every comfort), the Villa Ada (a 19th century residence adjoining the castle that is more modern but no less accommodating), and La Macina (a country house down the hill from the other two structures, and comes with complete apartments and has an adjacent pool).

All three offer the setting for an ideal vacation, but the castle is the place to stay because of its unique, one of a kind medieval setting. A perfect place to spend a honeymoon or simply have the vacation of a lifetime. Dinner is served nightly in the castle and the menu varies daily based on what is available in the local markets.

Where to Eat

7. LA TAVERNA, *Via delle Streghe 8. Tel. 075/572-4128. Closed Mondays, January 7-21 and all of July. All credit cards accepted. Dinner for two E60.*

Not to be missed. Excellent atmosphere (just getting here is like a walk back in time, located just off of the Corso Vanucci) with its vaulted ceilings and arched doorways, simply superb food, and the most attentive service. Come prepared to have a great meal in authentically medieval surroundings. Everything here is excellent and the waiter will be more than willing to help translate if need be. They make a tasty tagliatelle al ragu di anatra (pasta with duck sauce), linguini con pecorino e olio (pasta with pecorino cheese and oil), and crostini al tartufo nero (baked dough with black truffles). In fact if you come here in truffle season sample anything they make with them. Granted, most any dish with truffles will be the most expensive dish on the menu — as well as the most mouth-wateringly delicious — so be prepared for that.

This is an upper echelon restaurant — make sure you dress for the occasion — and most cognoscenti believe it the best in town. I concur.

8. IL FALCHETTO, *Via Bartolo 20, Tel 075/573-1775. Closed Mondays. Open 12:30-2:30pm and 7:30 - 10:00pm. All credit cards accepted. Dinner for two E40.*

Pink tablecloths, vaulted brick ceilings, soothing music, oil lamps on every table, and attentive service all set the scene for a serene meal. In back is where the locals congregate and is a little more boisterous, but both front and rear receive tasty local recipes made with exquisite care and presented with a slight flair. The grilled vegetable antipasto is perfect to start with and the tagliatelle ai porcini (with mushrooms) or al tartufo nero (with black truffles) are both tasty pasta dishes. For seconds they have a number of tasty grilled and oven baked meats and fish.

9. OSTERIA DEL BARTOLO, *Via Bartolo 30. Tel. 075/573-1561. Closed Sundays and January 7-25. All credit cards accepted. Dinner for two E75.*

An elegant but small place run by the effervescent and attentive Walter Passeri. They bake their bread in-house which makes it a wonderful complement to the meal. The pastas and desserts are also all made in-house. And as befits a restaurant in Perugia they too create quality truffle dishes. The menu here changes constantly, but be assured you will receive a superb gastronomical extravaganza. You need to make reservations and you must dress well. This is a very nice place, and if you are into that type of ambiance, as well as creatively prepared food at upscale prices, this is the place for you.

10. LA BOTTE, *Via Volte Della Pace 33. Tel. 075/572-2679. Open 12:30-2:30pm and 7:30-10:00pm. Credit cards accepted. Dinner for two E25.*

This is a small, simple, down-to-earth trattoria, off the beaten path, down in the basement of a medieval building down a small side street, that serves a vast array and tasty pasta and meat dishes at incredibly good prices. Locals and travelers alike flock to this little hole in the wall because of the tasty food and accommodating, relaxing family atmosphere. The entryway looks like a bar or café, but in the back under the while walls and vaulted brick ceilings you'll get some wonderful food, including penne alla vodka (with tomatoes, cream, meat and a touch of vodka), spaghetti alla carbonara (egg, cheese, bacon and peas), or my favorite, penne al panna e funghi (with a creamy mushroom sauce).

11. PIZZERIA LO SCALINO, *Via S. Ercolano 8. Tel. 075/5722-5372. Open 12:00-3:00pm and 7:00-10:00pm. Closed Friday afternoons. Dinner for two E20.*

A tiny local place whose entrance is located on the steps to the church of San Ercolano. A little cramped but comfortable, and frequented by the locals not only for the great pizza, but the warm and accommodating atmosphere. The pizza chefs prepare your pies in a small space in the dining area. Only a few varieties of pizza are available, a few salads, a couple of meat dishes, an excellent bruschetta for appetizer, but what the menu lacks in quantity, the food and local atmosphere makes up for in quality.

12. HOGANS BAR & GRILL, *Piazza Matteoti 20. Tel. 075/572-7647. Open 12:00-3:30pm and 7:00pm-2:30am every day. Dinner for two E20.*

This is a hopping place, packed every night, that serves American and Southwest style food such as burgers, steaks, burritos, sandwiches, baked potatoes, salads and appetizers of all kinds, as well as real American-style desserts like cheesecake and chocolate brownies. Inside you will find bits and pieces of Americana covering the walls such as license plates, photos of Michael Jordan, gas station signs and the like. For a fun time and taste of home, away from home, come here.

13. PIZZERIA MEDITERANNEA, *Piazza Piccinino 11/12, Tel 075/572-1322. Closed Tuesdays. Open 12:30-2:30pm and 7:30pm - midnight. Dinner for two E25.*

All they serve is pizza and it is so good and the atmosphere so electric that people line up to get it. Opening onto a small piazza just past the Duomo sits this festive little pizzeria. A small place with only two rooms, one of which has the pizza oven, this is the favorite hangout for the younger set at night. They only serve pizza, so if you are in the mood for it, give this place a try. If you do not show up early you will definitely have to wait. To get on the list of diners, flag down a waitress and she will give you a number. If you do not want to wait, La Botte is just around the corner.

Seeing The Sights
A. ROCCA PAOLINA
Piazza Italia.

A fortress built by Sangallo the Younger by the order of Pius III as the Papal States emphatic display of dominance over the city of Perugia. An entire medieval neighborhood, as well as the Baglioni Palazzi were covered over to create this ostentatious display of papal authority which even today makes Perugini leery of the influence of the Pope. In 1860 the fortress was destroyed and what remains underground is now used as a totally unique exhibition space, and a conduit for the escalators from Piazza Partigiani.

B. PRIOR'S PALACE,

Corso Vannucci. *Tel. 075/574-1247.* Closed the first Monday of the month. Open 9am-7pm, holidays 9am-1pm.

Home to the **National Gallery of Umbria** on the third floor, the Prior's Palace is also known as the Town Hall and is an outstanding example of medieval architecture. As such is considered one of the most elegant and famous in all of Italy. Begun in 1293, it was completed in 1443 after the building was consolidated with other homes and pre-existing towers all under one huge roof.

The entrance on Corso Vannucci is through a round portal, almost underneath an imposing tower and guarded by two Griffins – the symbols of the city – sinking their claws into two calves. The entire facade on the Corso is quite imposing and rather fortress-like. Before entering, take some time to check out the ornamental entrance with its friezes, twisted columns, sculptures and ornamental foliage. The Atrium is inside the entrance off of Corso Vanucci and is a covered courtyard with pillars and vaults.

The entrance on the Piazza IV Novembre is just to the left of the tourist information office up a flight of stairs and through a pointed portal. Above the portal are bronze statues of a Griffin and a Lion – the symbol of an old ruling family, the Guelphs. Through the portal is the Sala dei Notari (Lawyer's Room), an impressive hall that has some exquisite frescoes and grandiose arches. The frescoes are some scenes from the Bible and Aesop's fables. Other rooms in the building include the Sala del Consignio Comunale (City Council Hall), which contains a fresco by Pinturicchio, and the Sala Rossa (Red Hall) containing a mural by Dono Doni.

The National Gallery is the third floor and is a must-see in Perugia. It contains masterly examples of the paintings from the Umbrian school, which date from the 13 century CE to the 19th. Perugia's most famous artist, Perugino, is featured in rooms 12-14 with his *Adoration of the Magi* (room 12), *Miracles of San Bernardino* (room 13) and *The Dead Christ* (room 14). Also accessible off of the Corso Vanucci is the **Collegio del Cambio**. To the left of the facade of the Palazzo dei Priori, beyond the archway to the Via dei Priori are three portals, through which you can enter the fresco-laden room containing major works by the cities most famous artist, Perugino.

C. CATHEDRAL OF SAINT LAWRENCE

Piazza IV Novembre.

The steps on the left side of the building facing the Piazza IV Novembre is *the* place to hang out, whether it's sunny or not. You'll have to fight for space with the natives and locals alike, as well as some rather bold pigeons, but this is where you can sit and watch the life of Perugia pass by.

The building itself is an imposing Gothic church constructed between the 14th and 15th centuries CE. It still has an incomplete facade but nonetheless is beautiful. The main entrance is between Piazza Dante and Piazza IV Novembre and has a coarse stone facade with a massive Baroque portal and a large circular window above that. The left side of the building is decorated with ornamental masks by Scalza flanking the plain portal with its ancient wooden doors. Above the portal is the votive Crucifix placed here in 1539. To the right side of the portal is the 15th century pulpit of San Bernardino. To the left of the portal is the *Statue of Pope Julius III*, an intricate bronze by Danti from the 16th century.

The interior is divided by octagonal columns into one nave and two aisles. The Chapel of San Bernardino — to the right as you enter — which is enclosed by beautiful wrought iron railings, contains a stunning fresco by Federico Barocci. In the Chapel of the Holy Ring, enclosed by 15th century wrought iron railings — to the left as you enter — is a silver and gold plated copper tabernacle which contains the onyx wedding ring purported to have been worn by the Virgin Mary. Hmmm? A poor carpenter able to afford an expensive onyx ring? You be the judge of its authenticity.

Also please note the 16th century multi-colored stained glass windows by Arrigo Fiammingo and the 16th century carved choir seats. In the right transept are the tombs of Pope Martino IV, Pope Urbano IV and Pope Innocenzo III as well as the marble sculpture of Pope Leo XIII.

D. FONTANA MAGGIORE

Piazza IV Novembre.

The **Great Fountain** (Fontana Maggiore) is the monumental heart of medieval Perugia, built between 1275 and 1278 with the decorative sculptures created by Nicola and Giovanni Pisano. Topped by a bronze basin, the fountain has an upper stone basin held up by slender columns topped with a variety of capitals.

This basin consists of 24 red marble panels separating some of the Pisano brother's statues which depict scenes from the Bible, historical and mythological figures, and some saints. The lower basin has 50 panels on which are depicted the months of the year, the signs of the Zodiac, scenes from the Old Testament, the founding of Rome and Aesop's fables.

E. BASILICA OF SAINT DOMENICO,

Via Cavour. Open 7:00am-noon & 4:00-7:00pm.

An imposing Gothic church built in the 14th century then rebuilt in the 17th with a huge campanile (bell tower) and separate attached cloisters (not open to the public). On the bare facade is the elegant 16th century portal above a double flight of stairs. The interior is enormous and plain, a simplicity that gives it a peaceful and rather calming effect on the soul. Some elegant pieces include the 18th century organ and the splendid tomb of Pope Benedict XI. The apse is lit by a large, 23 meter high 15th century window. Most of the frescoes that adorn the walls have not survived the test of time. In every chapel there are exquisite paintings depicting a variety of religious themes, as well as a number of crypts containing personages of importance in Perugia.

F. MUSEO ARCHEOLOGICO NAZIONALE DELL'UMBRIA,

Via Cavour. Open 9:00am-5:00pm. Holidays 9:00am-1:00pm. E2.

To get to this museum go through the archway to the left of San Domenico, into the internal courtyard, go down the right portico to the entrance upstairs. The museum wraps around the 1st floor of the courtyard and contains many interesting archaeological relics culled from the many excavations in Umbria. You will find Etruscan, Roman and more recent artifacts. A simple, little museum that is worth a short visit.

G. BASILICA OF SAINT PETER

Borgo XX Giugno. Open 7:00am-noon & 4:00-7:00pm.

Located quite a ways from the centro storico through a rustic working class neighborhood, down the Corso Cavour past St. Domenico, through the Porta San Pietro and along the Borgo XX Giugno. The Basilica of San Pietro was built in the 10th century on the site of an even older cathedral. The church is dominated by a beautiful 15th century campanile. You enter the church through a rather run-down but at the same time elegant porticoed courtyard. Oddly enough there is a bar/café just off of the courtyard where you can grab a refreshment after your long walk over here.

The dark interior contains a single nave with two aisles divided by 18 Roman columns. This church, in contrast to San Domenico, is elaborate in its decoration — very much like San Ercolano — and has a wealth of art work, most of which is rather difficult to see without night vision glasses since the lighting is so poor even on the brightest day. Give your eyes time to adjust and take the time to view magnificent frescoes and paintings adorning virtually every inch of space on the walls. The sacristy contains some works by Caravaggio and Perugino, and the Chapel of the Sacrament has a *Pieta* by Perugino.

Behind the altar, through the intricately carved 17th century choir is a small terrace at the back of the church overlooking an incredibly panoramic view of the surrounding countryside. Take the time to get back here and admire the view, and savor the wood carved choir and doors that lead here.

H. ORATORY OF SAN BERNADINO

Piazza San Francesco. Open 7:00am-noon & 4:00-7:00pm.

The date this building was completed (1461) can be seen on the facade in roman numerals (MCCCCLXI). Masterly crafted by the Florentine Agoştino di Antonio di Duccio, the facade is a wonderful series of sculptures of saints in the Perugia-Renaissance style. The 15th century Gothic interior contains the Tomb of Beato Egidio and an ancient 4th century CE Roman-era Christian sarcophagus. In an adjacent building entered through the annex of the Oratory of St. Andrew you get to the Baldeschi Chapel, which houses the Tomb of Bartolo da Sassoferrato, an important 14th century Perugian leader, teacher and lawyer.

I. CHURCH OF SAN ERCOLANO

Via Marzia. Open 7:00am-noon & 4:00-7:00pm.

Dedicated to the patron saint of Perugia, San Ercolano, this church stands on the exact spot where he was martyred when the Goths seized the city in 547 CE. This 13th and 14th century Gothic church is a small octagonal structure with large pointed arches going around it. The interior is accessed through a beautiful double staircase built in 1607. Though more intricate in detail than the original structure, the staircase is the first initiation into the exceptional beauty of this medieval church. At the high altar is a noteworthy Roman-era Christian sarcophagus that contain the remains of San Ercolano. Around the dome are some exquisite frescoes dating to the 16th century which depict a number of scenes from the Bible. Every inch of these walls are covered with frescoes and bas-relief work.

J. THE ETRUSCAN ARCH

Piazza Fortebraccio.

Also known as the **Arch of Augustus**, the original structure was built in the 3rd and 2nd century BCE. Later there were Roman-era additions as well as some during the 16th century. This huge and imposing structure is bordered by some of the old walls of Perugia, clearly indicating the lengths attackers would have to go through to sack the city. Comprised of two powerful Etruscan towers, the right one lowered by an invasion, while the one on the left has an enticing patio on the top and a Roman fountain on the bottom. Above the gate is a sentinel arch, so named because that is where the guards for the city would keep watch. It has since been walled up and now is part of the structure to the left.

K. ROMAN AQUEDUCT

Via di Aquedotto.

What used to be a functioning aqueduct is now a pedestrian street. This may be your only chance to walk along an ancient aqueduct, so take it while you have it. Lining the aqueduct are quaint little homes. Also from this height you get to look down onto other streets and passageways, offering an interesting perspective of this mountain city.

Nightlife & Entertainment

The nightlife and entertainment in Perugia mainly consists of congregating in and around the **Corso Vannucci**, going for a stroll, grabbing an ice cream cone — the preferred social lubricant in Perugia — and meeting with friends at one of the many cafés that line the Corso. This lasts from before dinner through the meal hour and well into the evening, and is especially crowded on Saturday nights when everybody and their grandmother is out for a walk. It is beautiful to see every slice of life coming together for an informal community gathering. You will find young and old, well-off and beggars, wild and conservative, families and singles, all connecting despite their differences. You don't see this too often anymore in the US.

There was a time when the Perugini allowed cars to drive on the Corso Vannucci; but back in the '70s, realizing the detrimental effect it was having on their community, they put a stop to that practice by closing the street to traffic. Italians have not become overdependent on the automobile or let it dominate their lives. In fact on September 22, 1999, every major city in Italy joined other European cities in closing off additional sections of their cities to automobile traffic to show people how less frenetic life can be without cars cluttering up our lives.

Because of this understanding and appreciation for community, places like the Corso Vannucci thrive all over Italy. Along this street there are plenty of restaurants, cafés, and pubs in which to stop if refreshment is needed. Two that we recommend are listed below.

14. SHAMROCK, *Piazza Danti 18. Tel. 075/573-6625. Open 7:00pm - 2:00am.*

Great Irish atmosphere. Medieval vaulted ceilings coupled with dark wood furnishings, brass accents, and authentic Irish knickknacks gives this place a true feel of the Blarney. Definitely the best pub atmosphere in Perugia. Located down a dark medieval alleyway in the basement of one of the oldest buildings in the city, just across from the main entrance to the Cathedral. They serve a full complement of ales and have a good bar menu as well as snacks like chips, pretzels and peanuts – which you have to pay for. In the early evening, the music selection is contemporary but light. Later, the selection gets a little more techno and loud. They really don't open until around 7:00pm, so this would be a place to come before an 8:00pm dinner for a quick drink or afterward to see how the Italians like to celebrate life.

15. CAFFÉ SANDRI, *Corso Vannucci 32. Tel. 075/61012. Open 7:00am - 11:00pm daily.*

The perfect place to grab a cappuccino or a bite to eat on the Corso Vannucci. You may miss the place even though their window displays are tantalizingly spectacular with fruit tarts, cheeses and other delicacies enticing you inside. Sandri is Perugia's landmark café and, judging from the crowd, it is a local favorite.

The frescoed ceilings remain intact and the proprietors come from the same Swiss family, the Schucan's, who founded the café over 130 years ago, making it feel as if you've stepped back into a 19th century café. When in Perugia, you have to at least stop in for a look. And if this café doesn't appeal to you, fear not, there are plenty of others nearby.

Shopping

The main pedestrian street **Corso Vannucci** is also the best shopping street in Perugia. Along its route and around its periphery — mainly the parallel streets of **Via Baglioni** and **Via G. Oberdan** — you will find traditional little shops offering a wide variety native arts and crafts as well as local and international fashions.

16. I Legni di Giuseppe Baciocchi, Via Maeste delle Volte 8. *Tel. 075/57-26-080.* This artists' shop is located to the left of the Cathedral (as you face it from the Piazza IV Novembre) down the little passageway Via Maeste delle Volte, in the basement of a medieval building. Carved wooden figures are his stock in trade and they are simply wonderful. A perfect place to pick up some small gifts for friends, or buy one of his larger magnificent carvings.

Virtually right next to this store is **Talmone**, an excellent candy shop where you can get great gifts to bring home, or something to snack on later in the room. Inside this store are Etruscan walls dating to the 3rd century BCE, and the ruins of a Roman street from the 1st century BCE. Feel free to stop in and sight see or shop for candy.

17. Covered Market, Open 7:00am-1pm Monday-Saturday. Located off of the Piazza Matteoti and through the Palazzo Capitano del Popolo is the covered market of Perugia, which offers dry goods of leather and other crafts in the upstairs section, and fruits, vegetables and other foods on the downstairs.

18. Il Telaio, Via Bruschi 2B. *Tel. 075/572-6603.* Closed Monday mornings. Open 9:30am-1:00pm and 4:00-8:00pm. All credit cards accepted. This is a quaint little shop, off the beaten path, which sells local hand-crafted linens, pillow cases, sheets, tablecloths and everything associated with fabrics and textiles. Located past the Hotel Eden, and next to the church of San Angelo di Porta Eburnea, this is a wonderful shop to find unique products from Umbria.

19. L'Arte dei Vasai, Via Baglioni 32. *Tel. 075/572-3108.* Open 9:30am-1:00pm and 3:45-8:00pm. Closed Sundays. All credit cards accepted. If you don't want to venture all the way to Deruta to find ceramics, this store has by far the best selection available in Perugia. The perfect place to find hand-crafted, distinctively hand-painted ceramics, bowls, mugs, cups, plates and more.

20. Magazzini di Egidio Rastelli, Via Baglioni 17-29. *Tel. 075/57-29-050.* Open 9:00am-1:00pm and 4:00-7:50pm. Closed Mondays. Large cartoleria with all sorts of distinctly unique Italian notebooks, pens, calendars, day planners, sketch pads, and everything else for office, home or school. Italian stationery is world-renowned for its creative individuality and this store has everything you could want.

21. Casa del Parmigiano Reggiano, Via San Ercolano 36. *Tel. 075/573-1233.* All credit cards accepted. Open 7:30am-1:30pm & 4:30-8:00pm. This is the best place in Perugia to find those exquisitely tasty, pungently aromatic, uniquely Umbrian culinary delight, tartufi, not only because of their excellent price but also because they vacuum seal (sotto vuoto) them for you so that they stays fresh, if you ask, at no extra charge. You can also get all types of salamis and meats for sandwiches as the product that they are known for, Parmigiano Reggiano. You can get this hard cheese used for grating over pasta in the States, but what you probably did not know is that what we receive over there is not the top quality. The Italians keep the best for themselves, and the only way to get some is to buy it here and bring it back with you.

Books in English

22. Libreria C Betti, Via del Sette 1. Open 10:00am-1:00pm and 4:00pm-8:00pm. This tiny bookstore is located just off of the Piazza della Repubblica. It carries a small selection of English language books to the right just as you enter. Guidebooks are near the back, not that you will need another since you have this one.

Excursions & Day Trips

In actuality, the other towns listed in this chapter (Orvieto, Todi, Gubbio, Assisi and Spoleto) can all be considered day trips from Perugia, but at the same time, each of these places could be destinations in and of themselves. But Deruta is such a small location, and is so much closer to Perugia, that it is the only true day trip.

DERUTA

Located 15 kilometers outside of Perugia, **Deruta** is the generally considered the ceramics capital of Italy — something nearby Cortona over the border in Tuscany would dispute heartily. Let's just say that they're both good. Deruta is a quaint old town situated on a hill overlooking the valley of the Tiber. Unfortunately the new part of the town — which is parallel to and along the Via Tiberina — is a slip-shod, unplanned eye sore. But above from that is a beautiful little hill town filled with the largest selection of **fine ceramic pottery** anywhere.

The prices for the pottery created here is no less expensive than for pieces made here but sold in Florence or Rome, so don't come expecting any bargains. All you will get here is a large selection, not great prices. But what a selection it is. If you want to return home with some fine ceramic pottery, the best in Italy, and dare I say it — the world — come to the source, come to Deruta.

Not really a place to spend much time, except for pottery shopping. The best way to visit is to come and explore the little hill town first, see all the small family-run pottery businesses nestled in the winding cobblestone streets, maybe visit the small **ceramic museum**, buy your pottery, then head back to Perugia.

Getting There: By bus is the only way, other than by car, to get to Deruta. Pick up the bus schedule at the information office in Perugia. Buses are infrequent and as a result you need to plan to ensure that you can get there, have time to look around, then be able to catch a bus back.

Practical Information

Festivals
- **Good Friday procession** – La Desolata
- **Mid–July Rock Music festival** – Rockin' Umbria
- **First two weeks of September** – Sagra Musicale Umbria (musical recitals in Perugia's churches)
- **End of October/Beginning November** – Jewel And Antique show
- **2–5 November** – All Souls Fair

Laundry
Le Bolle, Corso G. Garibaldi 43. Open every day 8:00am-10:00pm. Attendant on duty from 2:00-4:00pm & 7:00-10:00pm. Self-service laundromat that is computerized and fully automated. Wash cost: E3 for 8kg (15lbs), E5 for 16kg. Wash takes 25 minutes. Drying cost: E3 for 8kg and E5 for 10kg. Free detergent. If the attendant is not present, call *075/41644* and she will pop down and give you some.

Onda Blu, Via Pinturicchio 102. Open 8:00am-10:00pm every day. Self-service laundromat located near Porta Pesa that is fully automated. Wash cost: E3 for 6.5 kg. Takes 30 minutes. Drying cost: E3 and takes 20 minutes. Detergent costs E3.

Money & Banking
There is only one money exchange shop in Perugia and it is in the Piazza IV Novembre but holds very erratic hours. The best bet to change money is at banks but they are only open 9:00am-3:00pm Monday through Friday. If you need to change money, but not travelers checks, on a Saturday go to the main post office at Via Mazzini 24, from 9:00am-5:30pm.

Tourist Information
The **tourist information office** is located in the Piazza IV Novembre next to the stairs leading up to the Prior's Palace. Open from 9:00am to 1:00pm and 3:00pm to 6:00pm, *Tel. 075/573-6458 or 572/-3327*. They have useful maps, and all the information you need for buses, trains, walking tours, etc.

Spoleto
Spoleto is by far the most stunning destination I have ever been to on this planet, and I have visited every continent except for Australia and Antarctica. What makes Spoleto so unique is a combination of different attributes, most of which would entice travelers by themselves, except that Spoleto has them all in one place: medievel charm, natural setting, excellent restaurants, cosmopolitan shops and art galleries, few tourists, and incredibly friendly and accomodating locals.

The ancient medieval town itself, with its winding streets, old buildings is like something out of a fairy tale. But even though this is one of the better preserved medieval towns in all of Italy, Spoleto is still only lightly touristed. During the world-famous **Spoleto Festival** held in June every year, tens of thousands of tourists descend here to savor a two week extravaganza of performing arts. When that is over, it seems that tourists leave the city alone, until the next festival. Spoleto has some of the best restaurants in all of Italy, quaint little artisans' shops selling exquisitely created local crafts, and little galleries and studios filled with locally produced painting and sculpture that is of top quality. But that's not all. Besides the fact that Spoleto is a serene medieval town filled with cosmopolitan distractions, the main distinguishing feature about Spoleto is that it offers instant access to inspiring natural settings.

Just across the **Ponte delle Torre**, an old medieval aqueduct turned walkway, from the centro storico and you are in untouched, pristine nature, laced with hiking trails that snake around the surrounding mountains, and through small local hill towns. Nowhere else in the world can you go from a quaint medieval town, filled with cosmopolitan amenities, to untouched natural settings after a five minute walk. Surrounded by lush, verdant hills, and dominated by the **Rocca fortress**, Spoleto also boasts a prolific artistic and cultural presence.

Situated on green hillside near the lower border of the Umbra Valley, Spoleto was founded by the original Umbrian people, Later it came under Etruscan influence and eventually was absorbed into the Roman Empire around the 3rd century BCE. Its claim to fame during that period came during the second Punic War, where it played a major role in repelling Hannibal's attacks. After the fall of the Roman Empire, Spoleto was a flourishing Lombard capital, then fell under papal influence and became one of the Pope's summer residences. During the rise of Perugia's power it came under that city's jurisdiction; and with Perugia and Todi in the 14th century it rose up against the excessive and abusive powers of the popes. During Napoleon's sojourn in Italy, Spoleto became one of his local capitals and eventually was absorbed into the newly formed state of Italy on September 17, 1860.

Arrivals & Departures

Spoleto has retained its wonderful medieval charm and preserved its raw natural beauty because it is not easily accessible from Florence or Rome, which means that the hordes of tourists that would come from those locations usually do not make their way here. From Perugia the train leaves every hour and takes an hour to get here. From Rome, the schedule is more erratic and the trip takes a little over an hour and a half. Check with your local information office for specific schedules.

Orientation

Spoleto is spread up a hillside with the defining structures being the spire of the **cathedral** and the imposing **Rocca** behind it. To the east up the hill is the **Duomo** whose **piazza** is a central focus of the town. The town's tiny roads twist and turn around the undulation of the hillside, so it's best to use a map or have a compass available to keep yourself on the right track.

Getting Around Town

Spoleto is made for walking, with twisting and turning cobblestone streets and winding staircases leading through quaint medieval passageways. Be prepared to hike up and down hills, but the effort will be worth it since the surroundings will instantly transport you back to a simpler place and time.

Where to Stay

1. CHARLESTON, *Piazza Collicola 10. Tel. 0743/223-235, Fax 0743/222-010. E-mail: info@hotelcharleston.it, Web: www.hotelcharleston.it/. 18 rooms. Single E50; Double E65. All credit cards accepted. Breakfast E6.* ***

In the centro storico of Spoleto, this 17th century palazzo represents a classic blending of the old and new. The common areas are very large and simply furnished and the rooms are comfortably sized with modern 'antique' furnishings. You will also have all three star amenities including TV, VCR, air-conditioning, heat, radio, phone and mini-bar. The bathrooms are small but come with hairdryer and complimentary toiletry kit. Buffet breakfast is served in two small rooms and consists of croissant, yogurt, juice and coffee or tea. In the summer this classical continental fare is served on a small terrace area.

Apart from the private garage, guests also have at their disposal a sauna, two bars, and a reading room. The hotel also offers hiking and biking excursions for those that request it at an extra charge. A great place to stay in Spoleto. And if you are wondering about the name of the hotel, Charleston SC hosts a Spoleto festival every year. The hotel's name comes from that connection.

2. CLITUNNO, *Piazza Sordini. Tel. 0743/223-340. Fax 0743/222-663. Web: www.venere.com/it/umbria/spoleto/clitunno/. 38 rooms all with bath. Single E65-80; Double E80-110. All credit cards accepted. Breakfast included.* ***

Located near the Teatro Romano and recently renovated (1994), the Clitunno offers a pleasant mix of the old and new. The best rooms are furnished with the 'faux' antiques with tiled floors and oriental rugs covering them. These rooms make for quite an ambient stay. The others are accommodatingly comfortable with more modern furnishings. The bathrooms are small but well appointed with all manner of amenities, including a phone. A good hotel in a good location.

3. AURORA, *Via Appolinare 3. Tel 0743/220-315, Fax 0743/221-885. E-mail: info@hotelauroraspoleto.it, Web: www.umbria.org/hotel/aurora/ita/default.html. 40 rooms all with bath. Single E40-50; Double E50-80.* **

A great two star right next to the Teatro Romana and just down from the Piazza del Mercato, the heart of the centro storico. This hotel is very obviously bucking for three star status and as such they are a superb two star, with clean and comfortable rooms and excellent service in an ideal location. The bathrooms are a little small and will need to be upgraded if they want to achieve that extra star, but in terms of price/quality this is a great find.

4. GATTAPONE, *Via del Ponte 6, 06049 Spoleto. Tel. 0743/223-447, Fax 0743/223-448. 14 rooms all with bath. Standard Single E85-95; Superior Single E112-125; Standard Double E95-135; Superior Double E155-180. Breakfast E12.* ****

This hotel is set in a magical location overlooking the green valley and the medieval aqueduct that traverses it. All the bedrooms overlook this picturesque scene and is the reason to stay here. The standard rooms are a little on the small side, but are comfortable and come with baths and showers so you can luxuriate in the tub after a long day of hiking through the mountains. I would suggest springing for the Superior rooms, which are located in the modern extension and offer more space. There are two comfortable bar areas (for guests and anyone who shows up and wants a drink while savoring the view — which is lit up at night), as well as two terraces below where sheep sometimes wander. A quaint rustic touch. This hotel, in its pristine natural setting, is only a short walk to the centro storico. If you are inspired and have the means, without a question, this is *the* place to stay in Spoleto.

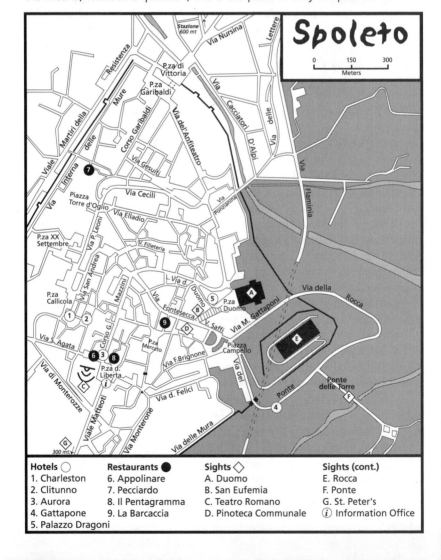

Hotels ◯	Restaurants ●	Sights ◇	Sights (cont.)
1. Charleston	6. Appolinare	A. Duomo	E. Rocca
2. Clitunno	7. Pecciardo	B. San Eufemia	F. Ponte
3. Aurora	8. Il Pentagramma	C. Teatro Romano	G. St. Peter's
4. Gattapone	9. La Barcaccia	D. Pinoteca Communale	ⓘ Information Office
5. Palazzo Dragoni			

5. PALAZZO DRAGONI, *Via del Duomo, 13, 06049 Spoleto. Tel. 0743/222-220, Fax 0743/222-225. Web: www.initaly.com/hisres/palazzo/palazzo.htm. 15 rooms, 9 suites. Double E125; Superior Double E150; Double Suite E265. Air-conditioning, parking. All credit cards accepted. Breakfast included. *****

This historic inn just steps from the Duomo, dating from the 14th century, has been lovingly restored and maintained through the years. In fact, the original stone foundations that you can see in the basement date from before 1000 CE, when the residence was two separate structures, with a street running between them! Ask to see it. The common room features vaulted ceilings, as do a number of rooms, with lovely rugs and a medieval feel. The rooms are spacious and charming, and the view from most rooms is incredible, looking out over the rooftops of historic Spoleto. You can see the spire of the Duomo and the walls of the Rocca from the lovely breakfast room on the top floor. Service is friendly and efficient. If you want to feel like you've stepped back into medieval times, this is the place to stay.

Where to Eat

6. APOLLINARE, *Via S. Agata 14. Tel. 0743/223-256. Closed Tuesdays. All credit cards accepted. Dinner for two E60.*

In the heart of Spoleto situated in what was at one time a Franciscan convent, in a short period of time this place has garnered a measure of culinary respect. The ingredients they use are all local but the way they prepare them is in the *cucina nuova* style. They get creative with their dishes so don't expect anything simple and traditional here. Do expect great atmosphere and imaginative food, though at elevated prices. A great place to come if you are into exploring the pleasures of the palate and are not concerned with the effect it has on your wallet.

7. PECCIARDA, *Vicolo San Giovanni 1. Tel. 0743/221-009. Closed Thursdays. No credit cards accepted. Dinner for two E35.*

Exquisite food, attentive service, great local atmosphere in a completely out of the way location, and all at prices that are easy on the pocketbook. This place is fantastic. A real slice of Spoleto. You have to come here if you are in town. Some of the simple but tasty dishes they serve include *gnocchi ripiena* (ricotta cheese dumplings), *stragozzi ai funghi* (local home made pasta with a spicy mushroom sauce) *pollo "alla Pecciarda"* (chicken stuffed with succulent herbs and spices), or a superb *arrosto misto* (mixed grilled meats). You'll come for the food and stay for the out of the way, off the beaten path, local atmosphere.

8. IL PENTAGRAMMA, *Via T. Martani 4/6/8. Tel. 0743/223-141. Closed Mondays and January 15-31. All credit cards accepted except American Express. Dinner for two E40.*

With a new owner and a new cook this place is going through a rebirth, not that it was bad to begin with. It's just that now it's fantastic. Located near the Teatro Romano this place has great local food and a serene musical atmosphere, at good prices. Try some of their frascarelli con pomodoro e basilica (pasta with tomatoes and basil) or tagliatelle ai funghi porcini (pasta with porcini mushrooms). For seconds the petto di tacchino e purea di fave (turkey breast with pureed fava beans) is rather tasty. They also make some great lamb dishes. To try a little of everything they have an abundant sampler menu for E25 per person, which gives you antipasto, pasta, main course and dessert. This is one of Spoleto's best restaurants.

9. LA BARCACCIA, *Piazza F.lli Bardier 3. Tel. 0743/221-171. Website: www.caribusiness.barcaccia. Closed Tuesdays. Credit cards accepted. Dinner for two E35.*

Located just off of the Piazza del Mercato, the heart of the centro storico, in an isolated piazza of its own, this restaurant offers typical local dishes at good prices. They specialize in cooking with truffles and grilling a wide variety of meats, especially veal. Everything they serve is stupendous and the ambiance is rustic and charming. For primo, try the tortellini al tartufo (meat filled pasta with truffle sauce), the tortellini panna e funghi (meat filled pasta with cream and mushrooms) or the spaghetti alla carbonara (with bacon egg, parmesan and pecorino). A great place to eat while in Spoleto.

Seeing the Sights

A. DUOMO

Rising up from the picturesque main square, the spire on the bell tower next to the Duomo acts as a beacon. The bell tower was constructed in the 12th century, with stone material removed from ancient Roman ruins. The Romanesque Duomo, built at the same time, has an imposing facade that is preceded by a portico built at the turn of the 16th century. The facade has five Rosetta windows and a mosaic created by Solsterno from 1207 above which are three more Rosetta windows.

The interior (open November-February 8:00am-1:00pm & 3:00-5:30pm; March-October 8:00am-1:00pm & 3:00-6:30pm) is simple with a nave and two aisles. You will find a variety of religious art including some magnificent works by Pinturicchio in the Chapel of Bishop Eroli.

B. SAN EUFEMIA

Located near the Duomo, this is one of the finest examples of simple Umbrian-Romanesque architecture. Constructed in the first half of the 12th century, the facade is basic but inspiring, with a portal window and a sweep of arches on the crown. The interior is white, austere and stark and is divided into three parts – one of which being the women's section above the main floor where women had to sit so as not to distract the men during services. Devoid of much finery, this church is a wonderful example of the piety and beauty of simplicity.

C. TEATRO ROMANO

A well preserved first century CE construction, located just off of the Piazza della Liberta and surrounded on one side by the stables of the 17th century Palazzo Ancaiani. The **church of Santa Agata** occupies what once was the stage area. Also included with the price of entry (E2) is access to the **Museo Archeologico Nazionale** (Via S. Agata, 9:00am-7:00pm; holidays 9:00am-1:00pm) which has a few interesting pieces, including artifacts from a warrior's tomb, jewelry, pottery and other material from the Bronze Age through the Middle Ages.

Outside, the Teatro Romano is a wonderful example of how architecture from different eras has been intertwined into the pastiche of daily life in Spoleto. Another example of that is the **Arco di Druso Minore** and **Arco Romano** nearby. These are two Roman-era arches have been completely incorporated into the surrounding buildings.

D. PINOTECA COMMUNALE

Up the Via del Municipio from the Piazza del Mercato — which used to be a Roman Forum — is the Palazzo Communale with its tall tower, small piazza and large flag out front. Begun in the 13th century and renovated in the 18th, this palazzo is now home to the Pinoteca Communale (admission E2.5, open 10:00am-1:00pm & 3:00-6:00pm, closed Tuesdays) which contains a small but captivating local museum. My favorite part is the display of old mint pieces that were used to make coins. As you enter, prior to going up to the museum, take a little time to admire the frescoes in the entrance way. Across from the palazzo are some delightful medieval houses set among winding little streets, which should be wandered if you are here.

Included in the price of entry is also access to the remains of an old Roman House, which I found infinitely more interesting than the little museum upstairs. Located to the left of the building, on the Via Visiale, is an excavated Roman home purported to be the home of the mother of Emperor Vespasian. Also included in the price of admission is access to the **Galleria Communale d'Arte Moderna** (Piazza Sordini 5, 10:00am-1:00pm & 4:00-7:00pm, closed Mondays) with a limited but interesting display of local modern art pieces.

E. ROCCA

This fortress stronghold dominates the view over Spoleto. Finished in the second half of the 14th century, from here you can get wonderful panoramic photos of the town and valley. Once a residence of the popes and other aristocracy, it has since been used as an army base and was a prison until 1982. In 1983 the process of restoring back to its former splendor began. Today you can go on brief guided tours (admission E5, open 3:00-6:00pm Monday-Friday, 10:00am-noon & 3:00-6:00pm Saturday and Sunday). The Rocca is being prepared to house a museum relating to the medieval duchy of Spoleto. The guided tour is well worth the price despite the limited material available.

F. PONTE DELLE TORRE

Past the Rocca is one of the most incredible sights I have ever seen in Italy, a medieval aqueduct spanning a gorge and leading to a pristine, verdant hill covered with hiking trails. This 13th century span connects two hillsides and is 230 meters long and 76 meters high and has towering piers and narrow arcades, which cast incredible shadows over the valley in the late afternoon light. It no longer carries water but serves as a foot bridge over the valley. Because of this sight and where it leads, it makes Spoleto a must-see destination when in Italy.

On the Via della Ponte on the way to the aqueduct, is a little bar, **La Portella**, that has tables set out on an overlooking with views of St Peter's. This is a good spot at which to relax anytime day or night.

G. ST. PETER'S

Located just outside of the old walled city, and visible from the Ponte delle Terme, is this fine church built between the 12th and 13th centuries. The beautiful but simple facade is embellished with numerous ornamental bas-relief decorations. There are three portals in the lower level, the center one surrounded by most of the ornamentation. The interior of the church is divided into three parts and was renovated and updated in 1669. This church, though plain, is one of the most important monuments in the region.

Other churches of interest inside the city walls are San Nicolo, San Filippo, and San Domenico.

Shopping

Spoleto does not have many international boutiques — yet — but what they do have are wonderful little shops selling typical works by local artisans. There are unique stores selling ceramics, fabrics, antiques, handmade note-books as well as shops catering to the needs of the locals like alimentari, salumerie and more. There are also numerous galleries and artists' studios filled with a diverse array of paintings and sculptures. The best shopping is along the **Corso G. Garibaldi**, up the **Via Salaria Vecchia**, and all around the **Piazza del Mercato**.

Practical Information

Festivals

Spoleto Festival, Mid-June to mid-July. *Email: tickets@spoletofestival.net, Web: www.spoletofestival.net*. A world-renowned festival filled with music, dance, cinematography, theater, art exhibits and more, that goes on every day for a month. An arts extravaganza that has no equal.

Other festivals include:
- **February and March** – Carnival of Spoleto
- **Week After Easter** – Week of the High Middle Ages
- **September** – Experimental Season of Lyrical Opera
- **December 14, 15, 16 and January 1** – Nativity and the Living Crib

Tourist Information

To arrange day trips, find out about bus tours, find train or bus information, get maps, or detailed walking tour information, book a hotel or simply get general information about Spoleto, the **tourist office**, Piazza della Liberta 7, *Tel. 0743/49890, Fax 0743/46241,* is the place to visit.

Gubbio

Gubbio is an ancient medieval town that majestically spreads out along the wind-swept ridges of **Mount Ingino**, with the **Torrente Camignano** river flowing through the town. This incredibly beautiful little town was founded by the ancient Umbrian people and eventually taken over by the Etruscans, as chronicled to in the **Eugubine Tablets** – the Rosetta Stone for ancient central Italian languages, culture and history – which are located here in Gubbio.

These seven bronze tablets give illuminating insight into how the city was run between the 3rd century and 1st century BCE, and are partially written in the Umbrian language – which is a derivation of Etruscan – and simultaneously in a rudimentary form of Latin.

In 295 BCE, Roman rule began and the town remained safe and secure until the end of the empire, like many of the towns in the region. Then it was destroyed during the Gothic wars of the 5th century CE and eventually came under Lombard control in the 8th century CE. By the 11th century the town was a free, independent commune and as such began to grow in power and importance. This situation instantly led to conflicts with Perugia, another strong city-state in the region, which conquered Gubbio handily in the 12th century. Then the city fell under papal control, which was not as benevolent as one might imagine – it was actually quite despotic. The Dukes of Urbino grabbed control for two centuries, then the Papal States reaffirmed their dominance in 1624 until the city was annexed into the new Italian state in the 1860s.

The layout of the town is very Roman with its structured grid pattern and is quite medieval with its ancient buildings, old city walls, and winding streets and steps flowing up and down the mountain. Also added onto this atmosphere are plenty of more 'modern' Renaissance towers and palazzi mingling with Gothic churches, making Gubbio a stunningly beautiful, 'can't miss' town if you are in Umbria.

The main handicrafts in Gubbio are ceramics as well as wrought iron work, carpentry, and copperware. The main flourish in the cuisine comes from the pungently aromatic white truffle that graces the local dishes mainly in autumn and winter. Gubbio loves a party and has a number of fun medieval festivals to enjoy, especially the **Corsa dei Ceri-Candle Tower Race** held on May 15th, replete with costumes and contests. This festival is on par with the best festivals in Italy. In this reenactment of an ancient tradition, separate sections of the city carry enormous wooden towers topped with wax statues of saints (Ubaldo, George, Anthony and Abbot) on their shoulders through the town, then up to the Basilica of San Ubaldo on Mount Ingino. Despite the Christian trappings, the festival is rooted in pagan rituals celebrating the coming of spring and each saint represents ancient pagan gods of fertility.

Another festival of note, this one on the last Sunday in May, is the **Palio della Balestra** – a crossbow competition. In this festival, archers dressed in period garb vie for an accuracy title. Complete with exciting pageantry, this is a fun festival to witness. Also, from July to mid-August, classical plays are performed in the Roman Theater outside of the main city walls.

Arrivals & Departures

Gubbio can only be reached by car or bus. There is no train service. The bus schedule from Perugia is not only infrequent, but erratic. Despite that, Gubbio is a great destination in and of itself, and can also be a quick day trip from Perugia. Listed below is the bus schedule from and to Perugia:

Perugia to:	Gubbio	Gubbio to:	Perugia
7:50	9:00	6:40	7:50
11:05	12:15	7:00	8:10
13:05	14:15	8:00	9:15
13:45	14:55	12:45	13:55
14:10	15:20	13:40	14:50
16:05	17:15	16:00	17:10
17:50 (Sunday)	19:00	18:15	19:25
18:40	19:50	19:15	20:25
19:40	20:50		

Orientation

Gubbio is 40 kilometers north-northwest of Perugia. It is separated into two different sections, upper and lower. In the lower section life revolves around the circular **Piazza Quaranta Martiri**. The upper town is centered on the **Piazza Grande**. Surrounding this piazza are most of the main sights of the city.

Getting Around Town

The best way to get around Gubbio, like most Umbrian towns, is by walking. Inside the old city walls the tiny medieval streets lend themselves to exploration by foot. But since it is nestled along a hillside, you should be prepared for some arduous climbs while you explore.

Where to Stay

1. GATTAPONE, *Via Ansidei 6. Tel. 075/927-2489, Fax 075/927-1269, E-mail: hotelgattapone@mencarelligroup.com, Web: www.mencarelligroup.com/ ing/hotelgattaponeing/gattapone.htm. Closed January. 28 rooms, all with bath. SSingle E65-80; Double E85-100. All credit cards accepted. Breakfast E3. ****

In an ancient building in the center of Gubbio, close to the Piazza Grande and the Palazzo dei Consoli, this old and respected hotel has recently been granted another star rating, and deservedly so. The general impression of the entire hotel is one of cleanliness, and every room is accommodatingly comfortable and come with air-conditioning, heat, mini-bars, telephones and TVs. Breakfast is either served in your room or at a nearby restaurant, Il Taverna del Lupo (see restaurant section below) that is owned by the same family, Mencarelli. The excellent hotel offers an additional asset for English- and French-speaking visitors, Beverly Goodwin. A transplant from the Caribbean island of Antigua, Beverly is helpful, knowledgeable and friendly. She can help you with all aspects of your travel plans in and around Gubbio, which can help make your stay that much more rewarding and memorable.

2. BOSONE PALACE, *Via XX Settembre 22. Tel. 075/922-0688, Fax 075/ 922-0552, E-mail: hotelbosonepalace@mencarelligroup.com, Web: www.mencarelligroup.com/ing/hotelpalaceing/bosonepalace.htm. 35 rooms all with bath. Single E65-80; Double E85-100. All credit cards accepted. Breakfast included. ****

Located in a 16th century building, this hotel is also run by the Mencarelli family. Like the Gattapone above, this hotel maintains an old world charm and ambiance while offering all modern amenities. The entrance is elegant with the aristocratic red divans and a stairway leading up to the guest rooms. Spacious and comfortable, the rooms are decorated with antique furniture and parquet floors covered with oriental rugs. Though on the small side, the bathrooms all have showers and come with a complimentary toiletry kit and hair dryer. An elegant hotel right in the middle of the old city.

3. AI CAPPUCCINI, *Via Tifernate. Tel. 075/9234, Fax 075/661-109. Web: www.venere.com/umbria/gubbio/aicappuccini/. 100 rooms all with bath. Single E160; Double E200-160. All credit cards accepted. Breakfast included. *****

Located a kilometer outside the walls of the old city but within walking distance, this hotel was once a convent back in the 1600's, complete with cloisters where the monks would go to meditate. While still maintaining the

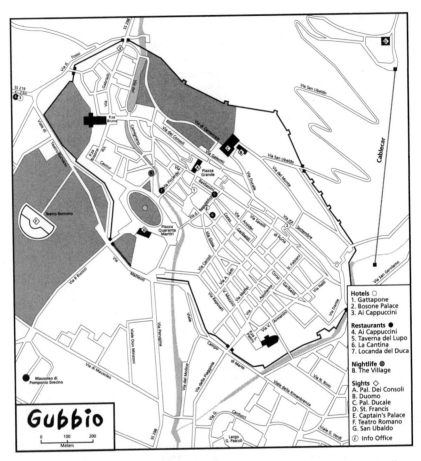

Gubbio

Hotels ○
1. Gattapone
2. Bosone Palace
3. Ai Cappuccini

Restaurants ●
4. Ai Cappuccini
5. Taverna del Lupo
6. La Cantina
7. Locanda del Duca

Nightlife ◉
8. The Village

Sights ◇
A. Pal. Dei Consoli
B. Duomo
C. Pal. Ducale
D. St. Francis
E. Captain's Palace
F. Teatro Romano
G. San Ubaldo
ⓘ Info Office

charm of the old structure, the renovations of 1990 have brought this excellent four star hotel into the modern era, with satellite TV (i.e. CNN and sports), air-conditioning, modern bathrooms with all amenities, updated telecommunications equipment, and more. Some of the rooms are the old cells the monks used, updated for your comfort of course, and some are located in a new addition to the older structure. Rooms are around the periphery of a quiet relaxing park area; all are spacious and perfect for relaxing, as is the swimming pool, sun deck and sauna. If you want to stay in the lap of luxury in Gubbio, stay here.

Where to Eat

4. AI CAPPUCCINI, *Via Tifernate. Tel. 075/9234, Fax 075/661-109. Closed Mondays. All credit cards accepted. Dinner for two E75.*

This is the restaurant of the excellent four star hotel mentioned above. The food here is superb so if you cannot afford to stay in the Park Hotel, at least come here for a meal. The cuisine is traditional Umbrian which means you'll find truffles, cheese and meats in most dishes. Try their maniche ripiene di ricotta zucchine peperoni e pomodoro (cylinders of pasta stuffed with cheese, zucchini, peppers and tomatoes). For seconds try their succulent petto di anatra tartufato (breast of duck with truffles). A charming atmosphere with seating inside and outside in the park terrace.

5. IL TAVERNA DEL LUPO, *Via G. Ansidei 6. Tel. 075/927-4368. Closed Mondays. All credit cards accepted. Dinner for two E70.*

Also run by the Mencarelli group that seems to have a firm grip on the accommodation and culinary options in Gubbio, beyond a doubt this is the best food and most welcoming atmosphere in Gubbio. I recommend trying the menu sampler at E35 per person since you'll get a full meal complete with antipasto, pasta, main course and dessert. The menu changes daily but each option is excellent. If you don't want the fixed menu you can also order a la carte and sample the staples of traditional Umbrian cuisine: pasta, truffles and meat. The ambiance is charming, romantic, and upscale. Come dressed appropriately and be prepared to pay for the privilege.

6. LA CANTINA, *Via Piccotti 3. Tel. 075/922-0583. Website: www.gubbio.com/lacantina. All credit cards accepted. Dinner for two E35.*

Great atmosphere and wonderful food. This place seems to be crowded all the time and for good reason – it is an excellent restaurant. There are some tiny tables set up just before the entrance in their own little cortile, but the place to be is inside in their expansive and rustic dining hall. Try some tasty tagliatelle al funghi porcini (with mushrooms) or al tartufo (with truffles). For seconds they have meats of all sorts, especially veal, as well as great pizza. A down-to-earth, fun place to eat.

7. LOCANDA DEL DUCA, *Via Picardi 1. Tel. 075/927-7753. All credit cards accepted. Dinner for two E25.*

This is a friendly and irreverent restaurant in a quaint old neighborhood, which serves tasty pastas and meats, but they are really known for their exquisite pizzas. The interior is rustic, set with a wood beamed ceiling; there's a small garden terrace overlooking the small river that flows through Gubbio. A good choice, a little off of the beaten path, and they are open until midnight if you need a late night snack. Even if you don't eat here, pass by and savor the ambiance of the location.

Seeing the Sights
A. PALAZZO DEI CONSOLI

Looking out over the town this imposing structure sits at the east end of the Piazza Grande and is the architectural and monumental core of the city. Ringed with some Renaissance *palazzi*, one of which is the **Palazzo Pretorio**, from this piazza you can get some stunning panoramic views.

The Palazzo dei Consoli is really two 14th century buildings, architecturally associated but clearly distinct. Simple and elegant, the palace is graced with a magnificent Gothic portal, in front of which are a set of steps that face out onto the piazza. The facade is divided by vertical pilaster strips, topped with turrets over which looks a small bell tower.

Also known as the Palazzo dei Popolo, the building now houses the **Picture Gallery** which has some paintings from Gubbio dating from the 14th and 16th centuries; and the **Archaeological Museum**, which houses the seven historically significant **Eugubine Tablets**, the Rosetta Stone for Central Italy. These tablets have a corresponding Umbrian language text, which evolved alongside the Etruscan, and a rudimentary form of Latin. There are also some interesting ancient archaeological finds like stone ceramics and coins. Not laid out and catalogued like the Smithsonian, but interesting and educational nonetheless.

B. DUOMO

A simple austere brick cathedral built in the 12th century, located up the hill from the older Roman town. The facade is graced with a plain circular window above a pointed portal. The interior is in a Latin cross plan and has one nave and many pointed arches supporting the ceiling. Simple and plain inside, except for the paintings and frescoes of the 16th century Umbrian artists along the walls, the church also has an incredibly detailed altar space, organ and choir. This cathedral is a wonderful example of austere medieval beauty.

C. PALAZZO DUCALE

Located directly across from the Duomo, this is a prime example of Renaissance architecture. Built in 1470 on the site of an older Lombard palace, this building contains a splendid internal courtyard surrounded by porticos. In the basement there is an archaeological excavation of the alterations made atop the building during the Renaissance. The palace's foundation can be seen as can segments of the original plumbing. Fragments of medieval ceramics found during the excavations are also on display.

The rest of the museum, upstairs, is really just a set of whitewashed walls, scattered antique furnishings, restored pieces from local churches, and an occasional modern art exhibit to fill up the space. Save the E2 cost of entry and buy a drink at The Village instead (see below under *Nightlife*), unless of course you are keenly interested in medieval plumbing.

D. CHURCH OF ST. FRANCIS

Located on the large Piazza Quaranta Martiri, this church was built in the 13th century with a bare facade, a Gothic portal and a small rose window. There is an octagonal campanile at the right side of the church.

The interior has one nave and two aisles. When the sun streams in through the large pointed windows along the sides and the colored windows in the apse, this church simply glows. The attached cloisters evoke images of times past and should be visited if open. Other churches of possible interest to visit in the town, though much simpler in ornamentation, are San Secondo, San Giovanni, and San Pietro.

E. CAPTAIN OF THE PEOPLE'S PALACE
Located on Via dell Capitano del Popolo #6, near the outskirts of this small town, this 13th century building is rather plain, but what's inside is memorable. Home to the **Museum of Torture Instruments**, you can just imagine the displays. They are educational, enlightening and a refreshing reality check concerning the relative safety of modern life.

F. ROMAN THEATER
Located just outside the old city walls, this ancient theater is considered to be one of the largest and best preserved in Italy. Now converted to a verdant park, this old theater is also home to live productions through July and mid-August. Separated into four wedge-shaped sections by flights of stairs with many of the ruins rebuilt and solidified, you really feel as if you've walked back in time.

G. BASILICA OF SAN UBALDO
At the summit of Mount Ingino lies the terminus for the traditional Corsa dei Ceri, the ancient tower up the hill. It can be reached by cable car from the station through the Porta Romana (an immense tower construction evoking a definite medieval feel) or by walking the length of the Corsa dei Ceri through the Porta San Ubaldo. I suggest that route only for the most fit.

Built in the 1514, worthy of note is the engraved marble altar and the glass coffin containing the well preserved body of St. Ubaldo. The three wooden towers used in the Corso dei Ceri festival are on display here year round. On the hillside above the church are the remains of the 12th century Rocca.

Nightlife & Entertainment
8. THE VILLAGE, *Piazza 40 Martiri #29. Tel. 075/922-2296.*
Art, history, architecture and the surrounding natural setting, coupled with a warm, friendly atmosphere make The Village is the place to come for late night festivities in Gubbio. Located in a renovated old church, I can't think of a better place to come with friends or to meet new ones. They serve Bass and Tenents on tap at E4 a pint and serve some basic Italian-style pub food.

Practical Information

Tourist Information

To arrange day trips, find out about bus tours, find train or bus information, get maps, or detailed walking tour information, book a hotel or simply get general information about Gubbio, the **tourist office** is the place to go, Piazza Oderisi 6, *Tel. 075/922-0693 or 922-0790, Fax 075/927-3409.*

Todi

An ancient and stunningly beautiful city surrounded by medieval walls, and filled with quaint winding streets, **Todi** rises up among green hills above where the Naia flows into the Tiber. This little town is a must see destination when in Umbria. Founded by the Tutere, an ancient Umbrian people, and heavily influenced by the Etruscans who settled along the banks of the Tiber, Todi eventually fell under Rome's control during the 4th century BCE and became known as Tuder. When the Roman Empire collapsed, the city underwent its share of destruction from the Goths and Byzantine Empire.

Beginning in the year 1000 it became an independent commune, during which time it extended its domain as far as Amelia and Terni in the 13th century. But then it became part of other empires again in the 14th century, eventually ending up in the hands of the Papal States. When Napoleon was in control of the Italian peninsula, Todi was an important government seat. After Napoleon it once again came under papal jurisdiction.

Todi is now mostly enclosed within the perimeter of the old town walls in a roughly triangular layout. Wonderfully apart from the advance of time, Todi has yet to succumb to the invading hordes of tourists. There is only one hotel in the centro storico, and a small bed and breakfast which means that the residents of the city still far outnumber the tourists, a situation you will find true all over Umbria, but especially so in Todi.

Todi, like all of Umbria, is not a place to pursue frantic sightseeing forays. Todi has a refreshingly gentle feel to it, and is still untainted by the hustle and bustle of frenetic tour groups trying to suck up the Italian experience as if it were a giant Slurpee. Todi is a town where you can fit right into the flow of real Italian life, wander unobtrusively among the friendly locals, sit with them in the parks as their children play, or smile with them in the piazzas as they pantomime one of the scenes in life's play. This is a place to undertake casual meandering, not only around the hilly cobblestone streets lined with medieval homes – some set into old Roman and Etruscan walls. Todi is also a place to rest and be rejuvenated in a fairy tale setting.

Arrivals & Departures

Todi is difficult to get to because the train and bus schedules are erratic. Also, the train station is a ways out of town (take the bus "C" from Piazza Jacapone) and is on a small regional line, which means the trains move much slower and stop at every town along the way. Check with the information office for schedules.

If you are taking the train into Perugia, be aware that Perugia has three different train stations. Trains from Todi stop first at Porta S. Giovanni station in Perugia, then go onto an even smaller station called **Perugia Santa Ana** (which is where you get off, since it is near the escalators up to the center), but they do not stop at the main train station in Perugia.

Orientation

Located 45 kilometers from Perugia, Todi is a small triangular shaped town sprawled along the crest of a hill. The skyline is dominated by Santa Maria della Consolazione in the lower part of town and the Chiesa di San Fortunato in the upper part. The Piazza del Popolo is definitely the central focus of the town around which are situated most of the major sights.

Getting Around Town

The only way to get around town is by walking. The town is small but even so, getting from the lower part of town to the upper can seem longer than it is because of the steep uphill grade. Be prepared to hike while here.

Where to Stay

1. RESIDENZA SAN LORENZO TRE, *Via San Lorenzo 3, Six rooms, four with bath. Tel. & Fax 075/894-4555, E-mail: sanlorenzotre@todi.net. Holiday Jan. 15 – Feb 28. Single E50-70; Double without bath E60-65; Double E85-90. Breakfast included. No credit cards accepted.*

Located on the upper floor of a quaint palazzo just off of the Piazza del Popolo, this is definitely the place to stay in Todi. If you simply must have a four star stay, go to the Fonte Cesia below, but you will be missing out on this amazing little residenza. Though not technically a hotel, I would categorize this bed and breakfast-style residence as a three star, despite the lack of mini-bar and TV in the rooms.

What this place lacks in unnecessary modern amenities is more than made up for with its charm, ambiance and incredibly scenic panoramic views. There are two rooms that open onto the most breathtaking vistas you can imagine. Each room is furnished with antique furnishings, which adds to the ambiance, but make sure you specifically request one of the two rooms with a view and your stay here will be stupenda (stupendous).

2. FONTE CESIA, *Via Lorenzo Leony 3, Tel. 075/894-3737, Fax 075/894-4677. E-mail: fontecesia@fontecesia.it. Web: www.fontecesia.it/. 37 rooms all with bath. Single E110; Double E130-150. All credit cards accepted. Breakfast included. *****

Situated in a noble and antique building in the center of Todi a few paces from the Piazza del Popolo and the Piazza Umberto, this is an excellent small town four star hotel. Opened in 1994, they have made the decor antique to add a touch of old world character. The rooms are spacious, very comfortable and come with every necessary modern comfort, though the bathrooms are minuscule. Their sundeck is a great place to relax as are the downstairs common areas. A good place to stay in Todi.

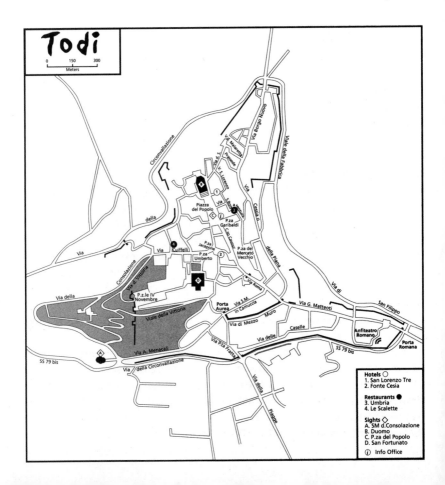

Where to Eat

3. UMBRIA, *Via San Bonaventura 13. Tel. 075/894-2390. Closed Tuesdays and at the end of December. All credit cards accepted. Dinner for two E55.*

This place has improved in the past few years. Where before the food was average, now it is really good. And before where the service was surly it has come to be professional. Now the atmosphere is local with a little pretense. I think you'll like the tagliatelle ai funghi (pasta with local mushrooms) or the spaghetti agli 'strioli' (spaghetti with an tasty herb only grown locally). For seconds the salami di cinghiale (wild boar) is a succulently tasty local sausage. An excellent choice while in Todi.

4. LE SCALETTE, *Via delle Scalette 1. Tel. 075/894-4422. Closed Mondays. Open 12:00-2:30pm & 7:00pm-1:00am. Dinner for two E35.*

This is a menu that has something for everyone, whether it's pizza, pasta, meats or vegetarian servings. They have terrace seating with some panoramic views, as well as a quaint medieval interior to add to this place's rustic charm. Located just past San Fortunato and Piazza Umberto I, at Le Scalette you will authentic local atmosphere, excellent regional cooking, attentive service, which will all translate into a wonderful meal.

Try their cappollini al tartufo nero (stuffed pasta with truffle cream sauce). It is the house specialty and is incredibly delicious. The pizza's overflow the plate and can be considered a meal in themselves. Not as formal or expensive as the Umbria, which — in my opinion — makes this a better place to eat.

Seeing the Sights

A. SANTA MARIA DELLA CONSOLAZIONE

Located a little ways outside of the city walls, this is a must see location when in Todi. A delightful example of Renaissance architecture, begun in 1508 and finished almost a century later, this lovely church, like San Fortunato, stands out from the diminutive skyline of the town. In the shape of a Greek Cross with a large central dome there are four apses each crowned with its own half dome.

B. DUOMO

This church dominates the Piazza Vittorio Emanuele II (also known as the Piazza del Popolo). The rectangular facade with three Rosetta windows and the same number of Gothic portals is simple yet refined. Flanking this facade is the robust bell tower that was once used as a military watchtower.

The interior is divided into three sections. In the left aisle is an interesting bronze of San Martino by Fiorenzo Bacci. The counter facade has a 16th century fresco of the *Last Judgment* by Faenzone. Unfortunately it has not been well preserved but is still powerful. Please also take note of the wooden choir behind the altar, as well as the two paintings portraying *St. Peter* and *St.*

Paul, to the left and right of the altar, done by Spagna. For E7.5 you can get a ticket to see the crypt which is a rather non-descript underground area but interesting for medieval history buffs.

C. PIAZZA VITTORIO EMANUELE II (PIAZZA DEL POPOLO)

Besides the aforementioned Duomo, also located in the extensive Piazza Vittorio Emanuele II (more commonly known as the Piazza del Popolo) are the Palazzo dei Priori, Palazzo del Popolo, and Palazzo del Capitano. An extensive piazza that is the heart of this small town, it is located on the site of an ancient Roman Forum and is one the most beautiful medieval squares in all of Europe. Dominated by the Duomo and surrounded by numerous monumental palaces. it transports you back in time.

Across from the Duomo is the turreted **Palazzo dei Priori**, built in the 14th century then joined together with some pre-existing buildings. The trapezoidal shaped tower was originally much higher, but through wars and erosion it remains in its truncated form today. The bronze eagle, the symbol of Todi, that stands out above the second order of windows was made by Giovanni di Gigliaccio in 1339.

The Palazzo del Capitano is a 13th century construction with a set of stairs leading to the second story entrance. The building is the site of the **Roman-Etruscan Museum and Civic Picture Gallery**. There are a number of Roman and Etruscan artifacts that have come from the surrounding area with terracotta and bronze work. In the Picture Gallery you will find fine paintings by many Umbrian and Tuscan artists, as well as gold and ceramic work.

D. SAN FORTUNATO

Rising up above the town this Gothic church (hours: winter 9:30am-12:30pm & 3:00-5:00pm; summer 8:30am-12:30pm & 3:00-7:00pm) was built between the 13th and 15th centuries. The half-completed facade overlooks the top of a scenic but fatiguing series of steps and their accompanying green space. There are three portals, the middle one richly decorated with a variety of colonnades, and is flanked by two statues of *Gabriel* and *Virgin Mary*. The other two are smaller versions of the middle.

The interior can be described as majestic but plain, with its three grandiose naves and the cross vaulting, and stark white walls. The wooden choir behind the altar is as extensive as in the Duomo but it is more accessible and visible here. Unfortunately some the fine frescoes are only in fragments now, as preservation work was not started until this century. But even if the interior art work is a little decayed, the serenity of the space is spiritually invigorating.

E. PARCO DELLA ROCCA

Near San Fortunato is the Parco della Rocca, where you have nice panoramic views, peace and quiet — when there aren't any kids running around — a place to picnic and cuddle, a rose garden to stimulate your nose, all of which make you feel as if you are on top of the world. The peaceful sense of continuity and permanence that Todi evokes is personified by this little park and the residents who frequent it.

Practical Information
Festivals & Fairs
- **March-April** – Antiquarian Exhibition of Italy
- **June-July** – National Antique Fair
- **September 8** – Festa di S. Maria della Consolazione
- **September** – Todi festival
- **October 14** – Festa di San Fortunato (Patron saint of Todi)
- **November 11** – Fair of St. Martin

Tourist Information
   To arrange day trips, find out about bus tours, find train or bus information, get maps, or detailed walking tour information, book a hotel or simply get general information about Todi, go to the **tourist office**, Piazza del Popolo 39, *Tel. 075/894-2526.*

Orvieto

   Umbria is Tuscany's understated cousin, quietly regal, unassuming, yet just as charming, and **Orvieto** is one of Umbria's best cities to visit. Umbria is a region of contrasts, where seemingly impenetrable, thick forests give way to sweeping, fertile valleys, where lush mountains and tranquil hills, dazzling waterfalls and still lakes mingle in a palette greener than any other corner of Italy. And just over the border with Lazio, the province that Rome is in, the stunning city of Orvieto rests picturesquely on the top of a hill bordered by protective cliffs, waiting for you to arrive on a day trip from Rome.

   Orvieto was a favorite refuge of the popes because of this defensible situation. One of the most beautiful towns in all of Italy, Orvieto has a rich array of winding medieval streets and stunning architecture. Its first inhabitants were Etruscan, after which the city became a protectorate of the Roman Empire.

   With the empire's decline, Orvieto underwent the inevitable spate of barbarian invasion. It then became a free commune in the 12th century CE and enjoyed a period of artistic and political advancement, until the Papal States suppressed it into their fold in the 14th century. When Napoleon Buonaparte conquered it, he made it an essential center of his dominion until Orvieto was absorbed into the Kingdom of Italy in 1860.

Known not only for its architecture and natural beauty, the town is also famous for the wonderful Orvieto wine that flows from the local vines, as well as the tasty olive oil from the nearby olive groves. Besides its culinary pursuits, the town also is a ceramic center. Local artisans, especially the immensely talented Michelangeli, also create intricate wood carvings as well as delicate lace.

Arrivals & Departures

Orvieto is accessible from Rome by a train which runs every two hours, starting at 6:12am and ending at 8:30pm, and takes an hour and twenty minutes or less depending on the number of stops along the way. Returns start at 9:00am and end at 10:30am. Once at the train station you then take the funiculare (cable car) up the hill, through an avenue of trees before tunneling under the Fortrezza to the Piazzale Cahen. By the funiculare station is where St. Patricks Well is located so stop there before you head up into town if you so wish.

From the station catch the bus 'A' — which should be waiting for you as you exit the funiculare since the bus is timed to its arrival — to the Piazza Duomo and the information office. From the Duomo you can get to all sights, hotels, and restaurants.

Orientation

Located on the top of a hill surrounded by cliffs, the **Corso Cavour** divides the city east to west. On the east is the **Piazzale Cahen** and the **Fortrezza** — built in 1364 and now a pleasant public garden with fine views over the surrounding valley — where the funiculare arrives, and at the west is the **Porta Maggior**e.

Getting Around Town

This town is easy to walk since being on the top of a bluff it is mainly flat. Once you take the funiculare up from the station there won't be many more serious hills to traverse.

Where to Stay

1. ITALIA, *Via di Piazza del Popolo. Tel/Fax 0763/42065, E-mail: hotelita@libero.it, Web: www.bellaumbria.net/grand-Hotel-Italia/. 42 rooms all with bath. Single E70; Double E100-110. American Express and Visa accepted. Breakfast E7.5.* *******

This 18th century palazzo in the centro storico of Orvieto offers you a pleasant stay right in the heart of things, adjacent to the Piazza del Popolo and just off of the Corso Cavour. The spacious rooms and relaxing common areas are furnished in a classic but comfortable style, with antiques and a floral

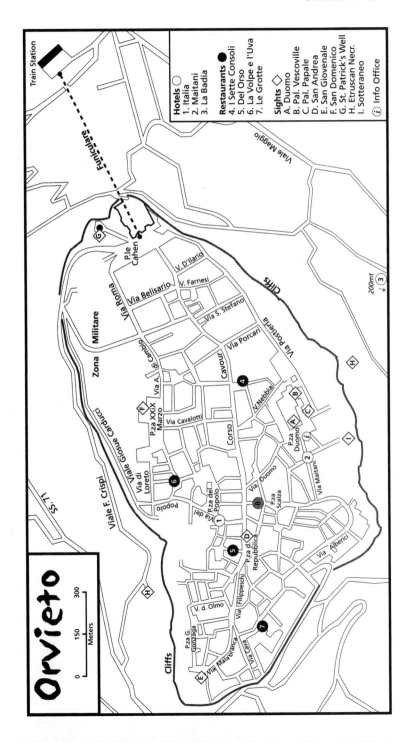

Orvieto

0 — 150 — 300
Meters

Hotels ○
1. Italia
2. Maitani
3. La Badia

Restaurants ●
4. I Sette Consoli
5. Del Orso
6. La Volpe e l'Uva
7. Le Grotte

Sights ◇
A. Duomo
B. Pal. Vescoville
C. Pal. Papale
D. San Andrea
E. San Giovenale
F. San Domenico
G. St. Patrick's Well
H. Etruscan Necr.
I. Sotterraneo

(i) Info Office

theme throughout. The best rooms are those facing the small courtyard (cortile), but all come with every three star amenity. The only real drawback other than that is the minuscule bathrooms . But besides that, this is a wonderful place to stay in Orvieto.

2. MAITANI, *Via Lorenzo Maitani. Tel 0763/42011, Fax 0763/660-209. Web: www.argoweb.it/hotel_maitani/maitani.uk.html. Closed January 6-26. 40 rooms all with bath. Single E80; Double E130. Suite E150-180. All credit cards accepted. Breakfast E10.* ****

If you want a serene atmosphere you'll find it here in this antique palazzo in the centro storico, only a few steps from the magnificent Duomo of Orvieto. The rooms are all different from one another but are furnished for comfort and style. The bathrooms are all modern, though a wee bit tiny compared to North American standards, and come with a complete complimentary toiletry kit. There is ample public space downstairs in the lounge/bar area, where you can put your feet up at the end of the day. A wonderful place to stay while in Orvieto, in an ideal setting.

3. LA BADIA, *1a Cat., 05019 Orvieto. Tel 0763/301-959 or 305-455, Fax 0763/305-396. All credit cards accepted. Single E125; Double E300.* ****

An unbelievably beautiful 12th century abbey at the foot of Orvieto is home to this incredible hotel that has only recently opened for business. You will be treated to one of the most unique and memorable experiences in the entire world. In the 15th century the abbey became a holiday resort for Cardinals, and today, through painstakingly detailed renovations, an ancient and noble Umbrian family, Count Fiumi di Sterpeto, plays host in this awe-inspiring environment.

The rooms are immense, the accommodations exemplary, the service impeccable, the atmosphere like something out of the Middle Ages. For a fairy tale vacation stay here, and make sure that you eat at least once at their soon to be world-renowned restaurant offering refined local dishes — many ingredients culled from Count Fiumi's farms and vineyards — in an incredibly historic and romantic atmosphere.

Where to Eat

4. I SETTE CONSOLI, *Piazza San Angelo 1/a. Tel. 0763/343-911. Closed Wednesdays and February and March. All credit cards accepted. Dinner for two E40.*

This is one of the best places in town with a comfortable local atmosphere, with a beautiful garden for dining during good weather. If you don't want to make a decision about the food you can order from a series of fixed price menu options that offer you a variety of dishes to sample, and all at good prices. Everything here is fresh and local, especially their salami and cheese, which come in a tasty antipasto platter.

5. TRATTORIA DEL ORSO, *Via della Misericordia. Tel. 0763/341-642. Closed Monday nights, Tuesdays and February. Visa accepted. Dinner for two E40.*

Deep in the heart of Orvieto, nestled down a small side street off of the Piazza della Repubblica, is a small trattoria passionately operated by Gabrielle (doing the cooking) and Ciro (greeting and seating) where you can find genuine and simple Umbrian cuisine. You should start with the magnificent bruschetta (garlic bread) and proceed to the luscious fettucine alfredo. For seconds there are plenty of meat and vegetable dishes, as well as omelets to choose from. The desserts are home made, so you have to save room for at least one. A great place to sample the local flavor.

6. LA VOLPE E L'UVA, *Via Ripa Corsica 1. Tel. 0763/341-612. Closed Mondays and From July 15 to August 15. American Express and Visa accepted. Dinner for two E35.*

You definitely have to make reservations, since their food, friendly atmosphere and low prices really packs in the customers. Lucio Sforza and his staff will do everything in their power to make your meal the best you have ever had. Their antipasto salami plate (salumi misti locali) features all sorts of local favorites. The gnochetti con olio pepe e pecorino is a superb mixture of pepper, oil and pecorino cheese over small potato gnocchi. For your entrée you should consider ordering the arrosto di maiale alle erbe (tasty roast pork marinated in herbs) that literally melts in your mouth, or the delicious pollo alla cacciatore (chicken hunter style) or agnello sulla griglia (grilled lamb). For dessert there is good selection of cheese and fruit as well as a rich, creamy chocolate mousse (mousse di cioccolato).

7. LE GROTTE DEL FUNARO, *Via Ripa Serancia 41. Tel. 0763/343-276. Closed Mondays. Dinner for two E40.*

Literally situated in a series of grotte (caves) carved into the tufo layer upon which Orvieto sits, this place offers you a unique dining experience to go along with their delicious food. The whole point of coming here is to eat downstairs in the caves, so avoid the terrace. The have a well rounded menu, but in truffle season that aromatic tuber is featured prominently and any dish seasoned with it should be sampled if you are here from October to December. Try Le Grotte when in Orvieto. You will not be disappointed.

Seeing the Sights
A. DUOMO

Stunning! Elegant! Mesmerizing! No words can really describe this amazing cathedral, located in the Piazza del Duomo, whose facade is covered with bas-reliefs, colorful mosaics, and radiating frescoes. The pointed portals on the facade literally jump out at you, and the rose window — flanked by figures of the Prophets and Apostles — is a treasure to behold. Bring binoculars to admire all the intricate detail, since the facade is an entire museum in and of itself.

Most of its ornamentation was created between the 14th and 16th centuries. The bronze doors are contemporary works by Emilio Greco (1964). A museum featuring more of his art is situated on the ground floor of the Palazzo Papale to the right of the Duomo. Above and beside the doors are the Bronze Symbols of the Evangelists. The exterior side walls are alternating horizontal layers of black basalt and pale limestone in the distinctive Pisan style. This same style is translated into the interior, covering both the walls, and the columns which divide the church into a nave and two aisles. The christening font is the work of several artists and is stunning in its intricacies. The apse is lit by 14th century stained glass windows by Bonino and contains frescoes by Ugolino di Prete Ilario.

In the right transept behind an artistic 16th century wrought iron railing is the beautiful Capella Nuova, which contains Luca Signorelli's superlative Last Judgment. It is purported to be the inspiration for Michelangelo's Last Judgment in the Sistine Chapel. A must see, since it is also considered one of the greatest frescoes in Italian art. The chapel also contains frescoed medallions depicting poets and philosophers ranging from Homer to Dante.

B. PALAZZO VESCOVILLE

Located to the right and at the rear of the Duomo, restored in the 1960s, it now houses the **Archaeological Museum** (open 9:00am – 7:00pm, Holidays 9:00am-1:00pm; admission E2), which has a collection of material excavated from the Etruscan Necropoli that are located nearby the city. A simple, basic introduction to the history of the region.

C. PALAZZO PAPALE

Situated to the right of the Duomo, this was once the residence of a long line of popes when they came to visit the city. This building dates back to the 8th century and is also known as the **Palace of Bonifacio VIII**. On the ground floor you can find the **Museum of Emilio Greco** (open 10:30am-1:00pm and 2:00-6:00pm in winter and 3:00-7:00pm in summer) exhibiting numerous works by this fine sculptor from Catania. On the first floor is the **Cathedral Museum**, which displays miscellaneous works of art, mostly from the Duomo or about the Duomo.

D. SAN ANDREA

On the edge of the Piazza della Repubblica, this plain church is best known for its dodecagonal campanile, a twelve-sided bell-tower. This masterful architectural complement to the church has three orders of windows and a turreted top section. Built between the 6th and 14th centuries on the site of a pre-existing early Christian church, the interior is a single nave with two aisles, a raised transept and cross vaults. The wooden altar by Scalza is worthy of note, as is the pulpit. Situated below the church and accessible by appointment are some ancient ruins dating from the Iron Age up to the medieval period.

E. SAN GIOVENALE
Originally a Romanesque building San Giovenale was reconstructed in the 13th century with Lombard features. The massive square bell tower dwarfs this plain and sturdy looking church. The interior is a simple design with one single nave and two aisles. Note the Romanesque high altar intricately decorated with bas-reliefs as well as the frescoed walls of the Orvieto school from the 13th to the 16th century. This part of town is the ideal location to take relaxing walks, filled with stunning panoramic vistas.

F. SAN DOMENICO
Set back from the Via Arnolfo di Cambio in a less inspiring part of town, this church is famous because St. Thomas Aquinas taught here, and the desk at which he performed his lectures is still inside. You should also take note of the 13th century Tomb of Cardinal de Bray by Arnolfo di Cambio, as well as the Petrucci Chapel built by Michele Sanmicheli, which is below the main church and entered from the a door on the south wall.

G. ST. PATRICK'S WELL
Open daily from 9:00am to 6:00pm, this well, **Orvieto Sotteraneo**, and the **Duomo** are the most famous sights in Orvieto. Built by Antonio Sangallo the Younger for Pope Clement VII, the well served as a reservoir for the nearby fortress if the city was ever put under siege. Hence it is also known as the Fortress Well. Its ingenious cylindrical cavity design was completed in the beginning of the 16th century. Going to a depth of 62 meters, there are two parallel concentric staircases (each with 248 steps ... go on and count them if you want). The water carriers with their donkeys used one spiral staircase for going up and the other for going down. Each staircase has a separate entrance and is ringed by large arched windows. In the public gardens above the well are the overgrown remains of an Etruscan temple.

H. ETRUSCAN NECROPOLISES
Located on either side of the city the foot of the tufa cliffs, the **Necropolis of the Tufa Crucifix** is to the north and the **Necropolis of Cannicella** is to the south. Each date from around the sixth century BCE. Well preserved but ransacked and looted a long time ago, these tombs nonetheless are something to visit while in Orvieto. It's not often that you can come face to face with something that was created almost 2,500 years ago. Inquire at the information office about the ways and means to visit them.

I. ORVIETO SOTTERANEO

If you do nothing else while here, make sure that you sign up to go on one of the guided tours of the subterranean passages that snake underneath the entire city. Guided tours are held every day starting at 11am and go until 6pm, and cost E5. Inquire at the information about the times for the tours in English. At last inquiry they were at 12:15 and 5:15pm. Recently excavated and opened for tourists, the tours of these caves under the city take you on a journey through history, including Etruscan wells, a 17th century oil mill, a medieval quarry, ancient pigeon coops and much more, all thoroughly narrated by well-trained guides. These tours are an extraordinary trip back in time and shouldn't be missed.

Shopping

In general there is great shopping in Orvieto, but without the same run-of-the-mill, cookie cutter, international name brand stores you find in most tourist locations. There are many small artisans' shops, unique boutiques, ceramics re-sellers, all of which add to the rich local flavor that Orvieto cultivates. One store in particular you simply must visit is:

8. Michelangeli, Via Gualverio Michelangeli 3B, *Tel. 0763/342-660, Fax 0763/342-461*. All credit cards accepted. An incredible store filled with intricately carved wooden sculptures, toys, figurines, and murals of the most amazing and appealing designs. A perfect store to find the perfect gift or keepsake. Michelangeli's work is slowly becoming recognized around the world. It is rustic but refined, and the very least you should stop in the store, check out the displays, take a look through his portfolios and treat the experience as you would a museum. A great store and a rewarding experience.

Practical Information
Tourist Information

To arrange day trips, find out about bus tours, find train or bus information, get maps, detailed walking tour information, book a hotel, get general information about Orvieto, or book a guided tour for Orvieto Sotteraneo, the **tourist office**, Piazza Duomo 4, *Tel. 0763/301-507 or 301-508, Fax 0763/344-433*, is the place to go.

Assisi

Dramatically situated on a verdant hill highlighted by olive groves and cypress trees reaching right up to the city walls, the beautiful medieval city of **Assisi** stretches majestically along the slopes of Mount Subasio. The home of **St. Francis**, Assisi is an original Umbrian settlement, after which it became a part of the Etruscan federation, and later was incorporated into the Roman Empire. In the 3rd century CE it became a Christian town, then after the fall of the Roman Empire it was destroyed by the Goths in 545 CE, conquered by the Byzantine Empire and eventually fell into hands of the Lombards.

Incorporated into the Duchy of Spoleto, it became an independent commune in the 11th century and achieved great success in the 13th century. During this period of freedom and economic success, St. Francis was born here in 1182 and **St. Clare** in 1193 (a daughter of a rich family, and a contemporary and disciple of St Francis of Assisi, she founded the order of Poor Clares. She died in Assisi in the convent she founded in 1253).

After the 13th century the city became part of the Papal States, then Perugia, then Milan, and finally fell under the control of the powerful Sforza family. And eventually, as a result of internal strife, Assisi was re-incorporated into the Papal States in the 16th century until it became a part of the new state of Italy in the 19th century.

Today Assisi stills bears the mark of a robust little medieval town, at least that part which is still encompassed by the old city walls. This stunningly beautiful little Umbrian hill town is a center for art and culture, a major religious pilgrimage site, and a heavily touristed location. As a result, be prepared for crowded streets, something that is unusual in the otherwise lightly touristed region of Umbria. Some of the town's charm was instantaneously leveled when an earthquake struck in 1997, causing severe damage to the city's structures, especially the Basilica of St. Francis. Many of Giotto's fine frescoes were destroyed in this natural catastrophe. An extensive renovation of the church has just been completed as of going to press. Assisi is a wonderful destination, but you may still find scaffolding and supports in place to secure certain structures of historic significance.

Arrivals & Departures

Assisi can be somewhat difficult to get to by train or bus, so if you don't rent a car, which is recommended so you can take in all the splendor of Umbria, expect at least a two hour train trip from Rome, or an hour and a half train or bus trip from Perugia. Buses and trains leave every hour and half to two hours from Perugia and are infrequent from Rome. Contact the local tourist office in Perugia for a more detailed schedule.

Orientation

Assisi is directly between Perugia and Foligno, about 13 kilometers from the former. The town is dominated by the **Basilica of San Francesco** on the northwest end. The core of the city surrounds the **Piazza del Comune** with many major sights in an around the square. All streets in the town seem to lead to this piazza, so it is almost impossible to get lost while in Assisi.

Getting Around Town

Assisi, like most Umbrian towns, is made for walking. Many or the smaller streets and the winding staircases are off-limits to cars, but you do have to contend with hills. So bring your walking shoes.

Where to Stay

1. SAN FRANCESCO, *Via San Francesco 48. Tel 075/812-281, Fax the same. 44 rooms all with bath. Single E70; Double E140. All credit cards accepted. Breakfast included.* ***

Located near the cathedral, this classic little three star hotel is right in the center of things. Some of the rooms have grand views of the cathedral. If you want one you need to request it with your reservation. All rooms have plenty of space and are comfortably furnished with a mixture of antiques and more modern furnishings. The bathrooms are minuscule but come with a complete complimentary toiletry kit. This is a good small town three star, a little on the rustic side, with an intimate terrace overlooking the cathedral, a quaint bar area, and a rather well respected restaurant.

2. FONTEBELLA, *Via Fontebella 25. Tel. 075/816-456, Fax 075/812-941. Web: www.venere.com/it/assisi/fontebella/. 43 rooms all with bath. SSingle E80-130; Double E105-235. All credit cards accepted. Breakfast E9.* ****

Almost in the center of Assisi with great views over the valley, this is a very nice four star that won the Premium Hotel Award in Italy for 1998. The common areas are spacious and accommodating. The bathrooms are not too big but do come with all modern amenities and a complimentary toilet kit. The rooms are relatively spacious and comfortable and are designed with a regal yellow and black color scheme. The breakfast buffet, served outside on the terrace in good weather, is quite a spread and is worth the extra money. A fine hotel with all the accoutrements of four star quality – plus their restaurant, Il Frantoio, is pretty good too.

3. SUBIASO, *Via Frate Elia 2. 075/812-206, Fax 075/816-691. Toll free in Italy 167/015070. 61 rooms all with bath. Single E115; Double E185. All credit cards accepted. Breakfast included.* ****

This is the place to stay in Assisi. Almost right at the foot of the Basilica di San Francesco this hotel has some breathtakingly panoramic views over the valley from the balconies of some of the rooms, as well as the sun terrace and garden terrace areas. All rooms are uniquely furnished with attractive antiques and are spacious and comfortable. There are a number of common rooms where you can relax and unwind, and the garden terrace, which houses the restaurant in the summer, is a perfect spot to grab a quiet meal.

4. IL PALAZZO, *Via San Francesco 8, 06081 Assisi. Tel. 075/816-841. Web: www.perugiaonline.com/ilpalazzo/. 40 rooms all with bath. All credit cards accepted. Single E55-65; Double E95-115.* **

The Palazzo Bindangoli-Bartocci — in which the hotel resides — was built

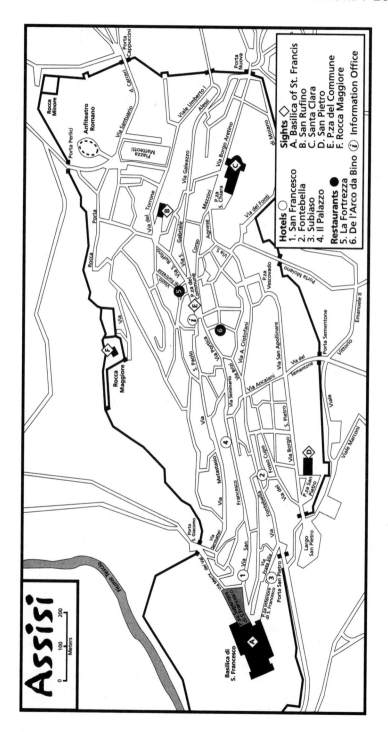

Assisi

0 100 200
Meters

Basilica di S. Francesco

Sights ◇
A. Basilica of St. Francis
B. San Rufino
C. Santa Clara
D. San Pietro
E. P.za del Commune
F. Rocca Maggiore
i Information Office

Hotels ○
1. San Francesco
2. Fontebella
3. Subiaso
4. Il Palazzo

Restaurants ●
5. La Fortrezza
6. De l'Arco da Bino

in the 1500s and still retains its quaint medieval charm. It is perfectly situated between the Basilica of St. Francis and the main square, Piazza del Commune. The foundation of the building is a mixture of stables, storehouses, and inns that were in use in the 12th century. Each room is different in size, shape and antique furnishings but all are decorative and comfortable. In some rooms you have the original oak and beams for ceiling supports. The third floor rooms enjoy a view over the Spoletana valley. Without a doubt this is the best two star in town, and is pressing hard for three star status.

Where to Eat

There are a large number of restaurants to choose from in this city since it is such a tourist destination and pilgrimage site. Listed below are what I consider to be the two best:

5. LA FORTREZZA, *Piazza del Comune. Tel. 075/812-418. Closed Thursdays and in February. All credit cards accepted. Dinner for two E40.*

In an ideal location right up a small side street from the main piazza, this is a superb local restaurant attached to a two star hotel of the same name (a good, inexpensive option while in Assisi). It has kept up its high traditional culinary standards. For appetizers, their prosciutto crudo con bruschetta (ham with garlic bread) is superb. For the pasta dish try the succulently rich ravioli alla ricotta e tartufo nero (ravioli with cheese and black truffles) or the tasty pappardelle alla ragu di agnello (pasta with lamb sauce). For the main course its tough to decide between their succulent meat dishes like filetto di vitellone al mosto cotto (veal), petto di faraone in crosta (breaded wild chicken breast), the coniglio (rabbit) or piccione (pigeon). A great atmosphere with a wide variety of superb food at more than acceptable prices.

6. TAVERNA DE L'ARCO DA BINO, *Via San Gregorio 8. Tel 075/812-383. Closed Tuesdays, January 8-31, and July 5-15. All credit cards accepted. Dinner for two E55.*

One of the oldest and definitely the best place to eat while in Assisi, and because it is down a small side street it is also one of the least visited by tourists. The specialty of the house is veal and lots of it. And they make it in a variety of different ways, including al tartufo nero (with black truffles), al gorgonzola (with gorgonzola cheese), alla brace (roasted), all'aceto balsamico (with balsamic vinegar), con funghi parmigiano e rucola (with mushrooms and parmesan), as well as a number of other preparations. To start off your meal try their bruschetta al tartufo nero di Assisi (garlic bread spread with black truffles). They also make an excellent fettucine al profumo di bosco (smoked wood-flavored pasta with mushrooms and truffles), which was my favorite, as well as other succulently tasty pastas.

A pleasant, upscale, local place with great atmosphere — vaulted brick ceilings and woodsy wrought iron decor — as well as simply scrumptious food. Try not to miss this place.

Seeing the Sights

A. BASILICA OF ST FRANCIS

Majestic and picturesque, the basilica and its accompanying cloistered convent have graced this rural landscape for many centuries. The basilica is split into two levels; the lowest is reached from the Piazza Inferiore di San Francesco which is currently being held up — after the earthquake of 1997 — with unsightly but necessary wood and iron brackets and scaffolding. In itself it is an enchanting open space, with a series of quaint 15th century arcades. The lower Church was built between 1228 and 1230 while the Upper Church was built from 1230 to 1253. The church is dominated by the huge square bell tower built in four layers, completed in 1239, with arches gracing the top section.

The **Lower Church** is entered through an intricate double portal surmounted with three rose windows. Inside consists of a single nave divided into five bays with a boule transept and a semi-circular apse. Even in the dim light the star-spangled blue vaults between the arches is stunningly beautiful. The remains of St. Francis are located in a stone urn in the crypt, which is down a staircase located in the middle part of the nave.

The side chapels are all wonderfully decorated with 13th century stained glass windows. On the right you can find the Chapel of St. Stephen, then the Chapel of St. Anthony of Padua and finally the Chapel of St. Mary Magdalene with frescoes by Giotto. In the Chapel of St. Martin on the left you can find some significant frescoes, including *Madonna, Child and Angels* by Cimabue as well as *Life of Christ and St. Francis* by Giotto on the right. The Chapel of St. Nicholas also contains some stunning frescoes by Giotto.

The **Upper Church** is reached — since the earthquake in 1997 it has been off-limits but may have reopened — by steps leading from the lower piazza. The facade faces the town of Assisi and looks over the wide lawn of the Piazza Superiore di San Francesco and has a pure linear Gothic look. The one embellishment is the large rose window staring out at the town. The interior of this level is bright and airy, in contrast to the lower section. It consists of one nave with a transept and a polygonal arch, with stunningly colorful frescoes by Cimabue decorating the walls of the apse as well as the transept.

The inlaid wood choir by the altar is a fantastic piece to admire. It was created between 1491 and 1501 by local artist Domenico Individi. The upper part of the nave is adorned with 13th century stained glass windows. Under the gallery, the walls were covered with some of the most magnificent examples of Giotto's work until the earthquake shook them loose and disintegrated them to powder. Sadly, this whole church is being pieced together, but work may well be complete by the time you visit – and these fantastic frescoes will be available for viewing once again.

B. CATHEDRAL OF SAN RUFFINO

Commonly known as the **Duomo**, the beautiful Romanesque facade is divided into three sections. The uppermost is triangular with a pointed Gothic arch; the middle is divided vertically by pilasters and is decorated with three fine rose windows and myriad carvings; and the lower section has three portals, the left of which is used to enter the church. To the side of the Duomo is the massive bell tower adorned with small arches at the top and an off-set clock on the same level as the top layer of the church.

The interior was renovated in the 16th century and consists of a nave and two aisles. The baptismal font in the right aisle was used to baptize St. Francis, St. Clare, St. Agnes, and St. Gabriel. Assisi definitely is a hotbed of sainthood. The apse contains an outstanding 16th century wood choir. The crypt is a must see. Situated underneath the cathedral, and once part of an earlier church, you can find a Roman sarcophagus which used to contain the remains of San Ruffino. Just down the road from here past Piazza Matteoti is a Roman amphitheater worthy of a short visit.

C. BASILICA OF SANTA CLARA

Simply, serenely, and classically Gothic, this 13th century church dominates the piazza of the same name. Attached to the left side of the building are three large flying buttresses with a slender bell tower rising up from the apse. The facade is decorated with two closed horizontal bands, is divided into three levels, and has a wonderful rose window and a plain portal flanked by two lions.

The interior is in the form of a Latin cross with a single nave and is as simple and bare as the outside. A good place to come for soul-enriching peacefulness. The crypt, reached by a flight of steps, contains the remains of St. Clare in a glass coffin. In the chapel of St. George is the painted cross which supposedly spoke to St. Francis when it was located in the Church of St. Domain. Located here beyond a lattice window are the remains of St. Clare.

D. CHURCH OF SAN PIETRO

Located just inside the city walls, near the Basilica of St. Francesco, this Romanesque-Gothic 13th century church is built on the site of a previous Catholic place of worship. The facade is rectangular with two orders and beautiful in a simple way. The upper level has three rose windows, and the lower has three portals. The interior contains one nave and two aisles, and has some 14th century frescoes and the ruins of some tombs of the same century. For simple beauty and peaceful serenity this is a fine church to visit.

E. PIAZZA DEL COMMUNE

Located in the heart of the old town, built on the site of an old Roman forum and in the midst of some ancient medieval buildings, is the center of Assisi, the

Piazza del Commune. The 14th century **Prior's Palace** houses the town council offices, the **Municipal Picture Gallery** contains Byzantine, Umbrian and Sienese frescoes, the turreted 13th century **Palazzo del Capitano del Popolo** has the 14th century **Municipal Tower** rising out from it.

Next to that is the **Church of Santa Maria Sopra Minerva**, built in the first half of the 16th century over the ancient Temple of Minerva. The facade is all ancient Rome from the Augustan period of the first century BCE, while the rest of the building is medieval.

F. CASTLE OF THE ROCCA MAGGIORE

Pass by the Roman Amphitheater as you go out the Perlici Gate to begin the climb up to this imposing fortress, which once served as protector over the city of Assisi. Built after the Lombard occupation, the fortress with its imposing ramparts and towers completely dominates the town below. A perfect place for kids of all ages to explore a medieval fortress.

Practical Information

Festivals

• **3rd and 4th of October** – Festival of St. Francis, Patron Saint of Italy
• **May Day celebration** – Calendimaggio
• **June 22nd** – Festival of the Vows
• **1st and 2nd of August** – Festival of the Pardon

Tourist Information

To arrange day trips, find out about bus tours, find train or bus information, get maps, or detailed walking tour information, book a hotel or simply get general information about Assisi, go to the **tourist office**, Piazza del Comune 27, *Tel. 075/812-450, Fax 075/813-727.*

Tuscany & Umbria Guide

index

Things Change!

Phone numbers, prices, addresses, quality of food, etc, all change. If you come across any new information, we'd appreciate hearing from you. No item is too small! Drop us an email note at: Jopenroad@aol.com, or write us at:

Tuscany & Umbria Guide
Open Road Publishing, P.O. Box 284
Cold Spring Harbor, NY 11724

Other Open Road Guides to Italy

We think this is the most comprehensive guide in English to *la bella Italia!*

Doug Morris takes you to his favorite restaurants, hotels, special sights, unique pubs and nightlife, and terrific area excursions.

We doubt you'll find another country in the world that is as welcoming and friendly to the bambini, and the number of family-friendly hotels and activities is incredible!

This comprehensive, compact 'menu-reader' will guide you through any Italian dining experience with ease!

See ordering information on the last page of this book.